THE STORY OF
COVENTRY

THE STORY OF
COVENTRY

PETER WALTERS

For Barb, Nick and Kate, with all my love.

First published 2013

The History Press
The Mill, Brimscombe Port
Stroud, Gloucestershire, GL5 2QG
www.thehistorypress.co.uk

British Library Cataloguing in Publication Data.
A catalogue record for this book is available from the British Library.

ISBN 978 1 86077 692 2

Typesetting and origination by The History Press
Printed in Great Britain

CONTENTS

ACKNOWLEDGEMENTS

I owe a huge debt of gratitude to all those who have written about Coventry's history, ancient and modern.

More particularly, I want to thank the following for their help in bringing this project to life – George Demidowicz, Iain Soden, David Fry, Martin Roberts, Christine Adams, Michael Hinman, Mark Radford, Chris Patrick, Marcus Lynch, Abigail Rhodes, Steve Bagley, Chris Ross, Andrew Paterson, Richard Briggs, Alun Thorne and David McGrory.

I am also indebted to The History Press for images from their own collection.

INTRODUCTION

There was a time when Coventry enjoyed a spotlight all of its own on the national stage. One of England's biggest and wealthiest cities, it had hosted more than one parliament and was effectively the seat of royal government for more than a year. Its celebrated cycle of mystery plays attracted crowds from counties around, while its equally famous city wall kept Coventrians safe when others suffered in troubled times.

Coventry's golden age was over long before Henry VIII's attack on the monasteries tore the heart out of the city, but the shine from that dimming spotlight lingered on.

England remembered the tale of saintly Godiva and the city's place in myth as birthplace of the legendary St George, patron saint and dragon-slayer. Shakespeare sprinkled the city's name through more than one of his plays, and true as Coventry blue, first coined to describe a dye that never ran, entered the language as a colourful way of admiring constancy. At Christmas people sang the *Coventry Carol*, a haunting refrain to loss, set in a biblical frame. At New Year, children were given Coventry god cakes as a special blessing from their godparents. They played card games like Peeping Tom or Moll of Coventry and in summer they picked the flowers of Coventry Bells, the popular name for the campanula.

Coventry gradually became a byword for quaint, a place of hallowed customs celebrated beneath the spires and gables of past glories as the world hammered away towards industrial revolution. In an age of machines it was still lost in a midsummer dream of crafts and guilds, until a farm boy from Sussex added the delicate skills of making bicycles to those other intricate crafts of watches and ribbons. In the dying years of the nineteenth century, his legacy spawned the first factory in Britain set up to make the motor car, a revolution in personal transport that changed the way we all lived.

Faced with trying to make this new industry fit into an old way of doing things and a medieval street pattern, Coventry became the only city in Britain to jump straight from the late Middle Ages into the twentieth century. Over the decades to come it was to reflect all the themes of the new century – rapid industrialisation, mass immigration, boom and slump, even total war. What emerged in 1945 was a different place, a city of the working man, by turns inventive and listless, that had not quite caught up with itself. But as one of the engineering dynamos of Britain it had a place back on the national stage.

Its pioneering Festival of Britain architecture, so widely admired in the postwar years, has managed to overshadow Coventry's remaining heritage in wood and stone and somehow erase the collective memories of the place, stretching back almost a millennium. This is the story of that 1,000 years, full of colour and incident but sadly little known at a time when the national spotlight has again moved away. For all that, it is a story worth telling.

one

IN THE BEGINNING

I n August of 1793, *The Gentleman's Magazine*, in its monthly digest of news from the provinces, reported an event of no little historical curiosity from Coventry.

Its correspondent 'Explorator' announced that he had two pots containing nearly 2,000 Roman coins, recently unearthed on the Bullester Field Farm in the neighbouring parish of Foleshill. And he went on to describe an earlier discovery, right in the heart of the old town: 'In the last summer the street in Coventry called Broadgate was opened to a depth of five or six feet when a regular pavement was discovered, and upon that pavement a coin of Nero.'

He added that it all gave further strength to his theory that a Roman road, linking the known Roman centres of Mancetter and Warwick, ran straight through where Coventry now stood. But could it also be evidence of a long-lost Roman settlement, from which the modern town of weaving and clock-making had sprung?

It appears not. More than 200 years later there is still no positive evidence of Roman occupation in what was to become Coventry. The pavement those eighteenth-century diggers discovered was almost certainly a floor of medieval origin and despite a string of finds by archaeologists, some made very recently indeed, proof that the Romans set up some kind of settlement in Coventry is still as frustratingly difficult to pin down as it ever was.

In some senses, this might seem surprising. In an area very close to the intersection of two major Roman roads – with Watling Street (now the A5) only nine miles away and the Fosse Way (A46) just six – we might expect there to be a settlement in such a well-watered and well-wooded area, where tradition suggests there had been an ancient trackway over the River Sherbourne, dating back into prehistoric times.

There's evidence nearby of occupation before the Romans arrived. A substantial settlement of fourteen Iron Age roundhouses was found on

Archaeologists working in Coventry city centre in 2006 found a Roman ditch. (Coventry City Council)

the University of Warwick campus, on the southern edge of the city, during work to lay a new university running track in 2002. The roundhouses probably dated from the third century BC.

What are believed to be boundary ditches from Romano-British farmsteads emerged from two further modern development sites to the east, during construction of the city's North-South Road (1987) and a new cinema site on the Cross Point business park (1991). As recently as 2006, archaeologists working on the Coventry University site off Priory Street in the city centre came across a ditch and scattered finds that might well have come from another farmstead.

However, the first-century Lunt Fort at Baginton, and the civilian settlement that grew up around it, are the only significant Roman remains to have been discovered in the immediate vicinity of Coventry. From the fort ramparts, reconstructed in the early 1970s, the modern city centre can be seen to the north, some four miles off.

The gateway of the Lunt Fort, reconstructed in the 1970s. (CV One/Coventry City Council)

First evidence of Roman occupation at Baginton began to emerge in the early 1930s, when extensive gravel-working around the edges of the village turned up large quantities of pottery, dating from the first to the third century, and other artefacts that suggested a military occupation there too.

Excavations in the summer of 1960 made the first discoveries of what turned out to be a sequence of military camps. The earliest of these are dated AD 60–61, when the Roman governor of Britain, Gaius Suetonius Paulinus, brought the rebellious Boudica, Queen of the Iceni, to her final reckoning.

That bloody and decisive engagement may well have taken place somewhere near Mancetter, more than twenty miles away at the northern edge of Warwickshire. It is believed that The Lunt was constructed by a unit of auxiliaries to deal with the many horses captured from the rebels by the victorious Roman army. Certainly the Gyrus, or horse-training corral, is its most important feature. No other quite like it has been found in the whole of the Roman Empire.

The Baginton Bowl. (Herbert Collections)

The Lunt was abandoned within twenty years, but the Roman army was back around AD 260 to build a further, short-lived fortification on the same site, and the civilian settlement that grew up around it continued long after the army had moved on.

It is that settlement that provides arguably the clearest archaeological link in this part of the country between the Roman and the Anglo-Saxon periods; the quarrying that churned up the village in the 1930s also disturbed an extensive Saxon cemetery, and bequeathed to us an extraordinary item found in one of the graves. The Baginton Bowl, a bronze hanging bowl dating from the sixth or seventh century and now on display in Coventry's Herbert Museum, is the most notable Saxon artefact so far discovered in Warwickshire.

Place names around what has become the modern city of Coventry suggest a steady advance for Saxon settlement right across the area. Allesley, Keresley, Corley and Binley, for example, are all Old English names, in notable contrast to Rugby and Princethorpe to the east, for instance, which betray clear Scandinavian roots.

The 'ley' word-endings of many of those Saxon place names, denoting a clearing in woodland, point to the looming presence of the legendary, now almost supernatural, Forest of Arden.

Coventry stands at the fault line between the great forest, stretching away to the west and north of the city, and the Feldon, a more open landscape of heath and rich pastureland to the south and east. There's evidence that Arden as a dense, continuous woodland, of the sort beloved by big screen outlaws, had already receded by Roman times, but the Saxon settlers and farmers who followed clearly still associated their new homeland with tree-clearing, and places like Allesley and Keresley are still classified as part of Coventry's ancient Arden landscape.

So where in all of this did the city itself get its name?

Over the past century of scholarship there have been a number of theories. At one time a connection with the Roman water goddess Coventina was thought likely. Another school of thought ascribed the name to a description of physical features of the site, principally a hillside and a cave.

But the balance of support has more recently settled around another sort of landscape feature – a tree employed either as a sacred object of veneration itself or as a boundary marker for lands held by a local Saxon landowner named Cofa.

While the use of trees as boundary markers was widespread in Saxon England, we have no idea who Cofa might have been. No information about

Woodland at Tile Hill, part of Coventry's ancient Arden landscape. (Chris Ross)

an individual who may be a key figure in the story of Coventry has come down to us. It is just another example of the shadowy nature of the city's beginnings.

Tradition, that long-established and widely quoted source that stands somewhere between rumour and evidence, identifies a female antecedent as the earliest known person with Coventry connections.

Her name was Osburga (or Osburg in modern parlance). She was in religious orders and one version of the story describes her as one of the famed sisters of Barking in Essex who left the security of their house around 675 to found other monastic settlements. She was later canonised.

Carved sandstone from an ecclesiastical building dated to around AD 1000. (Coventry City Council)

Osburga was abbess, it is said, of a nunnery established close to the River Sherbourne, somewhere in the Hill Top area of modern Coventry. This foundation, possibly with a small church included in it, was the earliest evidence of settlement in Coventry.

Reference to a nunnery at Coventry appears in some fly-leaf jottings on a bound set of anonymous sermons, dating from the late fourteenth century: 'In ancient times on the bank of the river called by the inhabitants Sherbourne, which flows right through the city of Coventry, there was formerly a monastery of young women dedicated to God.'

St Osburg herself remains an enigma, a virgin saint about whom very little is known, but the fate of her nunnery is perhaps a better known element of this old story. It was destroyed, the chroniclers wrote, in 1016 when a Danish army led by Cnut and the English traitor Eadric Streona ravaged Warwickshire.

Historically, this is not beyond the bounds of possibility. At that time Cnut was on the rampage in his ultimately successful campaign to seize the throne of England, and the Danes had long had a taste for pillaging monastic houses. Lying less than twenty miles from the Danelaw, the area of eastern and northern England over which the Danes had held sway since their treaty with Alfred the Great in 886, St Osburg's nunnery must have been at risk more than once in the dynastic struggles that erupted from time to time in this border country.

Another distant memory of those turbulent times may indeed have lingered on in the Hock Tuesday play, performed in Coventry on the second Tuesday after Easter from around 1416 until the early years of the seventeenth century. Traditionally, the play's origins are linked either to victory celebrations following a massacre of the Danes in England that took place in 1002, or to news of the death of the last Danish King of England, Harthacanute, in 1042.

There is no hard evidence that St Osburg's nunnery ever actually existed, but there are intriguing pointers as to some kind of ecclesiastical presence in the Hill Top area before the eleventh century.

A section of decorated sandstone moulding found in Palmer Lane in 1937, originally believed to be part of a free-standing cross, is now thought to be a door jamb or window moulding from an ecclesiastical building, dating from around the year 1000. A burial found during archaeological excavations (1999–2003) on the site of Coventry's first cathedral was carbon-dated to 875, while a second body discovered in a grave beneath the cloister has been dated to the tenth century.

St Osburg herself has certainly lingered in the city's collective memory. A shrine to her was established in the cathedral and her head, enclosed in copper and gilt, was listed as one of its most important relics. In 1408, the Bishop of Coventry and Lichfield, John Burghill, responding to public representations, commanded that her feast-day of 30 March was to be celebrated in the city.

Well beyond the Middle Ages, the name given to the marshy, riverine area now defined in the modern city as Pool Meadow was St Osburg's Pool, while the most central of Coventry's Catholic churches, with primary school attached, still bears her name.

The notion that St Osburg and her nuns were effectively Coventry's first identified citizens is contradicted by another long-held theory as to the city's origins. This argued that the first Saxon settlers established themselves, not around Hill Top, but on the other side of the river, on the south-facing slopes of Barr's Hill.

William Dugdale, the seventeenth-century Warwickshire antiquarian, firmly believed that this fledgling settlement lay on those slopes and had created Coventry's first church by the year 1003, named for St Nicholas. His was a view shared by many of the city's Victorian historians.

In fact, St Nicholas Church first appears in the records in 1183 and for much of its history it was a dependent chapel of Holy Trinity Church on Hill Top. By 1535, a full century before Dugdale was writing, St Nicholas was 'in decay and ruin' and within a generation had been turned into a store house. Exactly where the church stood is now open to conjecture, although human remains from its churchyard have regularly cropped up in successive waves of redevelopment since the nineteenth century.

An opportunity to test the tradition of early settlement on Barr's Hill came in 1965, when a cutting was driven into the hillside for an access road to serve Coventry's new inner ring road. But archaeologists found no evidence of human habitation whatsoever and it remains just another intriguing possibility.

The modest reckoning for Coventry in the Normans' great registry of interests, the Domesday survey, suggests that the place was scattered and rural in character at the time of the Conquest. It records a population of fifty villeins (tenants who could hold property but owed fealty, and service, to the local lord), twelve bordars (cottage holders who were often the younger sons of villeins) and seven serfs (little more than slaves) – with their families totalling around 300 people.

They were using twenty ploughs to work a significant area of arable land and they controlled a substantial area of woodland, covering about two square miles.

The consensus among historians now, however, profiles Coventry as a modest-sized settlement at the end of the Saxon period with a population of around 1,200, similar in size to the town of Warwick. There are plenty of towns known to exist at the time which do not feature at all in the Domesday survey. The ancient city of Winchester and even London itself are both examples, and the modern view is that Coventry was almost certainly the same, with merely the rural part of it recorded by inventory clerks.

There's some evidence that this settlement may have boasted a church too. In 1022, Archbishop Aethelnoth, while in Rome to be formally installed as Archbishop of Canterbury by Pope Benedict VIII, purchased a holy relic, the arm of St Augustine of Hippo. The chroniclers say that he paid 100 silver talents and one gold talent for it and, more importantly, that on his return to England he gave it to the church in Coventry.

Whether this was a church associated with St Osburg's nunnery or a later minster church established to serve the growing community remains a question that archaeologists might one day resolve.

However, there is no doubt that the earliest clear and unambiguous date in Coventry's history is the year 1043, when it is recorded that Leofric, Earl of Mercia, and his wife Godgifu (Godiva to us) dedicated a house of monks with the Benedictines in Coventry.

A sample from the Domesday Book. (THP)

Although they loom large in the story of early Coventry, neither Leofric nor Godiva could claim local antecedents. Godiva's origins remain obscure, although a fourteenth-century charter states that she was sister to Thorold, Sheriff of Lincolnshire, and if so may well have spent her early life in that part of eastern England. As a landowner she had extensive holdings in Warwickshire, including the fledgling Coventry.

History has downplayed the importance of Leofric in the story of eleventh-century England. He was one of the triumvirate of earls (Godwin of Wessex and Siward of Northumbria were the others) who held the ring in the turbulent years that followed the end of Danish rule in England in the early 1040s.

It was Leofric who represented stability when war threatened, backing King Edward the Confessor against the claims of the over-mighty Godwin, and somehow contriving to establish a truce which saw the Earl of Wessex and his family outlawed for a time, astonishingly without a drop of blood being spilt.

While he plays a subsidiary and brutish role in the story of his wife's legendary ride, Leofric's contemporaries regarded him rather differently. On his death in 1057, the eulogies described him as devout and illustrious, while the *Anglo-Saxon Chronicle* paid simple tribute to him as 'very wise in all matters, both religious and secular.'

Leofric was born, probably in the 990s, the third son of Leofwine, Ealdorman of the Hwicce, a Saxon tribal grouping who held sway over much of what is now

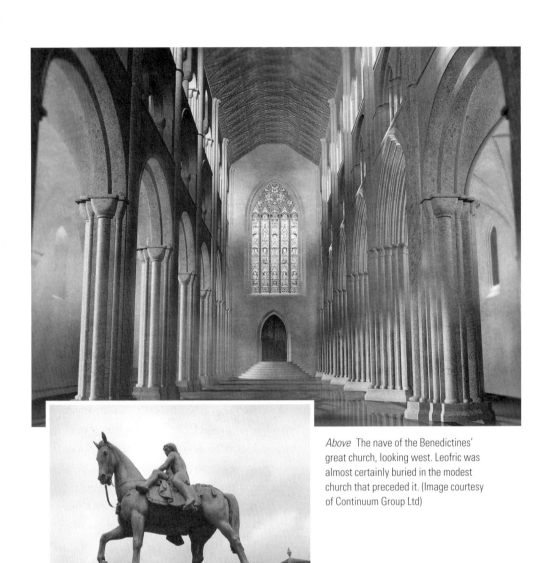

Above The nave of the Benedictines' great church, looking west. Leofric was almost certainly buried in the modest church that preceded it. (Image courtesy of Continuum Group Ltd)

Left Embodiment of a myth; the Godiva statue in Broadgate. (Chris Ross)

Worcestershire and south Warwickshire. Both his elder brothers died in war, the eldest, Northman, at the hands of the Danish warlord Cnut, on his way to seize the throne of England in 1017.

Yet it was the Dane to whom this shrewd and ambitious Saxon owed his advancement. Cnut clearly had a soft spot for Leofric, setting aside his usual practice of replacing Saxon nobility with Danes by making him Earl of Mercia around 1026.

When Cnut died in 1035, Leofric supported Harold Harefoot, the son of Cnut's first wife, against his half-brother Harthacnut. It is perhaps a sign of his gifts as a diplomat that he managed to hang on to the earldom when Harthacnut succeeded to the throne five years later.

Leofric faced a test of his loyalty within months when two royal tax-gatherers were set upon and killed by angry townsfolk in Worcester, right at the heart of his own family domain. An enraged Harthacnut ordered him to burn and pillage the town and there's every indication that he did – possibly accounting for the prominent reference to oppressive taxation in the later stories of Godiva's famous ride.

Ten years later, it was Leofric who devised a peaceful resolution when Earl Godwin threatened rebellion against Edward the Confessor. Despite some family troubles (his son Aelfgar was outlawed in 1055) he was still one of Edward's closest confidants when he died 'at a good old age' at his estate at Kings Bromley in Staffordshire in the early autumn of 1057.

He was buried, all the chroniclers agree, in a side chapel of his new abbey church of St Mary in Coventry, a foundation richly endowed with more than twenty estates, most in Warwickshire but as widely spread as Cheshire and Northamptonshire, and fabulously adorned with jewels and gold.

It may not have been the first time that Godiva had been widowed. There's some evidence, recorded in a twelfth-century history of Ely Abbey, that she had an earlier husband who was possibly an earlier Earl of Mercia. A persistent tradition also suggests that in the late 1020s she had had an illness from which she was not expected to recover. Could this have been the cause of her first husband's demise?

That she was beautiful and of a saintly disposition seems plausible – all the stories that emerged later agree on that point. And when she died ten years after Leofric, in September 1067, she made many bequests to churches, notably those possessing a shrine to the Virgin Mary of whose cult, a national obsession in the eleventh and twelfth centuries, she was a fervent follower.

That she rode through the town of Coventry naked, to rescue the townsfolk from taxes imposed by the 'grim Earl' her husband, is, however, myth.

The story, which emerged at the end of the twelfth century, owes something to the northern European pagan fertility rite that pairs in symbolic partnership a naked woman and a horse, and a lot more to inventive monks keen to promote their foundation and highlight the sanctity of this most appealing of benefactors.

Godiva's status (she was the only female Saxon landowner to be named in the Domesday survey) would not have

Image thought to be of Godiva from an early window in Holy Trinity Church, now lost. (Coventry City Council)

permitted her to make a public gesture of that kind, and in any event it is likely that she owned the estate on which the beginnings of Coventry were emerging and would therefore be entitled to any taxes raised there.

It is also true that Evesham was much closer to her heart than Coventry. The abbey there was where Godiva's friend and confessor, Aefic, had been Benedictine prior until his death in 1038. Although there is a tradition that her final resting place was a twin chapel alongside her husband's in their Coventry church, Evesham is where she almost certainly chose to be buried on her death in September 1067.

Almost 1,000 years later it is impossible to get any real idea of what Leofric and Godiva were like as people. A window image in painted glass from Holy Trinity Church in Coventry, now lost, was said to show him with a neat beard and short brown hair and her with long blonde tresses.

That Leofric could be the 'grim Earl' of popular imagining when he needed to be is self-evident. It went with power and high office in early medieval England. That Godiva, in her lifetime, acquired a reputation for good works and personal sanctity seems equally sure.

But even if they appear to us tantalisingly out of reach as real people, their decision to finance the Benedictines in establishing a house of monks at Coventry, and at the same time possibly re-founding an earlier church, was the catalyst that kick-started the place's rise to fame and prosperity.

As the Benedictine chronicler John of Worcester, writing nearly 100 years later, put it:

He [Leofric] and his wife, the noble Countess Godgifu, a worshipper of God and devout lover of Mary, ever-virgin, built the monastery there from the foundations out of their patrimony, and endowed it adequately with lands and made it so rich in various ornaments that in no monastery in England might be found the abundance of gold, silver, gems and precious stones that was at that time in its possession.

THE GODIVA MYTH

The story of Godiva's legendary ride first appears in an account by the chronicler Roger of Wendover at the end of the twelfth century, almost 150 years after her death. It begins:

> The Countess Godiva, who was a great lover of God's Mother, longing to free the town of Coventry from heavy bondage from the oppression of a heavy toll, often with urgent prayers besought her husband, that from regard to Jesus Christ, and his mother, he would free the town from that service, and all other heavy burdens.

It goes on to describe Leofric's exasperated challenge, that she should ride naked from one end of the market place to the other, and follows that with a brief description of Godiva letting down her long hair, mounting her horse and, accompanied by two knights, riding through the market place with only her bare legs showing.

Once the ride had been completed, it went on, her astonished husband gave her what she wanted and confirmed it with a charter.

The last few words are significant. The story, which has many factual holes in it, may well have been planted in the mind of the chronicler by the monks of Coventry's Benedictine priory, who at the time had been forced into exile by the monk-hating bishop, Hugh Nonant. And they were experts at forging charters to protect their own interests.

Peeping Tom, the hapless tailor struck blind for daring to take a peep at those long white legs, was a sixteenth-century invention, but the legend of saintly Godiva, freeing the townsfolk from an unjust tax levied by her husband, became embedded in Coventry imaginations. She featured regularly in the

Above A stained-glass image from the west window of the Benedictine's great cathedral. Could this be Godiva? (Image courtesy of Continuum Group Ltd)

Left Godiva and Leofric in anguished discussion, from a 1902 painting by Frank Albert Philips. (Herbert Art Gallery)

La Milo in Lady Godiva Procession Coventry, 1907.

The 1907 Godiva procession, the biggest of them all. (Author's Collection)

Great Fair processions of the late Middle Ages, although another character from local myth, the dragon-slaying patron saint, St George, took precedence.

It wasn't until 1678 that Godiva herself stepped centre stage with her own procession. This was dreamed up by commercial interests in the town, who wished to give a boost to visitor numbers in the face of an emerging Birmingham. She was played that year by a boy, the young son of one James Swinnerton, but by the nineteenth century the role was often taken by actresses, whose enthusiasm for the part among the ribaldry of the crowds often brought out senior clergy in a rash of condemnation.

Alfred Lord Tennyson went back to the chaste Godiva for his poem 'Godiva', written after he had made a railway excursion to Coventry in the early 1840s. Words from his poem were used on the imposing statue of Godiva, unveiled by the wife of the United States Ambassador to Britain in Broadgate in 1949.

More recently, the good lady has given her name to the Godiva Festival and to Godiva's Day, which falls on 10 September, the supposed date of her death in 1067. Godiva's Day celebrates selfless compassion and social justice, themes that still resonate in the modern world.

In 2012 she was brought to life as a twenty-foot high animatronic figure, making her way, by cycle-power, to London for the Olympic Games. There she represented the West Midlands region in the cultural Olympiad under the banner of Godiva Awakes.

The myth endures.

two

THE EARLY TOWN

Whatever the true scale of Coventry at the time of the Domesday Book, we know almost nothing about the lives of people we might characterise as early Coventrians. The records of how those villeins, cottagers and their families scraped a living from the land in their small settlement in the centre of England in the early years of Norman rule are simply not there.

We don't even know whether they resisted the imposition of what must have seemed like a brutal and alien regime. Leicester, only twenty miles away, lost many of its Saxon buildings after making a stand against the Norman takeover but, although the Conqueror himself was said to have passed through Coventry on his way from Warwick to Nottingham in 1068, there's no evidence that he had to put down an uprising as he did so.

There are reasons for the absence of documentary evidence. Coventry seems to have been particularly unlucky, or neglectful, in preserving the written record of its early history. The dissolution of the monasteries, which tore the heart out of the Tudor town, destroyed huge quantities of its earlier records.

A catastrophic fire in Birmingham Library archives in 1879 and Second World War bomb damage compounded these losses, and it has to be said that preservation of heritage has not always been a top priority with those who have ruled the modern city. So much has been lost from the early archive that serious scholarship now is too often reduced to informed speculation.

More importantly, Coventry's rise to become one of England's most powerful medieval towns happened fast and late. The boom town of the late fourteenth century was only just beginning to make its mark on England by the middle of the thirteenth century.

While other, much older, Midlands towns like Leicester and Worcester had already established a rich and stable archive in which their post-Conquest development can be clearly plotted, there is an echoing void where Coventry is concerned. As the

Victoria County History of Warwickshire somewhat snootily put it, 'there is little evidence for the social history of Coventry before the fourteenth century.'

Life in the late eleventh-century town remains largely a shadow play – except for the raucous, and to our eyes astonishing, chapter of conflict around the institution that Leofric and Godiva established with twenty-four monks and an abbot living under the rule of St Benedict.

Politics could well have played a role in the choice of Coventry in the first place – it clearly suited Leofric to establish a presence in a corner of Mercia fairly distant from his own power base. But it pales to nothing compared to the poisonous power struggle that erupted between the Benedictine monks of Coventry and the bishops to whom they were supposed to bow the knee in fealty.

The dispute had its origins in a new Anglo-Norman administration that favoured a clearly defined see, or diocese, in the charge of a bishop rather than a monastic foundation, however powerful and well-endowed. Coventry, because of its geographical location, fell into the Mercian see, with its episcopal centre located at Lichfield.

In the year 1075, Lanfranc, Archbishop of Canterbury, pursuing a further policy of moving episcopal sees out of villages into towns, ordered that the Mercian see should be moved from Lichfield to Chester, a much bigger town whose foundations had originally been laid by the old Roman legionary fortress.

Enter the first real villain in Coventry's story, the rapacious Robert de Limesey, a former chaplain to William the Conqueror with powerful connections to the heart of government who was consecrated Bishop of Chester in 1086.

The wealth of Coventry's Benedictine abbey – its manors alone were valued at £80 – caught de Limesey's acquisitive eye early. Before his death in 1089, Archbishop Lanfranc had felt cause to warn the bishop about his treatment of the monks in Coventry, ordering him to relieve the burdens he had imposed on them and restore what he had taken from them. He had been accused of breaking into the monks' dormitory by force, with armed men at his back, wrenching open their strong box and stealing the contents as well as horses and other goods.

But worse was to come. As the seat of his bishopric, Chester proved rather too close to the troublesome Welsh Marches for de Limesey's comfort, and in 1102 he petitioned Pope Paschal II in person to move the see back to the Midlands – not to Lichfield, described as a poor sort of place with a poor sort of church, but to the growing town of Coventry.

The success of this petition turned the Abbey of St Mary into a cathedral. This represented something of an instant demotion for the Benedictines in

Coventry, as their abbot (the first of whom had been Leofwine, thought to have been a nephew of Earl Leofric) immediately became prior, an office with somewhat less power and prestige. On top of that, they now had to come to terms with Coventry's first Anglo-Norman bishop, a man they already had cause to complain about, setting up his power base right on their doorstep.

The twelfth-century chronicler and historian William of Malmesbury, admittedly himself a Benedictine monk, did not mince words in his judgement of de Limesey. The bishop, he charged, was an embezzler who had stolen treasures from the abbey church, scraping, from one beam supporting a shrine, silver worth a staggering 500 marks (at a time when a mark was worth two-thirds of a pound).

Instead of restoring sagging roofs, he had allowed abbey buildings to collapse, spending money on projects of his own, possibly including a new bishop's palace. He had fed the monks inferior victuals and deprived them of learning so that they were unable to oppose his wishes.

Whatever the truth of these allegations, de Limesey clearly came from that branch of the Anglo-Norman clergy who believed that a comfortable life in this world was no disqualification from salvation in the next.

When he died in 1117, his bishopric was left vacant for four years, in what may well have been a deliberate move on the part of the king to harvest its lucrative rents, but which also gave the monks a well-earned rest from episcopal oppression.

For the ordinary folk of this modest place called Coventry, the arrival of the Benedictines in 1043 had been a milestone in the development of their town.

While other abbeys like Evesham managed to safeguard their records, details from the daily lives of the Benedictines in Coventry have been lost. All we know is how they looked, in a description set down by one of Coventry's later historians: 'A black coat, loose and divided down to their heels with a cowl or hood that is shorter than others use. Underneath a white woollen coat a hair shirt, with boots to the knees and heads shaved with a razor on top, called a corona.'

Ordinis Benedictini Monachus.

A Benedictine monk from the eleventh century. (Courtesy of the Thomas Fisher Rare Book Library, University of Toronto)

Their impact, however, was immense. The presence of the abbey, with its wealth and important seigneurial connections, immediately elevated Coventry in importance. Pilgrims were attracted to its shrine of St Osburg, while the monks, their officials and servants provided a ready market for the rural and farming part of the settlement, so carefully inventoried in the Domesday Book.

A triangular-shaped market place, some 150 metres long by 100 wide, was established outside the abbey gates, at which local folk could buy and sell their produce. At the time, Warwickshire appears to have had few markets beyond the old town of Warwick, so the new market would have enticed traders and customers from a fair distance around. The foundations for Coventry's commercial prosperity were being laid.

While the Benedictines had been instrumental in kick-starting the growth of an identifiable, urban Coventry, it was another Anglo-Norman force, this time secular, that gave it real acceleration.

Hugh d'Avranches, first Earl of Chester, nicknamed Lupus ('The Wolf'), acquired the estates once held by Godiva after, it was said, rallying to the cause of the Conqueror's son and heir, William Rufus, when rebellion threatened at the beginning of his reign in 1087.

Neither Hugh, his son Richard, nor grandson Ranulf I, paid much attention to Coventry, a small and insignificant land-holding in a fiefdom that ranged right across England and northern France. But the fourth earl, Ranulf II, who succeeded to the earldom in 1129, took a very different view.

Ranulf was, in the words of one chronicler, 'a consummate warrior, glittering with arms' whose exploits on the battlefield regularly found their way into popular street ballads. As a military man, he had a keen sense of strategy and no doubt saw the fledgling Coventry as very much part of his family's future, in large part, perhaps, because it lay in a fertile and peaceful area, well away from the troubled frontier country of his chief power base in England, Chester.

The instinct to build was always very strong in the Normans, and a castle would have been among Ranulf's first priorities, possibly as early as 1130. Initially it would have been a motte-and-bailey, little more than a defended mound, although exactly where it was and whether in time it became a more recognisable stone fortification is one of those Coventry uncertainties that still divide students of the place's history.

It certainly bequeathed to us place names in the centre of modern Coventry that are clearly associated with some kind of castle-building: Broadgate,

Bayley Lane, Castle Yard and even Hay Lane, from 'haeg' meaning enclosure rather than grass cut to feed livestock.

Archaeological excavations over the past forty years have repeatedly come across evidence of a network of twelfth-century defensive ditches that enclosed an area of up to seven acres and were up to six metres deep in places. The remains of a bakehouse discovered in what is now called Castle Yard, close to Hay Lane, have been linked to the castle, lying just inside the outer bailey or defensive perimeter.

With the important Norman strongholds of Warwick and Kenilworth so close, whatever Ranulf built was going to be modest in scale. The chronicler John Stowe, writing more than 400 years later, somewhat dismissively records the tradition that the earls of Chester had 'a fortlet, or pile standing in the Earle's Street' which had long since decayed.

A corner of modern day Castle Yard where archaeologists have found evidence of a castle bakehouse. (Mark Radford)

But the true significance of Ranulf's castle-building is that it signals his intention to take a stake in this place called Coventry.

He also seems to have erected a small chapel, later rebuilt in the fourteenth century as the imposing St Michael's Church, on the northern edge of his bailey. This was very close to the Benedictines' monastic boundary and their own small chapel, first recorded in 1113 and also later reconstructed as Holy Trinity Church.

With hindsight, this looks like the opening gambit in the struggle between the prior's half and the earl's half of the town that seems to dominate Coventry's pre-fourteenth-century history. Whether that struggle was as hostile and all-encompassing as historians have liked to characterise is open to doubt. But the reality of a new and powerful player in town must have troubled the Benedictines, who were, if nothing else, generally allergic to competition.

The hated Bishop de Limesey, for all his depredations, had almost certainly begun building work on the eastern end of the great cathedral church of St Mary, which was to replace the modest church of Leofric and Godiva's time by the end of the century. The monks had also been quick to protect their position with a series of forged charters that gave them, in the name of the saintly Godiva, full rights to trade, free from outside interference, whether bishop or earl.

For the townsfolk, the presence of such powerful competing interests must have offered the prospect of lasting prosperity, particularly as it had begun to give Coventry a regional and possibly even national profile as an emerging boom town.

Their hopes must have been considerably enhanced by a charter, formally confirmed by Henry II at Marlborough in early 1182, essentially re-stating an earlier grant of liberties issued by Ranulf, possibly as early as the 1140s.

In it, the earl states that the burgesses in Coventry may hold their property in free burgage, allowing them to pass it on to their heirs, with all the laws and customs that the citizens of Lincoln enjoy, and that they should have their own court (portmanmote) in which to settle disputes between themselves and the earl.

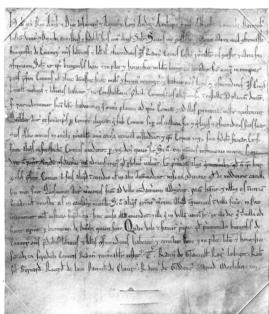

Furthermore, they would be able to elect one of their number to represent them in their dealings with the earl, they would have the right to bring before the court errant merchants and could expect security for any loans made to the earl or his men. Finally, newcomers to the town should be free of charges and taxes for two years, from the date they started building.

The formal and legalistic language of the time perhaps obscures the remarkable nature of this charter. In effect, it marks the beginnings of civic

Henry II's charter of 1182, confirming Ranulf's earlier grant of liberties. (Herbert Collections)

government for Coventry. The villeins of the Domesday survey, unfree tenants who owed their feudal lord military and agricultural service at his command, were now free men holding property in their own right, with their own town court and protection in their dealings with the earl.

The rights held by their equivalents in Lincoln, then England's fourth biggest town and another of the earl's principal estates, were to be the benchmark, as this Coventry charter would be in turn for other towns like Nottingham.

Perhaps most importantly, the lifting of all taxes for newcomers is a clear incentive for growth, aimed at encouraging inward investment from an expanded mercantile class. There is evidence that Coventry's population showed a marked increase around the middle of the twelfth century, and the Earl of Chester was clearly a principal promoter of it.

Sadly, just when these newly enfranchised burgesses could expect the benefits of this liberality to come rolling in, they found themselves caught up in the civil war, later dubbed the Anarchy, between Henry I's daughter Matilda and her cousin, Stephen, Count of Mortain.

As Henry's only surviving legitimate offspring, Matilda had a compelling claim to the throne. Through her mother, she also had Anglo-Saxon royal blood running through her veins, a distinction that her enemies among the Norman nobility were quick to seize upon, contemptuously dubbing her Godiva.

Stephen, Henry's favourite nephew, could not match his cousin's claim to the throne, but he was an energetic and capable soldier, widely admired for his intelligence and generous disposition. And he was a man. Many of the most influential Anglo-Norman magnates simply could not countenance the thought of England ruled by a woman.

Stephen struck the first blow, arranging to have himself crowned king at Winchester in December 1135, and by 1140 the cat-and-mouse game he was playing with Matilda, all shifting alliances, skirmishes and feints, was reaching something of a crunch.

At which point, Ranulf, Earl of Chester, having weighed carefully the strength of the competing parties, declared for Matilda. He laid siege to Lincoln Castle, overwhelmed it by a ruse – he sent his wife in to greet the lady of the house and then ambushed the guard when allowed in to 'collect' her – and finally captured Stephen when he arrived to lift the siege in early February 1141.

Stephen was to remain Matilda's prisoner for most of that year, but as the tide slowly turned in his favour he was freed in a prisoner-exchange deal and Matilda found herself repeatedly under threat of capture.

In the two years that followed, a war of siege and counter-siege among the fortified towns and castles of southern England left Stephen clinging precariously to the throne, without either side being able to land a decisive blow. And it was something of a side-show when in September 1144 one of Stephen's supporters in the Midlands, Robert Marmion, Earl of Tamworth, decided to attack Ranulf's Coventry castle.

Marmion, the war-like scion of a proud military family, once champions to the dukes in their native Normandy, seized the partly

Engraving of King Stephen being taken prisoner. (THP)

constructed buildings of the new cathedral, booted out the monks and turned what was a building site into a fortified camp from which to besiege Ranulf's own castle, literally no more than a stone's throw away.

As the outraged Benedictine chronicler William of Malmesbury put it:

> Robert Marmion, a ferocious and war-like man, almost unequalled for astuteness and audacity in his time, profaned the noble church (of Coventry) by locking out the servants of God and introducing to it the hired hands of the Devil, and he harassed the Earl of Chester, to whom he was particularly opposed, with frequent, heavy attacks.

So astute a soldier was Marmion that he managed to forget where he had placed some new defensive ditches. While riding out on a solo reconnaissance, he fell into one and was unhorsed. Rendered helpless by a broken thigh, he was promptly dispatched with a knife by a humble foot soldier (or even, one tradition says, a cobbler).

Centuries later, a detached skull discovered in an early archaeological excavation of the site was immediately proclaimed to be his. But the truth is that his body was taken away and buried at Polesworth in north Warwickshire, interred in unconsecrated ground as he had been excommunicated for his crimes against the Church.

The man himself may have come to a grisly end, but his small force of besiegers did manage to eject Ranulf from his castle. We have no first-hand account of how the fighting affected the townspeople – although there is evidence from a later charter that places of refuge were created for the poor 'during the hostilities' – but the incident must have been a setback to their hopes of a steady, and peaceful, rise to prosperity.

For Ranulf, losing his castle had clearly been a humiliation, but it wasn't until 1147 that he felt himself strong enough to seize it back. *The Gesta Stephani*, King Stephen's official history, described, in its usual highly partisan way, his attempts to starve out its defenders and then beat off the king himself, who had come to their rescue:

> And in front of the castle of Coventry, whither the King's men had withdrawn, the Earl himself fortified a castle and valorously checked their sorties over the country until the King arrived, escorted by a fine and numerous body of knights, gave the garrison fresh supplies, of which they were in the greatest need, and fought a number of engagements with the Earl, who had laid ambushes for him at the most difficult points in his journey... The King joined battle with the Earl and when a great many had been captured and not a few wounded, and the Earl himself put to shameful flight and almost killed, he at length obtained the surrender of the Earl's castle and demolished it.

Almost certainly, what was actually demolished was the temporary siege castle Ranulf had erected to help him mount an offensive against his own fortification. And seven years later, with Matilda, Stephen and Ranulf himself all dead, the new king Henry II returned estates and castles, including Coventry, to the earls of Chester.

After the destruction and uncertainties of the civil war, the 1150s would prove a more tranquil, productive decade for the people of Coventry, and the arrival of a significant new commercial force would help to usher in a period of rapid growth for the town.

In the year 1150, the Cistercian order, founded some fifty years earlier in France, established the beginnings of an abbey at Coombe, five miles east of Coventry. Four years later they added another at Stoneleigh, four miles to the south of the town.

The Cistercians were an austere offshoot of the Benedictine order, clad in white, rather than black, who preferred a life of manual labour and

self-sufficiency to the growing worldly sophistication of their mother order. They deliberately chose somewhat remote locations for their abbeys and kept themselves to themselves. But they possessed one great attribute that could unlock the key to real wealth in the early Middle Ages – they were *the* great experts at farming sheep.

As the two abbeys began to establish an almost industrial production line in wool, they needed a market through which to sell it, and Coventry was perfectly placed. Their arrival, it might be argued, was the single most important event in Coventry's early commercial history and one that set it on the path to becoming one of England's richest and biggest towns.

The place itself seems to have recovered quickly from the civil war. Until recently it was thought that Ranulf's charter, conferring its crucial liberties, applied just to those men living in his 'half' of the town, and it is certainly the case that the area he controlled grew more quickly in population. But now the consensus among historians is that the charter applied to all Coventry men of standing, those in the prior's half as well.

The Benedictine priors themselves, however, were not idle. The shrewd and powerful Prior Laurence, who was elected to the post in 1149 and remained in it for thirty years, also has a good claim to be regarded as one of the key founders of early Coventry.

Prior Laurence recommended work on the great cathedral church and in 1155 gave land 'between the bridges' (or Burges, as we know it now) on which

The fourteenth-century chapel of the Hospital of St John, now better known as the Old Grammar School and soon to be restored. (Chris Ross)

to build the Hospital of St John, 'for the reception and relief of indigent and infirm persons'.

The hospital, whose fourteenth-century chapel remarkably survives to this day as one of the city centre's oldest standing buildings, was the first institution to undertake active social welfare work in Coventry. It was to have a staff of ten, both men and women, offering temporary relief and lodging for poor wayfarers and permanent relief for up to twenty poor folk in Coventry who were old and sick.

The prior gave a gift of money to support it, but the moving spirit behind the actual building of the hospital was Edmund, Archdeacon of Coventry, a senior member of the bishop's staff and therefore traditionally someone who might have been regarded as an enemy of the Benedictines.

Between them, these two men founded an institution that says a lot about the condition of Coventry at the time. The town had become big enough, and of sufficient interest to visitors and those engaged in trade, to warrant such a hospital. It was also an all-too-rare example of priory and cathedral clergy working together in the interests of a wider Coventry.

Unfortunately, customary hostilities were to be resumed before too long. In 1121, four years after the death of the hated de Limesey, Robert Peche became the next Bishop of Coventry. He died only five years later, leaving few traces on the record but becoming the first to be buried within the developing cathedral precincts.

His successor, Roger de Clinton, the nephew of a powerful adviser to Henry I, was a strong supporter of King Stephen during the civil war. He was bishop when Robert Marmion, another of Stephen's supporters, attacked Ranulf, Earl of Chester's castle.

De Clinton, despite his personal loyalties, had already had dealings with Ranulf. Around the year 1140 he had issued a licence for the earl to build a small chapel on another of his estates a few miles to the east of Coventry. As the church of St Mary Magdalen, now in the Wyken area of the city, it still stands, and is the oldest standing structure in Coventry.

A very military sort of bishop, De Clinton died at Antioch on the Second Crusade in 1149. The next holder of the office, Walter Durdent, had actually been a Benedictine monk and immediately faced opposition to his appointment from the order's traditional enemies, the secular canons of Lichfield and Chester.

The church of St Mary Magdalen, Coventry's oldest standing structure. (Chris Ross)

In 1152, with his fellow Benedictine, Prior Laurence, at his side, he travelled to Rome to seek an audience with Pope Eugene III in an attempt to consolidate his authority. The Pope accepted his arguments and decreed that the episcopal chair should remain at Coventry, rather than being moved, as the canons wanted, to Lichfield.

Richard Peche, who succeeded Durdent as bishop in 1161, was probably the son of the earlier incumbent, Robert Peche. He was an able administrator, spending much of his twenty-one years in office restoring the diocese's finances to health, before retiring shortly before his death in late 1182.

His successor, Gerard la Pucelle, was a scholar and master of canon law who had been a member of Thomas Becket's entourage and was renowned for his skills as a diplomat. He might have been able to repair the fragile relationship between the Benedictines and the diocese, but died after just a year in office. Some said he was poisoned, but in reality he was probably just overcome by age. He was the last Bishop of Coventry to be buried in the developing cathedral.

The man who followed him was every Benedictine's nightmare come true. Canterbury-educated Hugh Nonant had also been in public service, as a diplomat in the service of Henry II, and although appointed in 1185, was unable to take up his duties in Coventry until 1188 as he was on royal diplomatic business abroad.

Nonant was almost certainly given the bishop's mitre as a reward for his service and was quite happy to buy his way into power and influence, purchasing the offices of Sheriff in Warwickshire, Leicestershire and Staffordshire and acquiring the rights and possessions of the Coventry Priory by paying the new king, Richard I, a bribe of 300 marks for his Crusader war chest.

As if this wasn't enough, Nonant was a man with a hatred of monks that bordered on the pathological. 'I call my clerks [the canons of Lichfield] gods and the monks demons,' he was reputed to have said, vowing that if he had his own way he would 'strip every cowled head in England'. He also declared his intention of moving his episcopal chair from Coventry to Lichfield and began calling himself Bishop of Coventry and Lichfield.

There was bound to be trouble and before long Nonant was accused of breaking into the priory with armed men and ejecting the monks, installing a community of canons from Lichfield in their place and giving away priory property as bribes for papal officials to turn a blind eye to what he was doing.

Nonant claimed that he had been physically assaulted by the monks, attacked and smashed over the head with a crucifix during a struggle in the cathedral itself.

And then there was the story that while supervising the continuing building works on the great church, he had narrowly escaped being brained by a huge block of stone that had mysteriously dislodged itself from a high wall above, killing a young monk standing next to him.

The monks, he claimed, had been 'contaminated with secular pollution' and he did manage to secure papal support for moves to expel them. But when he tried to persuade other bishops to mount a coordinated campaign against their own monastic chapters, his proposal fell on deaf ears.

When King Richard left England to join the Third Crusade, the duplicitous Nonant promptly switched his allegiance to his brother John, becoming an active participant in John's bid to seize power. Richard was taken prisoner on his way home from the Crusade, but returned to England after being ransomed in 1194, at which point Nonant was put on trial with other supporters of John. It cost him a huge fine of 5,000 marks to clear his name and have his bishop's seat returned to him.

Two years later, he retired to the Abbey of Bec in Normandy, ironically one of the greatest Benedictine houses in France, where he made his peace with the order, begging for forgiveness and repenting of a list of sins so long, it was said, that nobody could be found to absolve him. He died in March 1198, after a long and painful illness, thoroughly merited in the eyes of vengeful Benedictine chroniclers.

By that time, the monks in Coventry had reclaimed their priory and enjoyed a better relationship with Nonant's successor, Geoffrey de Muschamp, who held the post until October 1208. However, de Muschamp was buried at Lichfield when he died, a significant choice of final resting place that showed that Nonant's preference for Lichfield had stuck. The diocese was to remain double-centred until 1837 when it was split up and Coventry as the junior partner was transferred into the diocese of Worcester.

While work continued on the impressive new cathedral church, time was running out for another of growing Coventry's landmarks, the Earl of Chester's modest castle.

In 1173 the fifth earl, Hugh Kevelioc, in true family fashion, had joined a rebellion against the formidable Henry II triggered by the simmering resentments of his princeling sons, young Henry, Richard and Geoffrey. The king, with an army of professional mercenaries at his command, had little trouble in subduing the rebels and captured Earl Hugh in the process, shuttling him as a prisoner between Normandy and England for the next two years, while he decided whether to execute him or purchase his loyalty.

The Benedictines' great cathedral church as it might have appeared, dominating the early town. (Image courtesy of Continuum Group Ltd)

Luckily for Hugh, he decided on the latter. The earl received back his estates in England and went on to serve Henry on campaign in Ireland. But one of the prices he paid for this leniency was to have his castle at Coventry slighted, or damaged beyond reasonable repair.

At this point, the castle begins to slip away into history – within fifty years the earls had built a new base for their activities locally, Cheylesmore Manor, and the original fortification almost certainly quickly slid into ruin. There is, however, one odd footnote to its story.

In 1569, at a time of yet another baronial revolt, this time in the north of England, Elizabeth I decided to move the captive Mary, Queen of Scots, further south and settled on Coventry. Her first suggestion, in an imperious letter to the mayor announcing that Mary would be sent to Coventry (and they had better look after her!) was that she should be incarcerated in the castle. Monarchs have long, if not always very accurate, memories!

For the townsfolk, Hugh's involvement in this struggle between powerful people over distant causes was a serious setback. The slighting of the castle laid a cloak of suspicion over the whole town. Fines were levied on the citizens for trying to conceal from confiscation lands that belonged to the King's enemies, and it eventually cost them the sizeable sum of 200 marks to recover their fragile liberties from the Crown.

Hugh Kevelioc had left one positive legacy to Coventry by the time of his death in 1181 – a leper hospital and chapel built, as practice decreed, well away from the fledgling town, to the west. It was said that Hugh was prompted to do this out of sympathy for a knight in his household, William de Anneye, who had contracted the terrifying disease. He also paid for a priest to pray for the souls of the lepers, living or dead, and for men and women to look after them.

Dedicated to St Mary Magdalen, we know roughly where the hospital was from the suburb still known as Chapelfields that later grew up around it, but all traces of it have disappeared. What might have been statuary and decorative stonework from its buildings ended up in the garden of at least one of Coventry's nineteenth-century mayors and has now been lost, a depressing state of affairs that has happened far too many times in the city's post-medieval history.

If the ecclesiastical buildings in the emerging Coventry were built in stone, its domestic buildings were still generally constructed of wood. The town at this time was little more than an intersection of two straggling streets lined with wooden houses, but it was already beginning to develop some recognizable features of the city that it was to become.

From the market outside the gates of the rising cathedral church, Bishop Street struck north over the River Sherbourne to head up rising ground towards what is now Barr's Hill and on to Tamworth and Lichfield. Further south, on an east-west axis, the beginnings of Gosford Street and Spon Street flanked a central area, dominated by Smithford Street (the king's highway) and the street called Earl Street. By the 1180s the boundaries of the future city centre were already being laid, even if the buildings that lined these streets were still fairly primitive in scale and appearance.

The people who lived in them still laboured on the land; the imprint of oxen hooves from ploughing, laid on the ground more than 100 years after this period, has been found under fourteenth-century buildings in Gosford Street, less than 300 metres from Broadgate.

Yet they were starting to acquire other skills, and it is in the second half of the twelfth century that these new Coventrians, the ordinary folk of the town, begin to make their appearance in the records.

Bishop Street in 1913, showing its course up rising ground from the cathedral. (David Fry)

Among the first is Liulf de Brinklow, who in the 1150s is recorded as holding properties in Coventry in free burgage under charter from the Earl of Chester, for which he paid half a mark a year. He was granted the rights to two messuages (or dwellings) by the earl's constable, Eustace Fitzjohn.

From his name, Liulf was clearly an immigrant drawn into the growing town from nearby Warwickshire, persuasive evidence that early attempts to attract new inward investors to the town were working. He may have been a minor official working for the Earl of Chester, as his name appears as a witness to two of the earl's charters. More importantly, he was in Coventry to stay. By the 1220s, his family had acquired a substantial urban estate of fifteen messuages and a chamber. Within thirty years, their main tenement in Earl Street – already the smartest part of town – was known as the hall of Nicholas Liulf, his descendant.

Others were settling close to the market area. In a transaction from the year 1200, Alice de Corly is recorded as the owner of a messuage 'before the door of the Prior of Coventry'. We know nothing more of Alice, although she was plainly, from her surname, another immigrant to the growing town.

The market itself was developing, more permanent wooden structures replacing makeshift shelters that had done service as stalls for a growing number of traders attracted from some distance around. There's some evidence too that separate timber and cattle markets were established in Bishop Street and Cook Street by the year 1203, and that the first of Coventry's mills, Hill Mill, was already operating, fed by the Radford Brook close to what is now Naul's Mill Park.

Another construction project, the building of a road, West Orchard, directly from the prior's gate west to link up with the King's Highway, is possibly the development mentioned in a Pipe Roll of 1203.

A further Pipe Roll entry from this time indicates that enterprising townsfolk were already beginning to turn wool into cloth. It records that under a Royal Statute of 1196, the men of Coventry had to pay a 'fine' for their cloth-making – not a punishment but a levy that exempted them from the legal requirement that all cloth should be woven to a prescribed breadth (one and three quarter yards). In the interests of speed, weavers preferred to weave much narrower cloth.

Coventry's levy was £5, not one of the largest in England but nearly twice what the town of Warwick paid. The cloth in the Pipe Roll is referred to as 'panni tincti' (dyed cloths) which was of high quality. It is almost certainly the first reference to the emphasis on quality that was to make Coventry's fortune in the years to come.

The commercial life of the town received a further boost in 1218, when the men of the earl's half were granted the right to hold an eight-day fair and market, effectively the beginnings of what later became the famous Coventry Great Fair. In 1227, not to be outdone, the Benedictine prior Geoffrey purchased from the king the right to hold his own annual three-day fair in Coventry in early October.

By this time the industrial machine that was Cistercian sheep farming was whirring away at full pelt. Among the founding gifts for the abbey at Coombe in 1150 had been sandstone quarries at Harnall, now Hillfields, to the north of the Benedictine prior's half of the growing town.

By 1224, the monks had used that stone to complete their church and conventual buildings and were already taking a substantial stake as property owners in Coventry. Cistercian rule allowed its adherents to make a living out of only two things – farming and property – and by the 1250s the records show that the monks of Coombe owned around fifty properties, almost all of them in the earl's half, close to the 'enterprise zone' of Earl Street.

They were the biggest extra-mural investor in the town and had crafted a close working partnership with the emerging class of merchants who could market their wool, setting aside the order's traditionally uneasy relationship with towns.

The people they were keen to deal with were now taking on surnames that reflected the trades and crafts they were practising, alongside the ancestral agricultural activities of their forebears. The early records, from around 1200 onwards, name Ralph the weaver, Alexander the quareur (quarry-man), Pagan the miller, Ailwin le furner (charcoal-burner) and John le brocher (thatcher), among others.

They also put names to early Coventrians who were engaged in providing what might be described as the finer things in life – Adam le vinetur (vintner or wine merchant) and Geoffrey the goldsmith.

For the town to boast a goldsmith, there must already have been personal wealth to justify his business. Coventry's golden age was just beginning to dawn.

FROM THE BACKS OF SHEEP

A monastic drain, hidden for centuries, has provided the earliest evidence of the industry that made Coventry one of medieval England's most important towns.

Archaeologists working at Coombe Abbey in the 1990s uncovered a drain still partially clogged with limescale, soap-based carbonates and lanolin, all from the washing of fleeces.

The Cistercian monks who founded the abbey at Coombe in 1150 were sheep farmers of unrivalled expertise, but theirs was not the only monastic order to see potential wealth in wool.

The Benedictines at Coventry Priory were also substantial producers, managing huge flocks of sheep on their granges, or farms, in the countryside surrounding the emerging town. And it was to Coventry that these monastic producers naturally turned for a market in which to sell their raw product.

Most sheep in England at the time possessed coats of short-stapled wool, tangled and fluffy, and Warwickshire wool was prized for its quality. Until the 1250s, the trade in wool, with fleeces being exported all over England and even abroad, dominated Coventry's commercial life, making fortunes for many of the families involved.

But by 1200 the making of cloth was already on the increase, its techniques almost certainly introduced into Coventry by immigrants from the eastern counties of England, where skills had been learned from the Continent. The town's first full-time textile workers were probably servants, working for the monastic houses or for the Earls of Chester.

The trade received a huge boost early in the fourteenth century when the purchase of cloth for the Royal Wardrobe was switched from abroad to domestic markets, notably Coventry's.

By 1345, the incorporation year for Coventry, a drapery (or market hall for the assessment and sale of cloth) was operating in Bayley Lane. Within fifty years it was dealing with 3,000 whole cloths annually, enough work to give a living to up to eighty weavers and their families, working a two-handed horizontal loom.

Coventry blue is first mentioned around 1380. It initially applied to broadcloth dyed using woad, but later to blue thread. Sadly, no examples survive to show exactly what shade of blue it was.

Nevertheless, the fastness of the dye made it highly sought-after. 'True as Coventry blue' was the kind of high-end advertising that made many a fortune among the new ruling elite of merchants and drapers and gave them a route into

Medieval sheep farming. (Courtesy of the Thomas Fisher Rare Book Library, University of Toronto)

export markets all over Europe. Many of these powerful men were members of trading associations far from home, notably the Staple of Calais. And the links between that northern French town and Coventry were surprisingly close.

John Onley, Mayor of Coventry in 1396, was said to have been the first Englishman born in Calais after it was seized as an English possession by Edward III. Onley, the son of the king's standard-bearer, went on to be mayor twice of both Coventry and Calais.

Exporting could be risky. In 1398 allies of the Hanseatic League, with a grudge against English traders, seized a consignment of Coventry cloth marked with its elephant and castle stamp of quality, in the Swedish port of Stralslund. One Coventry merchant, William Bedford, lost cloth worth £200, while John Cross, one of the prominent citizens financing the re-building of St Mary's Hall at the time, lost merchandise to the value of £100.

By the middle of the fifteenth century, Warwickshire wool was no longer regarded as the ultimate in quality and Coventry's dominance of the cloth trade was under increasing and at times unauthorised pressure.

Regulations had been in place for more than a century to ensure that all cloth sold in the town was inspected for quality in the searching-house next to the Drapery in Bayley Lane. In 1455, after traders had been discovered selling cloth in the porch of St Michael's Church, it had been thought necessary to reinforce the rule that the Drapery and the Cloth Hall were the only places where cloth could be officially sold in Coventry.

The importing of alum, a vital ingredient in the process of developing Coventry blue, collapsed in the 1440s and it wasn't long before the supply of woad from Toulouse, used to intensify the colour, dried up too. Dyers struggled to find an alternative source.

It was left to the Elizabethan scholar and diplomat Sir Thomas Smith, writing more than 100 years later, to pronounce the last rites on the 'true as Coventry blue' brand that had helped to make Coventry great:

I have heard say that the chief trade of Coventry was heretofore in making blue thread and then the town was rich even upon that trade in manner only; and now our thread comes all from beyond the seas, wherefore that trade of Coventry is now decayed and thereby the town likewise.

three

A GOLDEN AGE

On 26 October 1232, Ranulf de Blondeville, sixth Earl of Chester, died at his castle at Wallingford in Oxfordshire. He was the last of his line.

News of Ranulf's death swept across Europe. As soldier and statesman he was a widely respected figure in the political and military circles of the Angevin empire, his exploits celebrated in ballad and legend.

In a life spent waging war and orchestrating peace across England, Normandy and much further afield, it is foolish to suppose that Ranulf spent much time at all on his Coventry estates; he had a carefully chosen small army of officials and administrators to manage them and promote his interests. Yet in a number of respects he showed a steady and personal interest in affairs in this small corner of a mighty earldom.

Ranulf's charter of the early 1200s had reinforced the rights given to his Coventry tenants by his grandfather, the fourth earl, half a century before, only omitting the clause giving new investors in the growing town freedom from taxes for the first two years. Coventry no longer had need of such enticements.

Another of his grants, from around 1204, had confirmed the right of the monks from the Benedictine priory to take two cart-loads of wood a day from his extensive woodlands for fuel and building repairs.

In 1226, Ranulf sought and received consent from Henry III to offer formal protection to the Jewish communities of Coventry and Leicester, an apparently altruistic act that threw light on the murky relationships between the Jews and their persecutors in England. His move may well have been prompted by a series of court cases, from 1218 onwards, in which Amtera the Jewess of Coventry successfully secured the forfeiture of lands by debtors who had failed to pay back her loans to them.

The hatred that this would have drawn down on her head was almost certainly the spur for Ranulf to act, and it is telling that after his death it appears that the small Jewish community in Coventry upped sticks and moved elsewhere.

The earl's concern for the Jews was, in truth, pragmatic as much as anything else, for with castles, estates and retainers all over England and Normandy, he had huge financial commitments, and would have borrowed from Jewish moneylenders on a regular basis.

One project that he may well have needed their finance for was the building of a new fortified manor house in Coventry to replace the severely damaged castle he had inherited from his rebellious father. Cheylesmore Manor, possibly completed by 1224, was built at the town end of his hunting park, featured a vivary (or menagerie) and was surrounded by a moat.

Ranulf's final act as lord of his Coventry estates had far-reaching consequences. In 1231, a year before his death, he invited the Franciscan order to establish a friary on the doorstep of his new manor in Coventry, a move perhaps inspired by his meeting twelve years earlier with its founder, the man destined to become St Francis of Assisi, on Crusade in the Holy Land.

The Franciscans, or Greyfriars as they were better known in England, were a mendicant order of street preachers, who preferred to rely on the generosity of well-wishers rather than on lavish moneymaking schemes to provide a living.

Dressed in a rough woollen habit and often barefoot, their humility and simple lifestyle, in sharp contrast to the more worldly and business-minded approach of the Benedictines, gave them an instant appeal. And the Benedictines didn't like it. The Benedictine chronicler Florence of Worcester (male despite the name) had greeted the arrival of the Franciscans in England in the mid-1220s with something less than enthusiasm, 'O sorrow! O worse than sorrow! A tiresome plague! The Franciscans have arrived in England.'

What really grated with the Benedictines was this new order's popularity when it came to presiding over burials. For many rich and powerful people, a simple interment by the Greyfriars, shorn of high ceremony and the accoutrements of wealth, quickly became the preferred route to salvation in the next world.

The order's new Coventry friary, formally established in 1234, was to become its most important outside London, and for 300 years provided a resting place for generations of the high-born and well-to-do from Coventry and Warwickshire and from further afield.

The Greyfriars' first church was a simple affair and roofed with wooden tiles, the product of a special grant of timber from Ranulf's estates. Meanwhile,

The surviving gate house of Ranulf's Cheylesmore Manor, restored in the 1960s and now Coventry's Register Office. (Chris Ross)

Coventry's two other monastic settlers were putting the finishing touches to much grander buildings.

In the early 1220s, the Cistercians at Coombe completed their own new church, built with stone from their Harnall quarries just north of the town. At around the same time, after more than a century of building, the great Benedictine cathedral church of St Mary was finally ready for occupation.

In the course of 100 years, the building's architectural style had changed, from Romanesque at its east end to Early English at the west end, and it had swallowed up the small church dedicated by Leofric and Godiva nearly two centuries before.

The records say the great church was completed by a master mason named Reginald, whose house stood just beyond the east end. He died shortly afterwards and the Benedictine prior, Geoffrey, offered the site of the dwelling to the Bishop of Coventry and Lichfield, Alexander de Stavenby, who had been particularly close to Ranulf. No trace now lingers of the bishop's palace that was subsequently built on it.

The passing of the Earls of Chester as a major hereditary force in the town led to a new surge of confidence among the class of merchants and skilled craftsmen who were emerging as leaders in a population of around 3,500.

They started to build more of their houses in stone, particularly around Well Street and West Orchard in the prior's half. Fellow tradesmen began to

How the west front of the great cathedral church might have looked in the early thirteenth century. (Image courtesy of Continuum Group Ltd)

cluster together in identifiable 'quarters' – smiths, dyers and weavers around Smithford Street, saddlers and goldsmiths along Broadgate, scabbard-makers and cutlers in Little Park and Much Park streets. This last area was also the centre for soap-making, a trade at which Coventry was to achieve a prominent, if passing, reputation.

The new property-owning class numbered men like Henry Baker, who as his name indicates, came from a family with roots in a fairly humble trade. He was probably an official working for the Benedictine prior, and from the 1250s onwards appears in many property transactions, acquiring over the next thirty years an impressive portfolio of properties ranging right across the town, from Bishop Street to Much Park Street.

Prosperity on this scale had already prompted prominent citizens to think a little more about defending themselves. To the ditches of the earlier fortified period, most of them now disused and clogged with rubbish, were added bars or chains at approaches to the town. More custom post than imposing barrier, the bar was nevertheless a way in which local officials could monitor, and impose levies on, traffic passing in and out of Coventry.

While the civil war between Stephen and Matilda a century earlier had shown how quickly a threat to peace and prosperity could materialise from without, it was the enemy within that was to prove a much greater challenge to these ardent moneymakers.

At his death, Ranulf, Earl of Chester's Coventry estates had been bequeathed to his nephew Hugh d'Aubigny, Earl of Arundel, the son of Mabel, one of his four sisters. Hugh, however, died in 1243, while still in his twenties, and the estates passed to his sister Cecily, who had married Roger de Montalt, formerly seneschal for Ranulf in Chester. In 1249 de Montalt decided to go on Crusade and, to fund the potentially ruinous expenses that faced him, was

Medieval houses in High Street, painted around 1820. (William Henry Brooke, Herbert Art Gallery)

persuaded by the entrepreneurial Benedictine prior, William de Brightwalton, to sell all of his Coventry holdings (except Cheylesmore Manor and park, the house of the Greyfriars and the leper hospital) to the priory, receiving in return a 'pension' of £100 a year.

At a stroke, the Benedictines had secured control over that part of Coventry they had long coveted, and it wasn't too long before they took steps to consolidate their grip on Coventry's commercial life.

In February 1267, by charter of Henry III, the prior was granted the right to appoint a coroner, and even more importantly, to set up a guild merchant for his tenants, a formal association that gave them privileges and exclusive rights to trade. In effect, this shut out many of the traders and craftsmen from the earl's half. There was bound to be trouble.

Rioting flared on the streets and the crisis reached its flashpoint when officials working on behalf of the newly appointed coroner tried to view the body of a man in the earl's half of the town, possibly a victim of the riots. They were prevented from doing so by angry traders and called for help in carrying out their duties from the Sheriff, the King's official representative in Warwickshire.

What happened next was set out in a later report, 'Certain men from these parts, with others, armed with force, took Gilbert, clerk to the said sheriff, sent hither to this end, and imprisoned him, and broke the royal rolls and charters and beat and ill-treated the men of the prior and convent.'

The protest, in part at least, seems to have been successful. While the office of coroner was established and continued in Coventry, nothing more was heard of the prior's guild merchant. Neither is there evidence of a follow-up court case, bringing to justice rioters and the destroyers of the royal rolls and charters. Punishment for such offences would have been severe. Although the Lateran Council of 1216 had abolished trial by ordeal, a hated Norman innovation that had never found favour with the native English, the law had at its disposal particularly harsh penalties for defying the king, and Coventry already had at least one jail. It was attached to the priory and the first recorded inmate was a chaplain, Robert de Rode, who had been incarcerated there for the murder of his servant, Gervaise, in 1221.

The failure of the prior to pursue his guild merchant must have given his opponents in the town grounds for confidence, and they took a further step in town building in 1285, securing from Edward I the authority to take a toll from all saleable commodities brought into the town, to help pay for the streets to be paved.

The toll amounted to one halfpenny for every horse-load of corn and every horse, mare, ox or cow entering Coventry. The paving was almost certainly cobbles – the idea of pavements was still a long way in the future. It wasn't quite the money-spinner they had hoped for and they needed another royal licence to impose a toll in 1305, but it was a significant step forward in municipal pride.

Coventry's sharply rising prosperity was starting to be noticed. The town had not been invited to send representatives to the rebel Simon de Montfort's groundbreaking parliament of 1265, but in 1295 two of its burgesses, Aunketil de Coleshull and Richard de Weston, did go to Edward I's Model Parliament, in effect becoming its first Members of Parliament. It was the first time that Coventry had been given a democratic voice in affairs beyond its own parochial concerns.

Edward's motives were undoubtedly fiscal, as he was desperately short of money to fund his wars against the Scots, and in 1301 he summoned two Coventry merchants, Thomas Ballard and Lawrence de Shepey, to attend a council at York, for much the same purpose. Over the next five years, a string of fundraising councils convened by the king included at least two Coventry burgesses on the list of those summoned to attend.

It wasn't surprising. For decades, Coventry's mercantile class had been making a name for itself as manufacturer and purveyor of luxury goods and services in a way that none of its Midlands rivals could match.

The town boasted more goldsmiths than Leicester or Nottingham and had a higher percentage of merchants in its population than even Norwich, already one of England's most important towns. Among the list of trades being practiced were brooch makers, spice dealers, silk sewers, and dealers in venison and salmon, all occupations geared towards the luxury end of the market.

The records show that up to fifteen wine merchants were in business in Coventry before 1236, the year in which one of them, Jordan de Coventry, had his ship laden with wine impounded by bailiffs in the Sussex port of Winchelsea. The following year he was importing wine belonging to a French dealer named Arnold of Perigord.

The pavage grant of 1285 further revealed that goods to be taxed included cloth of silk with gold and baudekyn, a very expensive material used for altar cloths as well as fashionable clothes.

Merchants and craftsmen involved in trades like these had a lot to lose and deeply resented interference from the Benedictine prior, now Coventry's undisputed landlord. Furthermore, in Prior Henry de Leycester, elected in 1294, they found a compelling target for their anger.

In 1302 and again in 1307, Prior Henry went to the law to stop men in the earl's half of the town selling goods from their own premises on the day on which the market was being held in his part of the town. They in turn argued that under charter they had the right to stage their own market, but the court found against them and levied a fine of £60, a huge sum of money at the time.

Whatever else he did, Henry de Leycester made sure his own family benefitted from his tenure in office. A Thomas de Leycester appears as a land agent in Coventry in 1299 and over the next twenty years the records show many transfers of land between the de Leycester family and the priory. Henry de Leycester died in 1322, but his successor, Henry Irreys, was no more sympathetic towards the townsfolk and within a year they were ready to take desperate and startling action, in a way that resonates vividly down the centuries.

In December 1323 a group of powerful Coventry merchants, led by Richard le Latoner, approached John de Nottingham, a necromancer then living with his assistant Robert le Mareschal in a dilapidated old house in Shortley Park, close to the town. Their proposal was brutal in its simplicity. Using wax and canvas supplied by the merchants, Nottingham and Mareschal would employ sorcery to kill Prior Irreys, his steward Nicholas Crump, King Edward II (who had backed Irreys' election) and the king's hated favourites, Hugh Despenser and his son, also named Hugh. The pair were sworn to secrecy and told that they would be paid £35 when the job was done.

One of the prior's underlings, Robert Sowe, who had probably made himself unpopular as well, was chosen as a trial victim. A waxen image was made of him and a sharpened feather was driven into its forehead. The next morning poor Sowe was raving and within days he was dead.

At this point Robert le Mareschal, a humble tailor by profession, appears to have panicked and confessed his part in the plot. John de Nottingham was arrested by the Sheriff's officers, as were a number of Coventry's most important and wealthy citizens. The younger Hugh Despenser was sufficiently rattled to appeal to the Pope for protection against 'magical and secret dealings', and was told, somewhat peremptorily, that all he needed to keep him safe was faith and proper confession.

Fellow merchants in London and in Warwickshire stood bail for the conspirators, an indication perhaps of the sympathy that they were attracting in their struggle with the prior. In 1325 they were brought to trial in London, but the authorities were unable to bring the chief suspect into court. Rather conveniently, John de Nottingham had died in prison. A jury promptly brought in not guilty verdicts on the other defendants and they were released. The report on the case, in the Parliamentary Writs, remains the earliest account of a witchcraft trial in England.

Despite the acquittals, prospects did not look promising for the prior's opponents in Coventry. He was very much in the ascendancy and modern commentators have even speculated that the witchcraft plot was all a set-up, with the prior's hand behind it in a subtle attempt to flush out his enemies.

But then, out of the blue, those enemies enjoyed a stroke of quite astonishing good fortune. In 1327, Robert de Montalt, owner of Cheylesmore Manor and grandson of Roger who had acquired it more than eighty years before, drew up a formal deed, bequeathing the manor to Queen Isabella, widow of Edward II, if he and his wife Emma died without issue. Within three years, they had indeed both succumbed without heirs and the formidable Isabella was suddenly a force to be reckoned with in Coventry.

Aged thirty-five in 1330, the queen spent the final months of that year under house arrest at the court of her son Edward III, after being overthrown by him

as she tried to rule England with her lover
Roger Mortimer. Widely suspected of having
had her husband, Edward II, murdered three
years earlier – a crime for which her many
enemies dubbed her 'she-wolf' – Isabella spent
the next two years with the king at Windsor,
before being allowed to settle at Castle Rising
in Norfolk.

Supposedly 'in retirement' she was intent
on enjoying a lavish lifestyle and took a
close interest in the income generated by
her estates, including Cheylesmore Manor.
Having spent a lifetime of intrigue with whole
kingdoms at stake, a little local difficulty with
a grasping Benedictine prior was not going to
trouble her much, and she was to prove an ally
without compare to the townsfolk, unlocking
the key to the next phase of the town's
development. From then on, the currents of
history would shift in favour of Coventry's
ambitious and acquisitive merchants and
craftsmen, and they were quick to exercise
this new sense of power against the prior.

Before long, he was complaining vigorously
about townsfolk stealing wood, breaking
down fences and refusing to pay him his

Edward II's widow Isabella, 'she-wolf' but
a good friend to Coventry. (St Mary's Hall/
Coventry City Council)

rightful dues. And on one occasion, moves to enforce the status quo ended
with a frightening reverse, as a contemporary account records. When the prior's
bailiff, Simon Pakeman, came to demand the rents of certain tenements, 'up
came Peter of Stoke and other mad folk, and assaulted the said Simon with
force of arms, and beat and ill-treated him, saying that if the prior and the
monastery ever made any demands of the kind in the earl's half they would
make their heads fly off.'

In 1337 Prior Henry Irreys petitioned Edward III, claiming that 'Madame'
(his description of Isabella) had allowed her officers to seize profits from
his fair. Furthermore, people from Coventry had thrown down hedges and
ditches in his park and felled and taken trees. One hundred of the prior's fat

cattle had been stolen and two cart-loads of corn being driven to the priory were 'attached and arrested' in the middle of the streets of Coventry.

He got nowhere, for the king had already shown where his sympathies lay, granting a licence in 1332 for the men of the earl's half to erect a common conduit twenty feet long and ten feet broad 'in such of their streets as they think fit.' In effect, this was the town's first public water supply and it said much about the growing self-confidence of a place where wealth was being generated, not just nationally, but from abroad too.

Back in 1273, Coventry merchant Roger le Chamberlyng had secured from Henry II a licence to export twenty sacks of wool to any place beyond the seas, except Flanders, whose countess had quarrelled with the unforgiving Henry.

In 1328, Andrew le Pynner (a pin-maker) and his servants received royal protection for their journeys around the kingdom and to Ireland, and in 1334 the merchants of Coventry were given freedom from toll on all their goods and merchandise. This applied to all major towns, including Bristol, England's fastest-growing port and already the most important collection and distribution centre for Coventry's exporters.

Six years later, much against the will of the prior, they were given the formal right to establish a merchant guild of their own to protect their interests. St Mary's Guild, regarded initially as a focal point for opposition to the priory, was quickly followed by others: St John the Baptist Guild (1342), the Guild of St Katherine (1345), Corpus Christi (1348) and finally Holy Trinity Guild (1364), which, by the 1390s, had united all but Corpus Christi within its ranks.

Coventry was moving rapidly up the list of England's most important towns – an assessment for tax in 1334 rated it the twelfth wealthiest in the kingdom, equal to Salisbury – and it was on the threshold of an unprecedented building boom.

Work on the Guildhall of St Mary, a home for the first of the guilds, was nearing completion by 1342. Two years later, Queen Isabella gave

The seal of the Guild of St John the Baptist. (Herbert Collections)

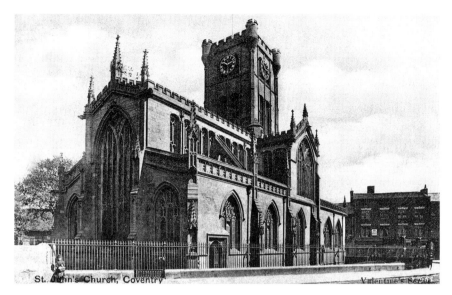

The church of St John the Baptist, built on land given by Queen Isabella. (Author's Collection)

the St John the Baptist Guild a parcel of land at Bablake, to the west of the town, to build a collegiate church where priests could live and study together, while singing the praises of their benefactors.

As St Mary's Hall was opening its doors, another monastic order was arriving in Coventry, looking to settle. The Carmelite order of friars, known as the Whitefriars because of the colour of their habit, relied on alms to earn their living and owed this new foundation to the generosity of a private benefactor, Sir John Poultney, four times Mayor of London and one of the capital's most powerful merchants.

In 1342 he gave them ten acres of land and a dwelling house close to what in time would become the London Road into Coventry. A further grant of land quickly followed from the Benedictine priory, a move perhaps designed to encourage the establishment of a rival to that other order of mendicant friars, the hated Greyfriars. The church they began building would be almost cathedral-scale in its ambition, with an impressive preaching nave, a slender tower and, unusually, resonance passages cut into the floor to improve the acoustics for singing.

With paved streets, a public water supply and now a new generation of imposing stone buildings, Coventry had reached a level of urban sophistication enjoyed by few other towns. The stage was set for its next great leap in self-government.

Above What remains of Whitefriars today. (Chris Ross)

Left Coventry's 1345 Charter of Incorporation, the first of a new kind in England. (Herbert Collections)

On 20 January 1345, Edward III granted the men of Coventry favours and privileges, 'that they and their heirs and successors may henceforth have a commonalty (or corporation) among themselves and may annually elect and create from among themselves a fit Mayor and Bailiffs.' It was a Charter of Incorporation, the first of a new kind in England, supported in name by Queen Isabella herself and 'purchased' or negotiated by twelve prominent citizens, many of whom later went on to hold the office of mayor. Their new privileges included the right to settle all pleas and disputes among themselves, to build a prison for the 'chastisement of malefactors' and to have their own corporation seal.

Coventry's first mayor, John Ward, was elected in January 1346, but the collective sense of achievement that this must have prompted was to be short-lived. In the early summer of 1348, a ship docked at a port on the south coast of England, probably Melcombe Regis in Dorset, bringing with it a deadly contagion.

By the middle of August, the plague, or the Black Death as it was known, was spreading rapidly north, terrifying whole communities into a helplessness bordering on paralysis. There seemed no defence; even prayer failed against a foul contagion that many believed had been spawned by the Devil.

It is impossible to say when the Black Death reached Coventry. Even though the death toll really got into its stride in March and April of 1349, the disease may have been present in the town the previous autumn. It is a characteristic of this type of bubonic plague, spread by fleas that hibernate, that it can lie dormant over winter.

The Benedictine prior, William Irreys, who had succeeded his namesake Henry seven years earlier, was a victim in the summer of 1349. As was Coventry's second mayor, Jordan de Shepey, and one of the newly appointed bailiffs, Richard de Keresley, who had been one of the twelve cosignatories to the Charter of Incorporation. His replacement, William de Happesford, disappeared from the records that October, almost certainly cut down too, and the plague also took the life of the Whitefriars benefactor, Sir John Poultney, who became one of the first to be buried in the order's new church in Coventry.

Exactly what the death toll was, in a population of around 7,000, is hard to gauge, although some estimates have put the death rate among clergy at 40 per cent; they were uniquely exposed to plague as they gave succour to the sick and dying. It is likely that up to a fifth of all people in Coventry perished, the unimaginable equivalent of more than 60,000 deaths among the city's population today.

The City Annals, a not completely accurate account of Coventry history as it was written in hindsight, declared that when churchyards were not large enough to bury the dead certain fields were purchased for the purpose.

Land remained uncultivated. Several of the town's mills, including Hill Mill, were left untended for want of a miller, while it was said that the majority of the prior's tenants in the farming communities of Exhall, Keresley, Willenhall and Coundon – the heads of upwards of 100 families – had died. Poorer areas of the town like Spon Street, where housing was more crowded and insanitary, suffered worst.

The impact of the disaster can be seen most clearly in the property transactions for Coventry in 1349. There were 175 deeds that year, compared to just 42 the year before and 31 the year after, and the unemotional detail of these legal transfers of goods and land masks the tragic stories contained within.

John de Arthingworth was a wealthy Coventry merchant, appointed the first town coroner in 1346, and a property owner of some magnitude. He died of the pestilence in late March 1349, bequeathing his property, in part, to his widow Lucy and only daughter Joan. Yet by the middle of April young Joan had passed on her share to her mother and also disappears from the record, without doubt another victim.

Yet in the midst of all this horror, there were signs that Coventry's stability and prosperity would endure. Transactions like those of the tragic Arthingworths were not the panicky reactions of wealthy people fleeing a trouble spot, but the considered bequests of men and women who knew that they may not have long to live and wanted to leave their affairs in good order.

The coming of the Black Death was to prove an early test for the fledgling merchant guilds, set up to protect and sustain their members just a year or two before. In the event, the guilds, through their trustees, became the repository for many properties from plague-ravaged families and played a vital role in preserving stability out of chaos, often letting property out to former owners at favourable rates.

There is no doubt that the establishment of these guilds, just in time, allowed Coventry to recover remarkably quickly.

Just six years later, in 1355, Queen Isabella, the prior (by now William de Dunstable) and the new mayor signed the Tripartite Indenture, bringing to an end the disputes and conflicts that had scarred the recent history of the town.

In truth, the men of the earl's half had never quarrelled with their fellow citizens in the prior's half, with whom they traded and intermarried at will.

Their problem had always been with the priory itself and the sway it sought to hold over their lives. Indeed, two of the ringleaders of the riots that followed the prior's attempt to create a merchant guild back in 1267 actually owned property in his half of the town.

It was not the case that Coventry had been governed as two entirely separate entities as it had long been considered one place for all important purposes, and the Tripartite Indenture was intended to bind that emerging civic relationship even more strongly together at a time of crisis.

In the same year another great unifying force made its appearance in the townscape. As far back as January 1329, in the wake of a national crisis brought on by successive harvest failures and increasing lawlessness, King Edward III had issued letters patent to the prior and the 'good men' of the town, giving them the right to levy murage, a tax to raise money to build a wall. In the summer of 1355, Richard de Stoke, the town's ninth mayor, in great ceremony laid the first stone, close to where the Whitefriars had built their new friary.

It was a slow start. The first mile took forty years to complete and it was to be almost 180 years before the town was finally encircled, but Coventry's town wall was to become one of the wonders of the late Middle Ages – two and a quarter miles long, at least twelve feet high, up to nine feet thick and furnished with thirty-two towers and twelve gates. Its tiny image appears, under construction, on the first modern map of England, dated around 1360.

Others were building in stone too. In 1358, Edward the Black Prince, who had that year inherited his grandmother Queen Isabella's Coventry estates, gave the Greyfriars the right to quarry stone from his Cheylesmore Park to build their new church, the spire of which still stands.

Before her death, Isabella had made a further significant contribution to the expansion of the town, leasing quarter-acre plots of land in her Little Park for an annual rent of five pence to eighty-eight wealthy citizens, including all twelve who had negotiated the Charter of Incorporation. Based on a new thoroughfare, Queen Street, the proposed development of what was effectively an up-market residential area ultimately failed because of the Black Death. But it is believed to have been the earliest attempt at town planning in Coventry.

It was left to one of Isabella's henchmen, her sub-bailiff William Walshman, to make the crucial intervention that pushed Coventry into the ranks of England's most important towns.

Walshman (or Welshman) was an immigrant, as his name suggests, as were half of all those living in Coventry in the year of the Black Death. He had been instrumental in helping the St John the Baptist Guild develop their collegiate church at Bablake, using stone from an uncompleted oratory building dedicated to the Virgin Mary on Isabella's estate at Cheylesmore.

He also operated an important drapery merchandising cloth in Bayley Lane, a highly lucrative venture which he and his wife Christiana would eventually bequeath to the Holy Trinity Guild.

With Isabella's strong backing behind him, Walshman's greatest achievement was to get cloth purchases for the Royal Wardrobe transferred from London to Coventry, giving the town a huge boost in trade. The impact of such prosperity is plain to see in the will of Coventry merchant John Prest, one of only three final testaments so far discovered from the town before 1370.

Prest, who died in 1361, just a dozen years after the visitation of the Black Death, was a founder of the Corpus Christi Guild and was elected one of Coventry's Bailiffs in 1356. Mindful of his civic duties, he left money to the guilds he belonged to and to 'mend the way' below his orchard and repair the road surface of Dogge Lane, which would later become Coventry's main road out towards Leicester. In addition to bequests to family and friends, his will made significant donations to monastic foundations and churches, not only in

Drapers Hall, an 1832 gentlemen's club built on the site of the city's first drapery, established by William Walshman. (CV One/Coventry City Council)

Coventry, but as far away as Worcester and Lichfield. In total, it amounted to well over £100, an impressive fortune at the time.

There were quite a few like John Prest. By 1377, when tax assessors came to look at every important town in England, Coventry was rated the fourth wealthiest in the kingdom, after London, York and Bristol. Astonishingly, the population had recovered too, presumably with further immigration, and stood at around 9,000.

Coventry had managed to cope with the havoc wrought by the Black Death, and at least two further outbreaks of the plague in 1361 and in 1376. But elsewhere the devastation had sewn discord and instability throughout England; some places having lost half their population. A settled order, where many were still tied to feudal lords and virtually living as serfs, could no longer be sustained. Rebellion was in the air.

It exploded in south-east England in the summer of 1381, with the Peasants' Revolt which for a few weeks seemed to threaten the notion of kingship itself, then personified in the fourteen-year-old Richard II.

There is no evidence that Coventry felt directly threatened by the Peasants' Revolt, although a contingent of the peasant army had made it into the East Midlands before the revolt collapsed, but it does feature in an intriguing footnote to the story. After the rebellion had been crushed, one of its leaders, the charismatic renegade priest John Ball, was found hiding in a ruined house in Coventry.

Ball, born in St Albans, was a powerful speaker and fiery agitator, whose belief in democracy and social justice was summed up in his most famous epithet, 'When Adam delved (dug) and Eve span, who was then the gentleman?' Plucked from his hiding place, he was unceremoniously hauled off to his home town and there, on 15 July, 1381, was hanged, drawn and quartered in the presence of the king. Why he should have sought refuge in Coventry is still an unanswered question. Did he have family in the town, or was it that there were citizens in Coventry who shared his radical views?

In the same year, the last monastic order to arrive in Coventry, the Carthusians, established a new foundation on land at Shortley, just to the south of the town. It was not an auspicious beginning for the Carthusians, an austere order of cloistered monks who spent their lives in prayer and contemplation. Within a year, their patron Lord William Zouche, of Harringworth in Northamptonshire, had died, and his heir, also William, seems to have become embroiled in a plot against the young king, Richard II, not long afterwards.

Coventry's Charterhouse. What remains is the prior's residence and guest accommodation. (CV One/ Coventry City Council)

With just a handful of monks, the new house appeared doomed to fail, but then the king himself declared that he and his young queen, Anne of Bohemia, would be the founders of the new Charterhouse. On 6 September 1385 he came in person to lay the foundation stone of the Carthusians' simple church.

A mile away, in the centre of Coventry, work was already underway to rebuild and expand the churches of Holy Trinity and St Michael's. Details of the development of Holy Trinity remain sketchy. The Norman church built for the tenants of the Benedictine priory had been largely destroyed by fire in 1257. Keen to make a fresh start, it was the priory that had appointed the first recorded vicar, Ralph de Sowe, in 1264.

The north porch that was incorporated in the rebuilding, and which survives today, is almost certainly the only survivor of the earlier church. Beginning in the 1380s, major works lengthened the chancel and refashioned the crossing, giving Holy Trinity something of its modern appearance.

A few yards away, another porch, this time to the south, appears to have been the only survivor of an earlier St Michael's church, which had been Early English in design. Work to rebuild this in Perpendicular style began in 1373, largely funded by the wealthy Botoner family of wool merchants.

William and Adam Botoner, each of them Mayor of Coventry three times between 1364 and 1385, were credited with paying for the church and tower, employing the renowned master mason Robert Skyllington, while sisters Mary and Anne Botoner, presumably from a later generation of the family, gave money to build the spire in the 1430s.

Richard II's interest in Coventry was not confined to the Carthusians. In May 1385 he gave the men of Coventry the right to quarry stone from his Cheylesmore Park to continue their wall-building, which after almost thirty years had reached the boundaries of his estate. A condition was that the wall had to enclose the royal manor.

In September 1397, the King again favoured Coventry, choosing it as the location for what he planned to be a startling demonstration of his royal powers after a troubled reign beset by rebellion and treachery.

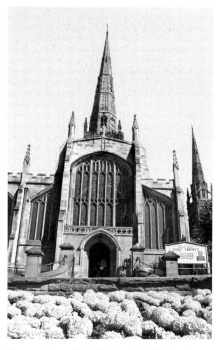

The west front of Holy Trinity today. (CV One/ Coventry City Council)

The event was a duel or trial by combat, between his cousin, Henry Bolingbroke, Duke of Hereford, and Thomas Mowbray, Duke of Norfolk, one of his closest advisers. Former friends, they had fallen out after Henry alleged that, in private conversation, Mowbray had told him that he expected both of them to become the subject of the king's retribution, a clearly treasonous statement if true. Mowbray fiercely denied it but failed to get the suspicious Richard's support in setting aside the charge and it was decided that they should meet to settle their quarrel. The duel to the death, on horseback with lance and sword, was to take place on open ground to the east of the town. On 17 September, St Lambert's Day, the King of England arrived with his entourage on what is now Gosford Green to bear witness.

It must have been a truly astonishing sight. The King, it was said, had brought with him his entire royal household, protected by 10,000 men in armour – perhaps an exaggeration but nevertheless a mightily impressive show of force.

Mowbray, whose family had acquired nearby Caludon Castle more than forty years before, bore his colours of crimson velvet, embroidered with silver

Above Richard's herald rides out to stop the duel. (Nineteenth-century engraving, courtesy of THP)

Right Richard II chose Coventry for the duel that never was. (St Mary's Hall/Coventry City Council)

lions and mulberry leaves, on his glittering armour. At the far end of the list, Hereford prepared to meet his charge in armour specially acquired in Lombardy, decked in his own livery of blue and green velvet, embroidered with swans and antelopes. Just as they were beginning to close with one another, Richard called a halt, deliberated with his advisers for two hours and then announced that Hereford would be exiled for ten years and that Mowbray would be banished from England for life.

It was a fateful decision. Within two years, Hereford was back to usurp the throne as Henry IV. Richard was captured at Lichfield and brought under guard to Coventry briefly before being taken on to London, where the following year he died in prison. It has been suggested that he was deliberately starved to death.

For the people of Coventry, the glamour of this royal visit to end all royal visits must have represented a heady hour on which to fret and strut themselves on the national stage. It would not be the last time this happened, but the town's fortunes would be tied increasingly into the politics and brutal conflicts of the troubled century to come. And that would mean an uncomfortable ride.

AN ELEPHANT AND A CASTLE

The earliest surviving image of Coventry's highly distinctive civic insignia comes from a circular seal, dated around 1250. The reverse side shows St Michael slaying a dragon, but its main face depicts an elephant bearing a triple-towered castle on its back and standing in front of an oak tree.

The tree may be a reference to the conjectured origin of Coventry's name (Cofa's tree) and from a very early date St Michael was a saint very much associated with the growing town. But why use something as exotic as an elephant?

The elephant and castle motif was almost certainly adopted as the centrepiece of Coventry's new coat of arms in 1345, following the town's Charter of Incorporation. But exactly what it represents remains something of a conundrum. Nobody in Coventry at the time would have seen a living elephant. That much is clear from a decorative fifteenth-century chair, now in St Mary's Hall, that was made by an unknown Coventry wood carver. His version of an elephant sits somewhere uncomfortably between a pig and the real thing.

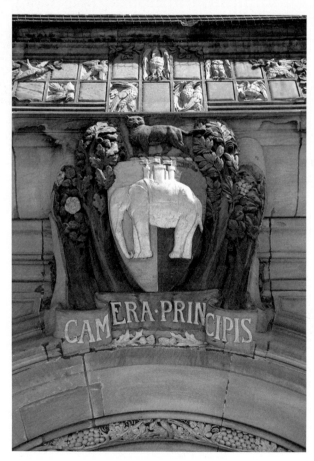

Coventry's medieval crest, still visible in handsome detail above the entrance to the Council House, opened in 1920. (Mark Radford)

But there were elephants in England. In 1255 King Henry III was given a present of one by the King of France and kept it in the Tower of London. They were known through the Bestiaries, books of fabulous beasts, whose activities and characteristics were used to highlight human qualities and frailties. The elephant represented strength and purpose, slaying a dragon to protect its young. But it was also believed to lean against trees as it slept and could be rendered defenceless when the tree was chopped down. Was the castle on its back an attempt to evoke memories of the Earl of Chester's modest 'fortlet' in Coventry? We shall probably never know.

Nevertheless, the elephant and castle as a distinctive 'badge' for Coventry was highly valued. In 1398, Coventry cloth worth more than £200 was recorded as lying in the Baltic port of Stralsund. As a mark of quality, it bore the stamp of the elephant and castle, as all of Coventry's quality cloth did.

The other elements in the medieval coat of arms are easier to interpret. The cat at the top spelled watchfulness and was widely used. Coventry's civic colours were red and green and splitting them on the background could well have been a reflection of the town's long episcopal associations with Lichfield.

The Black Prince. Coventry was anxious to flatter him. (St Mary's Hall/Coventry City Council)

The motto *Camera Principis* is translated as Chamber of the Prince and is a clear and deliberately flattering reference to Edward the Black Prince. He succeeded his grandmother Queen Isabella as Lord of Cheylesmore Manor in 1358 and took an interest in his Coventry estates, although there's no proof he ever actually visited them.

four

DARKENING SKIES

I n early January 1394, a few days before the Feast of Epiphany, a triple murder stunned the prosperous and civic-minded community of Coventry.

The bodies of John Cristleton, his son William and their servant Ralph Giffard were discovered in the sextern's house at the priory, where they lived. They had been hacked to death and robbed of a large sum in cash and jewellery worth a very tempting £10. The murderer, Geoffrey Wytles, was long gone, leaving behind him the murder weapon, an axe valued at 2*d*.

It wasn't by any means the first Coventry murder case to find its way into the records. More than a century before, the Warwickshire Eyre, the court where Crown Pleas were heard, was dealing with a steady stream of killings with axe, dagger and bludgeon. Most were quarrels that got out of hand, like the altercation in early 1262 between Geoffrey de Bygginge of Stoke and Mabel le Hucstere. He eventually threw her to the ground, the court was told, so that she burst internally and died on the fourth day following.

In a world of barely rudimentary medical attention, death came in many guises. At the same session of the court, two of Coventry's bailiffs were brought before the justices to explain their treatment of one Hugh Russell. They accused him of stealing a horse, it was reported, and threw him into the stocks for eight days so that his feet went rotten, fell off and he later died.

Coventry's boom in prosperity brought its own lethal disputes. In 1380, the mason Thomas de Whateley killed another mason, John de Lyveden, in what appears to have been a craftsman's quarrel that turned bloody.

Crime had been a constant thread as the town developed and Coventry's growing wealth put temptation in the way of many. In 1382, John Ray, an alnager, or collector of excise duty on cloth, was accused of a large-scale fraud against the king, by stealing 900 cloths brought to the Coventry Drapery for him to inspect and seal.

What happened to Ray isn't known, but if he was found guilty the range of alternatives open to his accusers would not have been huge. Between a fine and execution lay only prison – a punishment that had yet to adopt the idea of specific sentences and seems to have been extraordinarily easy to escape from.

Time and again, the court reports reveal that a criminal had escaped from jail and either disappeared or sought sanctuary in one of the town's churches, where if he admitted his crime and agreed to voluntary exile from the realm, he might go free to seek passage abroad – as long as he could stay clear of vengeful victims!

By the time of the priory triple murder, Coventry at least had its own machinery of justice in place. In 1374, the town had appointed its first six Justices for the Conservation of Peace; John Perce, Adam Botoner, Henry de Keel, Simon de Lichfield, John de Herdcoyhe and John Toftes. At around the same time, Coventry appointed its first Recorder, or local legal adviser.

These appointments, strongly opposed by legal officers in Warwickshire, were a result of the pioneering Incorporation charter of 1345. They also had an impact on the Leet, a legislative assembly designed to draw up, and enforce, local by-laws governing life in the town.

The Leet, which met twice a year in January and September, with the mayor and bailiffs acting as presidents, was a replacement for the old feudal system of justice, administered by the Lord of the Manor's Steward. But in Coventry it increasingly took on a legislative function, more akin to a town parliament than a tribunal of justice. To the Leet can be ascribed the idea, in 1422, of inviting commoners to represent the ten wards of the town: Bayley Lane, Bishop Street, Broadgate, Cross Cheaping, Earl Street, Gosford Street, Jordan Well, Much Park Street, Smithford Street and Spon Street. It first makes reference to a Town Clerk in 1430 and to Aldermen in 1469.

Its record of activity, the Leet Book, which survives from 1421 onwards, offers a tantalising account of life in fifteenth-century Coventry, recording the creation of new by-laws and regulations on a whole host of important municipal concerns, from street cleansing and refuse disposal to protection of the water supply and the regulation of food prices. The Leet concerned itself with public hygiene, ruling, for example in 1421, that no animals except pigs should be slaughtered within the town walls, and later ordaining fines for anybody caught sweeping rubbish into the river. It had an eye to public safety too, forbidding, on pain of a heavy fine, the use of thatched roofs in the town in 1474 and ordering householders to keep the pavement in front of their homes in good repair.

Perhaps more surprisingly, education too was a focus for the Leet's interest. The Benedictines had founded a school for the children of their tenants and officials as early as 1303, and there was another run by the Carthusians at their Charterhouse in Coventry, set up shortly after their arrival in the 1380s. In 1425, the Leet appointed John Barton as master of a town grammar school and followed him with a successor, John Pynchard, in 1429.

Ten years later it felt the need to chide the Benedictine priory for trying to force tenants to send their children to the priory's school. A man, it decreed, could send his children to whichever school he wished.

But to think of the Leet as in any way inclusive or democratic would be wrong. It was in the clearest sense of the phrase, a self-perpetuating oligarchy. The Leet appointed the mayor and bailiffs, but in turn its twenty-four members, or 'jury', were appointed by them. And they were all men who had been, or still were, prominent in trade and in the Coventry guilds.

The mayor himself (there were to be no women mayors of Coventry until the second quarter of the twentieth century) wielded formidable powers, aided by his council, numbering the twenty-four members of the Leet jury, known locally as The Scarlet, plus a handful of close advisers or 'brethren', who acted as an inner cabinet.

With such power could come public exposure when things went awry. In 1387 angry townsfolk stormed St Mary's Hall, already the base de facto for civic government in Coventry, and threw loaves of bread at the head of the mayor, Henry de Keel, for not enforcing the rules that governed the quality and price of bread.

Three years earlier the people of the town had objected to members of the powerful Trinity Guild taking control of four fields that were regarded as common land. In what is the earliest surviving reference to the Leet in Coventry, it ordered that men should be convened from every street in the town, a total of sixty-eight in all, to decide what to do.

They found in favour of the Trinity Guild, but the suspicion remained that they were probably placemen, acting in the interests of that powerful oligarchy who, from their membership of the most powerful guild in Coventry, ruled the place. It would not be the last dispute over common lands between the ordinary citizens and their betters. The seeds of discord were being sown.

While divisions between the town's elite and its common people were widening, by contrast Coventry itself was increasingly attracting royal attention and patronage.

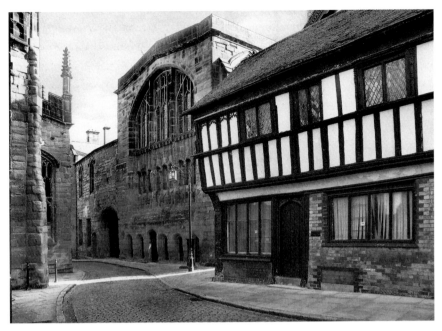

The men who ruled Coventry deliberated in St Mary's Hall (centre) and worshipped in St Michael's Church (left). (CV One/Coventry City Council)

The wealth of its merchants and the importance of its powerful Benedictine foundation had long made it a place of some note. The Dictum of Kenilworth, the peace treaty that had finally come up with a face-saving compromise following Simon de Montfort's rebellion in 1265, had actually been hammered out by a council of all sides, not in Kenilworth but within the imposing precincts of Coventry's great priory.

In 1330 the town took another leap into the royal spotlight with Queen Isabella's somewhat fortuitous acquisition of the Cheylesmore estates from the de Montalts. Later on, to both Edward the Black Prince and his father Edward III after his death in 1376, Coventry represented a small, but lucrative, element in the never-ending struggle to keep the royal coffers in reasonable shape.

Richard II maintained a close interest in municipal affairs, contributing stone from his Cheylesmore quarries to a number of the major building projects. And Coventry was on the radar too for his usurper, Henry Bolingbroke, or Henry IV as he became.

In 1400, the financially hard-pressed Henry borrowed a hefty sum of £300 from local merchants, and never actually got round to repaying £163 of it.

A few years later, in early October 1404, Coventry became the focus of national attention when the king called a parliament to meet there, with royal finances high on the agenda. It was called the Unlearned Parliament, because the king forbade lawyers from attending as members. It met in the Great Hall of the Benedictine priory and the atmosphere was, to say the least, poisonous.

The Commons, the eighty-three knights and burgesses who represented the shires and towns, were bitterly resentful of the burdens being imposed on them and argued that the Church was not contributing its share. The knights complained that while they put their bodies on the line for the kingdom in foreign wars, the clergy 'sat safe and quiet at home.'

Anti-clerical feeling was everywhere. When the Archbishop of Canterbury, Thomas Arundel, encountered a procession bearing the host through the streets to a sick man's bedside (dysentery was rife in the town) he bent the knee in homage, and was outraged to see a party of the king's knights turn their backs on it without even breaking off their conversation. 'Never before,' he raged, 'was the like abomination beheld among Christian men.'

The archbishop had to deliver a stern lecture and even voice the threat of excommunication before the Commons would reconsider their favoured solution – confiscating revenues from Church lands for a year to meet the king's needs. In the end, after more than a month of debate, the Unlearned Parliament granted Henry IV the taxes he sought, with the proviso that war treasurers should be appointed to make sure that the king made progress in defending the realm against its enemies.

The impact on Coventry's provincial resources of hundreds of Lords, Members of Parliament and officials spending five weeks in the town would have been severe. Although money had been made, it must have been with a sigh of relief that the townsfolk said farewell to them. As one account put it, 'victuals were growing scarce and lodgings scanty.'

Thomas Arundel, Archbishop of Canterbury, from a stained glass window in St Mary's Hall. (St Mary's Hall/Coventry City Council)

For the host, Coventry's Benedictine prior Richard Crosby, it had all been a bit of a disappointment. He used the presence of many of England's most important people to seek recompense for damage he said townsfolk had done to a water conduit built to serve the priory, but the parliament had weightier matters on its mind and brushed his complaint aside.

Although the prior had long since lost the battle to control his secular neighbours, disputes were rumbling on and it is clear that the Benedictines increasingly viewed those they lived among as little more than a criminal rabble.

In a document dating from 1410, the priory was even forced to make mention of those earthly pleasures to which as monks the brethren were forbidden, when an area to the north of the town in Radford was singled out as a place where amorous couples were accustomed to go to enjoy some privacy. The Benedictines preferred to call it Closegrove. To the townsfolk it was simply Fuckers' Fields.

Public order was plainly an issue too and by 1421 the prior was calling for a special watch to be mounted to deal with rowdy crowds who filled the streets during religious festivals.

In 1421, the first year for which Coventry's Leet Book survives, law and order seems to be very much on the minds of Coventry's ruling class. The Leet forbade the carrying of weapons in the streets, a useful by-law at a time when rough justice was still the first resort for many an injured party. And in a telling reference to a new set of institutions that might be regarded as a threat, it commanded that no Coventry craft guild was to be allowed to draw up its own by-laws.

The creation of the quasi-religious merchant guilds from the 1340s, to which the town's most powerful men belonged, had prompted others to seek their own associations based on the trade they pursued. Complete with a structure of master, journeyman and apprentice, these craft guilds were created for self-protection and quickly became powerful in their own right.

Perhaps the earliest was the Guild of the Shearmen and Tailors, founded in the early 1390s. In 1395 the records show a newly formed Weavers' Guild building the Chapel of St James and St Christopher alongside Spon Bridge with the interests of travellers in mind. A guild for Dyers in the town was established around 1400, while the rules of the new Pinners and Tylers Company (as the guilds were known in Coventry) were formally agreed in 1414.

Even in the craft guilds, the lot of the journeyman was not always a contented one, and in 1406 the Leet ordered the suppression of the first purely

The Chapel of St James and St Christopher, set up by the Weavers' Guild to minister to travellers entering Coventry from the west. (David Fry)

journeymen's guild, the Fraternity of St Anne, which had been set up some years earlier. Unrest among weavers in particular, often over wages, was a regular occurrence and the Fraternity clearly attracted considerable support. A second suppression order had to be issued in 1412 and third in 1425, by which time the organisation was calling itself the Guild of St George and was meeting in a chapel of that name adjoining Gosford Gate in the new wall.

For the wealthier citizens, protected by the powerful Holy Trinity and Corpus Christi Guilds, the journeymen's organisations may have represented a tangible threat to stability, but they still felt confident enough in their own power to extend the privilege of membership of their own guilds to sisters as well as brethren. Margery Russell, a member of the Trinity Guild, was only one of many wealthy women active in trade in fifteenth-century Coventry. In 1412 the formidable Margery sought lawful permission through the English courts to equip ships to seize back goods worth a staggering £800 from Spanish merchants, after claiming that she had been robbed of a cargo worth that sum by pirates operating out of Santander.

In a town that owed so much of its historical development to two women, Lady Godiva and Queen Isabella, and possibly even to a third, St Osburg, the success of women like Margery may have seemed fitting. Her considerable wealth would have come in handy too when royalty came Coventry's way and lavish municipal gifts were demanded. In March 1421 the victor of Agincourt, Henry V, brought his young queen Catherine to Coventry and was given £100 in hard cash. The young couple were each then presented with an ornate gold cup, a tradition in Coventry that its merchants felt would be sufficient to send anybody away satisfied.

Contented the king may have been, but trouble was brewing much closer to home from the followers of the religious reformer John Wycliffe, who had been Rector of Lutterworth, only fifteen miles from Coventry, before his death in 1384. Dubbed Lollards, or mutterers by their enemies, they were viewed as dangerous heretics by the established monastic orders.

The gable end of St George's chapel, painted shortly before its demolition in the 1820s. (Herbert Art Gallery)

Local sympathy for the views of Wycliffe, who advocated the translation of the Bible into English and opposed corruption in the Church and the influence of the Pope and clergy over secular affairs, may well have been what prompted the renegade priest John Ball to seek refuge in Coventry after the failure of the Peasants' Revolt in 1381. The following year, the Lollard preacher William Swynderby, known as William the Hermit, tried to preach in Coventry but was driven out by the clergy.

Another prominent Lollard, Nicholas of Hereford, a former pupil of Wycliffe, had translated part of the Old Testament for his old teacher but had later recanted and for many years pursued his former colleagues as heretics. As an old man, he joined the community of monks at the Coventry Charterhouse, where he died in 1417.

Seven years later, in late November 1424, Lollardy made its presence felt again in the town. This time the preacher was John Grace, a former monk and friar, who claimed he had permission from the bishop to preach for five days in Cheylesmore Park. Grace was a popular figure, admired for his modest, saintly lifestyle and oratorical skills, and to the horror of the Benedictine Prior Richard Crosby he attracted large and enthusiastic crowds to hear him speak.

Crosby was determined to expose this heretic, and accompanied by an unlikely ally, Friar John Bredon, Master of the Greyfriars in Coventry, went to Holy Trinity Church to denounce Grace and those who flocked to the park to hear him. Whether justified or not, both men feared that an angry mob gathering outside in the churchyard would tear them limb from limb and refused to leave the church until the mayor, John Braytofte, arrived with a small escort to rescue them.

In due course Grace was arrested, sent to London and imprisoned in the Tower, but the authorities in Coventry had seemed reluctant to act against him. The following spring, when securities were demanded from around fifty Coventry artisans that they should obey the mayor and bailiffs and not favour Lollardy or 'make riotous congregations to the disturbance of the peace', the orders came from London, not the Coventry Leet. More than half of those in the firing line were also called upon to answer to contempt of the peace for having participated in unlawful assemblies.

The truth is that there were many in Coventry who sympathised with Lollard ideals and offered support to them. Along with Northampton, the town was regarded as a Midlands centre of Lollardy by its opponents and it was inevitable that when real trouble flared in 1431, there would be Coventry people involved in it.

The trouble, when it came, was known as Jack Sharpe's uprising and it spread from the town of Abingdon in Berkshire, where Sharpe and his fellow townsmen sought to throw off the yoke of the abbot. The detail is sketchy, but in the wake of what the authorities clearly chose to regard as a dangerous rebellion, a number of Coventry folk followed the hapless Sharpe in being indicted and condemned to death. They included a woman who, intriguingly, was said to be the wife of a mayor. Her identity remains a mystery, but she may have been the wife of wealthy Coventry mercer Ralph Garton, never mayor but a prominent Lollard sympathiser in the town.

Right in the middle of all this religious ferment came an event that the God-fearing in Coventry would certainly have viewed as a sign of heavenly displeasure. On 28 September 1426, the City Annals recounted:

> between one and two in the morning, began a terrific Earthquake with lightning and
> thunder and continued two hours. It was universal; men thought ye Day of Judgment
> was come. The beasts of the field roared and drew to the towns with hideous noises,
> and the wild fowls of the air cried out

The Coventry Doom. Was an earthquake the trigger for it? (Holy Trinity Church)

This event, terrifying but not, in Coventry at least, all that destructive, may well have been the spur for the 'Coventry Doom', an astonishing depiction of the Day of Judgment painted high on the chancel wall of Holy Trinity Church by unknown local artists, early in the 1430s.

Arguably the finest surviving wall painting of its kind in Britain, the Doom teems with detail, showing sinners, including recalcitrant ale-wives who had been watering the beer, being dragged by demons to the mouth of hell, yawning open with huge fangs, while the godly rise from their graves to sit at the right hand of God. But might the painting's finger-wagging message of warning also owe something to the displeasure shown by the Church authorities towards those in Coventry who showed such worrying support for the Lollard manifesto?

The quality of the painting suggests another specialist Coventry craft from the late Middle Ages that remains shadowy, but was to boast its finest exponent in John Thornton, a glass painter born in the town, probably in the early 1360s.

Very little is known about Thornton's early life, although he may have come from a line of accomplished glass painters. A John de Thornton recorded as the holder of a tenement in 1371 may have been his father. Not much of his painted glass survives intact in his native city either, but his greatest work certainly does – the Great East Window in York Minster, the biggest and generally regarded as the finest work in stained glass in medieval England.

As a Coventry craftsman, Thornton most likely secured his lucrative contract in December 1405 through connections with Richard Scrope, Archbishop of York, who had been Bishop of Coventry and Lichfield until 1398 and probably knew his work. After meeting his three-year deadline for the work, Thornton stayed on in York, becoming a freeman of the city in 1410. He was back in Coventry by 1413, with a workshop and house close to the Burges, but later returned to York and was still living there in the early 1430s.

Before heading north to the bright lights of York, Thornton may well have designed the windows of the new church of St Michael in Coventry, back in the 1390s. Fragments that survive certainly betray his trademark style of white glass and yellow stain, set against blue and ruby patterned backgrounds, and his highly distinctive modelling of faces.

While Coventry could not boast the career opportunities and cultural richness of York, its own success as a commercial centre had embedded a growing sense of civic pride and cultural ambition. In 1423 the Leet Book made its first reference to the 'waits', or town band, recording the appointment of four musicians, led by a trumpeter and paid quarterly, 'as others have afore them', who would be expected to play in the streets at night and on important occasions.

At the time, music would not necessarily have been the ordinary Coventry citizen's first choice of entertainment. Animal-baiting seems to have

A commemorative plaque to John Thornton, close to the site of his Coventry workshop in the Burges. It takes the shape of his greatest work, the Great East Window in York Minster. (Chris Ross)

had rather more adherents, with cock-fighting particularly favoured. And in the same year the Leet ordered that no butcher in Coventry could kill a bull, unless it had been first baited at the accustomed place. The following year it gave orders for a new bull-ring to be established in the market place close to Holy Trinity Church, so that 'bulls may be bayted as they have been heretofore.'

Nevertheless, the town waits were a sign of cultural aspirations. Provided with rent-free cottages by the Trinity Guild and decked out in their livery of coats of green and red, with silver escutcheons, they entertained with trumpet, pipe, drum and strings at festivities of all kinds. They became so sought-after that a later command of the Leet restricted them to appearances at religious houses no more than ten miles from Coventry.

The waits' most important work was to help provide the soundtrack to the pageants, plays with a biblical framework performed by the craft guilds in the streets at the Feast of Corpus Christi, on the Thursday after Trinity Sunday in early June. The first reference to a pageant house in the town dates from 1392, but the plays themselves had almost certainly been in existence for some time before, possibly from the foundation of the Corpus Christi Guild itself, back in 1348.

There were ten of them in all, bringing to life New Testament stories, from the Annunciation to the Last Judgement. And even though the craft guilds at times chafed at the responsibility and expense of staging them, over the next 200 years they were to make Coventry's name famous and do wonders for the local visitor economy.

Paying for pageants was one thing. In 1449 the craft guilds were called into action for a very different purpose – raising men to defend their town. In the general muster of that year, the companies raised more than 600 able-bodied men, their contribution reflecting the scale of each craft in Coventry – ranging from the tailors and shearmen with sixty-four, the drapers (fifty-nine) and the weavers (fifty-seven), right down to the masons (seven) and the cooks (five). It was a timely demonstration of readiness, for a coming storm was beginning to darken skies over England and Coventry, still fairly prosperous but nervous behind its half-finished wall, was not immune.

In May 1448, shocked bystanders witnessed a 'great fray' in the heart of the town between long-standing enemies Sir Humphrey Stafford and Sir Robert Harcourt and their retainers, in which a number of combatants on both sides, including Stafford's eldest son Richard, were killed.

These were no ordinary brawlers, Stafford had held the office of Royal Commissioner and Governor of Calais, and their feud reflected the taking of sides in the approaching conflict between the houses of York and Lancaster. That nobody was brought to trial for the killings only deepened the sense of a society spinning out of control.

In July 1450, Coventry was placed on a high state of alert when the Kentish rebel Jack Cade, fuelled by real injustices, raised an army of 5,000 men and stormed and looted London. For a moment it looked as though the rebellion would spread and in Coventry the Leet deployed forty armed men to keep watch all night, from the closing of the town gates at 9 p.m. to the daybreak bell, sounded at 7 a.m. Four brass cannons were also hurriedly purchased from Bristol, then the country's leading centre for iron manufacturing, and mounted on the town walls at the new Bablake Gate.

They weren't needed. Cade was quickly defeated; he died of his wounds in captivity and his quartered body was scattered around the kingdom, part of it almost certainly ending up on one of Coventry's gates. But his uprising had been a test for a man who was about to become very involved in Coventry's story. And it was a test that he had failed.

Henry VI had been an infant when his warlike father Henry V had died of dysentery on campaign in France. After long years of regency he had come of age in May 1445, first marrying a bride eight years younger than himself, the teenage but already strong-willed Margaret of Anjou, and then being crowned king on 30 May.

Standing five foot nine inches and with a build strong enough to enjoy the hunting field, Henry cut a suitably regal figure. But he lacked the determined facial cast of his father, whose war-like visage had no doubt been enhanced by a scar from a crossbow bolt, taken full in the face when he was sixteen.

To his contemporaries Henry VI had a wondering, distracted air and appeared utterly uninterested in ruling as a king ought to do. One described him as 'a saint or a natural fool.' By 1450 his passivity as commander-in-chief had helped throw away almost all of England's final remaining possessions in France, even Normandy. As a consequence, England was suddenly full of a defeated, embittered soldiery, who clearly blamed the king and his government for their plight and would be the brutal instrument of the coming war.

Henry was at Leicester when word came of the Cade rebellion and was persuaded to travel with all haste to London to try and persuade the rebels to give up. He failed miserably and quickly fled back to his stronghold at Kenilworth Castle. Well aware of the importance of securing allies for the Lancastrian cause in the forthcoming struggle, the king and his advisers took steps to woo the Midlands' most important town and in late September 1451 he arrived in Coventry, greeted by the mayor and his brethren on the road from Leicester.

Henry lodged at the priory and celebrated mass at St Michael's – his presence was widely seen as an appropriately regal consecration for the extraordinary new spire. He told the mayor, Richard Boys, in private audience that Coventry was the best governed town in the kingdom. He stayed for two weeks and on the day of his departure for Kenilworth announced that he would confer the status of city and county on Coventry, divorcing it from the old county of Warwickshire in an administrative break-away that would endure until the local government reforms of 1842.

Scarcely believing their good fortune, the mayor and his brethren acted swiftly, sending Coventry's recorder, Thomas Littleton, and half a dozen of its most important citizens hotfoot to London to get the king's promise confirmed by charter. Issued on 26 November 1451, the charter they secured incorporated outlying hamlets like Radford, Keresley, Foleshill, Caludon, Wyken, Stoke, Whitley and Whoberley into the new county, but went further, granting Coventry merchandise freedom from tolls, not only throughout England but Ireland too. No longer a town, but now the city and county of Coventry – it must have been a gold-medal moment for those involved, although more cautious heads would have realised this meant the new city's colours were, for now at least, firmly nailed to the Lancastrian mast.

The coming conflict would initially centre on two rivals: Richard Plantaganet, Duke of York, who claimed a direct line from Edward III, and Edmund Beaufort, Duke of Somerset, Henry's head of government, who was descended, albeit illegitimately, from Edward's brother John of Gaunt. When the king's mind gave way in August 1453, after news of a devastating English defeat in Gascony, it was York, Henry's cousin, who persuaded the lords to make him protector of the realm, despite opposition from the queen who believed she should rule in her husband's place.

It was Christmas 1454 before Henry recovered from what was clearly some form of catatonic illness, recognising for the first time his young son Edward, born more than twelve months earlier. But it was too late to prevent the first vicious encounter of the Wars of the Roses, a bloody skirmish at St Albans in May 1455, in which Somerset was killed.

Coventry men may well have fought on the Lancastrian side at St Albans, going into action beneath the standard of the Black Ram, and when the king's health suffered a relapse it wasn't long before Queen Margaret came to the conclusion that London was a dangerous place for him to be. It was at this point, in the summer of 1456, that she decided Coventry would serve as an alternative centre of royal power. She spent so much time in the city over the next year or two that it began to be called, not always with affection, 'the Queen's bower'.

While pro-Lancastrian sentiment was strong in Coventry, there was always a significant minority who favoured the Yorkists, focused on the wealthy merchant quarter around Little Park Street and an inn called the White Rose, or Roebuck. There were plenty in the new city for whom such a close association with a damaged king and his cause was regrettable.

Henry VI and Margaret of Anjou are the central figures in St Mary's Hall's 500-year-old tapestry.
(St Mary's Hall/Coventry City Council)

The royal household arrived on 14 September, greeted by the mayor and council who had already decided that the habitual gifts of silver-gilt cups and money worth in total £100 were in order. Carefully planned pageants, with characters decked out in the richest materials that the guilds could afford, were staged to sing Margaret's praises, comparing her to the queen of heaven. Margaret might have been flattered, but there was business to be done and she moved quickly to pick up the reins of power. In October 1456 a Great Council met at Coventry to try to find some common ground in a conflict that had already horrified contemporaries with its savagery. It elected new royal officials – Chancellor, Treasurer and Keeper of the Royal Seal – who were acceptable to all sides, and the Duke of York swore a public oath of loyalty to the king.

When Margaret left Coventry the following spring she was preceded out of the city in procession by the mayor and sheriffs, a signal honour only ever given to the reigning monarch. Yet York had already refused to attend a second council in the city, and the next time that Coventry featured as a venue for national debate, the final die would be cast.

A sign of warlike times? The Coventry sallet, made by Martin Rondelle of Brussels around 1460 and purchased by the city's Carpenters' Guild. (Herbert Collections)

By early 1459, Margaret was back in the city, this time with an army raised in the north as the stand-off with her enemies hardened. At another Great Council, called in June, Richard of York and his nephew and right-hand man, Richard Neville, Earl of Warwick, failed to appear and after a series of running skirmishes fled abroad.

At the parliament of 20 November, the second to be held in Coventry and the last to be held outside London, thirty-two lords met in the priory's Chapter House and 120 Commons assembled in the Great Hall. York, Warwick and their chief supporters were declared traitors and 'attainted', with their property and lives forfeit to the Crown. After the Devilish Parliament, as the Yorkists dubbed it, there would be no going back.

By the following spring unease at the abrasive Margaret's high-handedness and the very idea of government from provincial Coventry was beginning to turn the tide against the Lancastrian cause. York and Warwick landed back in England with an army, defeated Margaret's forces at Northampton on 10 July 1460 and made a captive of Henry, who was found quietly sitting in his tent while battle raged. Richard of York's subsequent attempt to have himself declared king was regarded with horror by all but the most partisan of his followers and instead he had to settle for a deal, in which Henry ruled on until his death, at which time York would succeed to the throne. It was an arrangement that Margaret, as the mother of the next rightful king, could never accept and as the fighting continued York was killed at the battle of Wakefield in December. It seemed a decisive blow, but turned out to be simply the next instalment of a grisly horror show of brutal pitched battles and tit-for-tat atrocities as the English nobility tore itself to pieces over the next decade.

Coventry's role as the Lancastrians' chief headquarters and rallying point had much diminished, no doubt to the heartfelt relief of its tradesmen, forced to deal with a royal household that was notorious for not paying its bills. But the war was not finished with the city yet. In late 1465 it looked as though Coventry might come under siege, as York's clever and imposing second son, now King Edward IV, advanced on the city. He had a force that included 200 archers to arrest his family's erstwhile ally, the Earl of Warwick, and his own brother the Duke of Clarence, who had taken shelter within its walls after being accused of treason. Disaster was averted when the charges were found to be spurious, and the party spent a presumably jolly Christmas together in the city as their hosts gave thanks for deliverance.

In early 1471, Edward blockaded Coventry with his army in an attempt to flush out Warwick, who turned out to have switched sides after all, and was holed up with his own forces inside the city.

Edward's attempt failed, but at the battle of Barnet in March, Warwick was killed by a dagger thrust through his visor. The final defeat for the Lancastrian cause came two months later at Tewkesbury, when Margaret and Henry's young son Edward was killed in battle and the queen herself was taken prisoner nearby. She was brought to Edward IV at Coventry, once her 'bower' but now a place of bitter failure and bereavement.

For the citizens of Coventry, this meeting with the king was to prove unsettling and expensive. Recalling the city's recent role as a shelter for the turncoat Earl of Warwick and still smarting, no doubt, from that Devilish Parliament, Edward confiscated Coventry's ceremonial sword as a punishment. He also removed the city's liberties, including what appears to have been a newly granted right to mint coinage. Certainly no coins from Coventry's fledgling mint, active in the late 1460s from a site on Hay Lane, have been discovered bearing a later date.

Coventry had to work hard to get back in the king's good books and within a year Edward had restored the city's liberties, redeemed at a price of 500 marks. Three years later, the city fathers were very careful to treat his four-year-old son, the ill-fated 'Prince in the Tower' otherwise known to history as Edward V, with special reverence, presenting the little boy with lavish gifts and entertaining him with pageants and music on 'harp and dulcimer and small pipes' performed by the city waits.

Edward IV never entirely trusted Coventry, and in 1477 the Leet Book recorded his warning to the mayor not to harass John French, an alchemist living in the city, who was trying to turn base metal into gold 'for the king's profit and pleasure'. It was a fleeting reference to French, whom the authorities clearly suspected of practising the dark arts. What became of him isn't known. In all likelihood he made a discreet withdrawal from a place where he was obviously not welcome.

After Edward IV's untimely death in early 1483, his usurper brother, Richard III, was in the city in October en route to crushing a rebellion in the south. While keeping Whitsuntide at Kenilworth Castle in May 1485, Richard was again in Coventry, this time to see the mystery plays. There is a tradition too that he had decided on the fate of the hapless Princes in the Tower during one of his earlier visits.

Whatever the truth of that, the city managed to steer itself clear of the final major clash of the Wars of the Roses; Richard lost his crown and his life to another usurper, Henry VII, at the battle of Bosworth Field in Leicestershire, less than twenty miles away.

Henry was in Coventry just two days after the battle, staying at the house of the mayor, Robert Onley, in Smithford Street and receiving, of course, a gold cup and £100 in readies from a city desperate for his favour. Onley was later knighted for his hospitality. Among the prominent citizens contributing provisions to entertain the king and his entourage was John Smyth, one of nineteen bakers listed as members of the Baker's Company in the muster of 1449.

Richard as Duke of Gloucester in the St Mary's Hall tapestry. The coin he grasps in his fingers suggests treachery. (St Mary's Hall/Coventry City Council)

Smyth's appearances in the Leet Book illustrate clearly the careful line that wealthy men in Coventry had been treading during those turbulent years and the commitment they were repeatedly asked to make to defend the city. In 1461 he is recorded as a collector in the Much Park Street ward, helping to raise contributions towards the military costs of the Earl of Warwick as he pursued the remnants of the Lancastrian army after their terrible defeat at the battle of Towton. Seven years later he's one of those contributing to the city's costs of entertaining Elizabeth Woodville, wife of Edward IV. In 1469, the Leet Book lists him as Captain of the Much Park Street ward, ready to defend the city, and the following year he's raising money again, this time to pay the wages of city men fighting in Edward's army in skirmishes at Exeter and Nottingham. In 1471, as collector for the Gosford Street ward, he's one of the contributors towards a loan offered to Edward IV.

Smyth survived the years of war – the last reference to him is in 1495, when he was among those appointed to a jury to hear a land dispute involving the Hospital of St John. But for Coventry itself, the sheen of its golden age had been well and truly tarnished. A further outbreak of pestilence, possibly cholera, in 1479 had carried off a significant chunk of the city's population; it was alleged up to 3,000 people at the time although that seems far-fetched.

Law and order was being stretched in a number of directions. In the 1460s the Leet Book makes its first reference to 'vagabonds' haunting the city, ruling that to avoid immediate expulsion and qualify for alms, all bona fide beggars in Coventry must have an elephant and castle stamped on their filthy bags.

Disturbingly, the city had also acquired an unenviable reputation as a place of execution. In August 1469, the Earl of Warwick had had another member of the Woodville family, Richard, 1st Earl Rivers, and his son John summarily put to death on Gosford Green. The following year, a man named Clapham, who had, it was claimed, led the 'rabble' from Northampton at the battle of Edgecote, was beheaded and his head stuck on Bablake Gate, and in 1487, the shadowy rebel Thomas Harrington, taken prisoner at the Battle of Stoke, Henry VII's final reckoning with the Yorkists, was beheaded on the conduit opposite the Bull Inn, watched by Henry himself from the window of the inn, where he was staying.

Worryingly, despite its best efforts to concentrate on business, the war had cost the city more than £2,000 in loans and bribes to the warring parties. It was a financial drain it could ill afford.

COVENTRY'S MYSTERY PLAYS

It is a Thursday in June, the Feast of Corpus Christi, and between the cobbles and the eaves of Gosford Street the procession of Coventry pageants is gathering at their first station.

There are ten of them in all, covering the story of the world from Creation to Domesday, and each is a source of pride to the craft guild that has created it – from the Shearman and Tailors with their account of the Nativity, to the Weavers telling the story of the child Jesus and the Doctors in the Temple, and the Drapers presenting their extravagantly mounted Domesday play.

The streets are buzzing with excited crowds. Corpus Christi marks the beginning of an eight-day annual fair in Coventry and local people in festive mood have been joined by thousands more revellers drawn from near and far by the spectacle, a beguiling mixture of the sacred and profane.

The pageants themselves were the wagons on which the plays were performed, two-storey constructions of wood and iron, manhandled through the streets to each 'station' or performing site. The first reference to a pageant house, where one of these contraptions was stored, was in 1392, but the plays had probably already been in existence for at least forty years.

Other cities, like York and Chester, boasted mystery plays, but none enjoyed a greater level of royal patronage. Henry V and VI both saw them – the latter's wife, Margaret of Anjou, making a special visit to see them in 1457, after which she and her entourage dined on, 'three hundred loaves, a pipe of red wine, a dozen fat capons, pippins, oranges and a pot of green ginger.'

Richard III was a spectator at Corpus Christi in June 1485, just two months before meeting his fate at Bosworth. A year later his conqueror, Henry VII, was in the audience. Henry VIII, a man with a great love of theatre, came to Coventry in 1511 with his wife Katherine of Aragon to see them,

Representation of a Pageant Vehicle and Play.

The state, and reverence, and show,
Were so attractive, folks would go
From all parts, ev'ry year, to see
These pageant-plays at Coventry.

A Coventry pageant in performance. (Coventry City Council)

as did his daughters Mary – who in 1526 saw a special performance of the Mercers' play, which depicted the later life of the Virgin Mary – and Elizabeth, who in August 1565 watched four plays, surrounded by her entourage and respectful crowds, in Earl Street in the heart of the city.

Of the men who wrote, performed and produced these plays, we have only tantalising glimpses. In 1523 Japheth Borseley, although a member of a prominent family of Coventry cappers, was granted leave to take a role in the Weavers play, a clear case of having the right connections. Contrast him with poor John Careles, a weaver jailed for his Protestant views but released in June 1556 to perform in the guild's play. Afterwards, he was sent in chains to London, where he died in prison and his body was 'cast on a dunghill.'

In the 1450s the Smiths Guild employed Thomas Colclow, a skinner, to organise their pageant for them. In the 1530s, Robert Crow, the most prominent impresario of the Coventry mysteries, re-wrote the Weavers' and the Shearman and Tailors' plays.

By Crow's time the writing was on the wall for the Coventry mystery plays. In an increasingly Protestant and anti-theatrical city, it became harder and harder to justify the lavish staging of plays associated with a Catholic tradition. Traditionalists like the master upholsterer Thomas Massey fought a rearguard action to preserve them but the last complete cycle of the plays was performed in 1579.

The Shearman and Tailors' Nativity play is the only one to have survived in any substantive form, and its blend of earthy humour and raw emotion allows us to see the characters as medieval audiences would have seen them – querulous and ridiculous Joseph, comic shepherds and a ranting, violent Herod. Those characters may well have made a deep and lasting impression on one young audience member from the sixteenth century. In *Hamlet*, Shakespeare's sweet prince mocks an actor in Elsinore whose ranting style, he says, 'out-Herods Herod'. Could that have been a memory lodged in the mind of a writer who as a boy had seen the plays performed, not twenty miles from his native Stratford?

five

A FANATIC TOWN

As the son of a former mayor and a member of both Holy Trinity and Corpus Christi guilds, the dyer Laurence Saunders was on the fast-track to advancement in late fifteenth-century Coventry. Intelligent, resourceful and well-connected, he was a man heading for eminence and his appointment as one of the city's two Chamberlains in early 1480 was the first rung of the ladder.

To the Chamberlains fell the responsibility for building and maintaining the town wall and overseeing the city's common land, and it wasn't long before those who had nodded through Saunders's appointment realised the error they had made. His first act of rebellion, reported by the Leet Book, was refusing to pay weekly wages to labourers quarrying stone for the town wall, as custom dictated. Instead, he announced, those who had set them to work should pay them.

For this, Saunders and his fellow Chamberlain, William Hede, who later recanted, were confined to prison for a week and ordered to pay a stiff fine. But that was just the beginning. Before long, Saunders was being accused of levying excessive fines on those whose livestock had exceeded the quota permitted to graze on the commons. The accusation shattered the uneasy truce between rulers and ruled in Coventry over use of the common lands that surrounded the city. Disputes could be traced back more than a century and a flashpoint had been reached in 1469, the year that Laurence's father, William Saunders, had been mayor.

In November 1469, the landowner William Bristowe moved to wall in allegedly common land at Whitley that his own father, John Bristowe, had 'acquired' forty years before. When the citizens got to hear of it, a 500-strong crowd led, it was claimed, by the mayor and 'arrayed in jacks and sallets' (leather jerkins and helmets) marched out of the city, demolished the wall and returned in high spirits, serenaded by the waits, playing triumphal airs.

One week later on 6 December, St Nicholas Day, they sallied out again to another piece of disputed land, known as the Prior's Waste, and destroyed hedges. On this occasion the authorities, nervous of the Benedictine prior's reaction, hastily moved to compensate him with other property. But in a subsequent court case, William Bristowe's attempt to sue the mayor and commonalty for trespass and annexe common lands as his own was rejected.

In 1477, in the wake of this lengthy dispute, it was decided that in future the chamberlains would ride out annually to inspect the commons in person and make sure they were properly accessible. Three years on, it was 200 of William Bristowe's sheep that Saunders now seized for exceeding the grazing quota, along with 400 animals belonging to the prior, among others.

In the uproar that followed, Saunders travelled privately to the Prince of Wales's council at Ludlow and presented a petition alleging that the prior, the recorder, Harry Boteler, and other powerful officials were withholding common lands from the citizens, instead allowing a favoured few to graze as many animals as they liked there. The royal councillors demanded the presence of a deputation from Coventry to put their side of the story, and after hearing the case found in their favour. Saunders was jailed briefly, had to kneel before the mayor and council in St Mary's Hall to plead forgiveness and was ordered to pay the deputation's travelling expenses, a hefty £15 11s 1d.

The fine was a heavy burden, but it didn't shut him up. Two years later, when the final decision in the Bristowe court case was made known, he was accused of bursting into 'untoward speech' about enclosures and was briefly imprisoned again, until friends secured his release. Forced to recant, Laurence Saunders was silent for more than a decade, but on Lammas Day (1 August) 1494, in the wake of a dispute over apprentice fees between the mayor and council and some of the craft guilds, he was heard by witnesses to say, 'We shall not have our rights until we have stricken off three or four of these churls' heads that rule us.' He also urged a crowd in the market place to seize oats belonging to William Boteler, son of the former recorder, and treat them as their own.

Flung into jail for seven months, he was stripped of all offices and his membership of the guilds and warned that if he fomented rebellion a third time he would be hanged. It didn't stop him. In July 1496, now elderly and impoverished, he submitted a petition to the mayor, John Dove, demanding that enclosures of common land should be stopped. When the petition was rejected, he threatened Dove with a revolt and was again arrested. In November, his case was sent to the Star Chamber in London for trial and he was committed to the Fleet Prison to await the verdict.

At this point, Laurence Saunders disappears from Coventry's history. What became of him isn't known, although it is probable that he died in prison. But the old rebel's story – the fullest account of a municipal controversy to survive from the fifteenth century – illustrates the underlying mistrusts and tensions in a place where the golden age was long past and the city's staple industry of cloth manufacturing had been in decline for some time. 'The commons in Coventry arose,' had become a phrase used all too frequently by those who chronicled events in Coventry, and disruption and disorder was not confined to the mob.

In 1484, a dispute with the mayor and council led the Masters of the Bakers Company to call their members out on strike and decamp en masse to Baginton, outside the city's jurisdiction, a further act of rebellion for which they were fined £10. The following year the most powerful of the Coventry guilds, Holy Trinity, recorded 135 of its 387 houses and cottages empty, a worrying reverse in fortunes for one of the city's biggest landlords. It is probable that from a peak of around 10,000 earlier in the century, Coventry's population was now no more than 8,500.

It had not lost its taste for religious nonconformity, however. In March 1485, eight Coventry men – John Blomston, alias Master John the physician, Richard Hegham, Robert Crowther, John Smith, Roger Brown, Thomas Butler, John Falkes, and Richard Silwyn – were brought before the Bishop of Coventry and Lichfield, John Hales. They were accused of heresy, in particular of mocking the veneration accorded to sites of pilgrimage, notably the Whitefriars' chapel of Our Lady in the Tower.

It was a very Lollard thing to do, and after confessing their guilt, the perpetrators were made to walk barefoot from St Michael's Church to the market place, and then to the chapel in the wall, each carrying a faggot on their shoulder to symbolise the burning that surely awaited them if they transgressed again.

As Coventry entered the final decade of the fifteenth century, there was the odd pinpoint of light amidst the economic gloom. A new craft, using wool to make caps and other headgear, was experiencing a meteoric rise, giving immigration something of a boost and ensuring that in the century to come cappers would enjoy a high profile in the city, with a number becoming mayor. But in 1494 the Leet was admitting that many of the crafts which had, from the beginning, borne the cost of the city's pageants were finding it hard to continue doing so.

For the Benedictines in Coventry, no doubt fearing the rise of Lollardy once more, there was at least some consolation in the shape of recognition from within their order. The Coventry priory had succeeded Northampton as the periodic venue for the provincial chapter of the Benedictines in England, and in July 1498 it hosted representatives from all of the order's English houses. The four-day meeting began with a formal greeting from the mayor, Thomas Bond, and his brethren, and Bond ordered that a list of regulated food prices in the city should be nailed to the south door of St Michael's church, so that visitors could see they were not being conned by local victuallers.

Using a church door as a message board was not new in Coventry. Back in 1446, Friar John Bredon of the Greyfriars, a champion of the people and no friend to the Benedictines, had nailed up some words of rebuke on the door of Holy Trinity. He urged citizens to throw off the yoke of the prior 'as the thraldom of Pharoah', a risky suggestion for which he was thrown into jail, forced to repent on his knees and then expelled from the city.

And in 1495, at the height of the final controversy surrounding Laurence Saunders, an anonymous hand pinned verses in his support to the door of St Michael's Church. They began:

> Be it known and understand,
> This city shudd be free and nowe is bonde,
> Dame goode Eve made it free,
> And now the custom for woll and the draperies
> Also hit is made that no prentis shall be
> But thirteen pence pay should he

The reference to Godiva shows how strongly the idea of her freeing the people from burdens had taken root in Coventry and the warning tone reflects something of the anger of the ordinary people, in tough times, against those who were in charge.

Life for the ordinary citizen of Coventry at the turn of the sixteenth century was relatively short, often brutish and always tightly controlled by the governing elite of the mayor and his council, steadily beginning to acquire powers that had formerly been vested in the Leet.

The day-bell was rung at 4 a.m. from St Michael's and Holy Trinity, at which the night-watch stood down, the city gates were opened and the water conduits unlocked. By 5 a.m., unemployed craftsmen had to be at the city's central crossroads (Smithford Street and Broadgate) ready for hire if needed. With so many men in the streets, the mastiffs widely used to guard property had to be chained up by this time.

For most people the working day began at around 6 a.m., and in an age with only crude oil lamps and tallow candles to provide artificial light, its length was dependent on the time of year. Winter officially began on 1 November and lasted until 2 February, during which the waits played longer in the streets at night as a kind of reassurance that all was well. In a curiously modern touch, the working day did have times laid down for meal breaks, but probably lasted in most cases for fourteen hours.

Children, regarded as fledgling adults and often referred to as 'manikins' and 'womankins', had to play their role in that. Even though there were schools for Coventry children to attend, one or possibly two town 'grammar' schools, and small establishments run by the Benedictines and the Carthusians, the concept of childhood was a somewhat alien one. It belongs to later centuries. Most boys, except the sons of the elite, were at work by the age of twelve, while girls, if they weren't already in service, were expected to contribute their labour to household chores.

At the end of the working day, curfew was sung in the central churches at 8 p.m., the city gates were locked an hour later and by that time the lanterns which hung outside the doors of inns and the houses of the better-off had to be extinguished.

Strict regulations governed the basic transactions of daily life. Corn could be sold at market on Monday, meat and hides on Tuesday. On Wednesday bakers were allowed in from outside the city to sell their wares, and it was also the day on which the mayor and council would receive petitions from their fellow citizens about their concerns and disputes. On Thursday, meat could again be sold at market, while the sale of fish, corn and bread was permitted on Friday, chief market day and also the day on which the drapery, or covered cloth market, operated. Meat and hides were sold on Saturday, which was also pay day for most people and the only day on which the working man could resort to an alehouse or, if he belonged to the right guild, to one of the city's more upmarket inns, like the Cardinal's Hat in Earl Street or the Crown in Broadgate. Sunday, of course, was meant to be a day of contemplation and religious observance. Even so, the street outside every tenement had to be swept clean before inspection on Sunday afternoon, while the city aldermen, between compulsory attendance at service after service, were tasked with keeping a constant eye out 'for all them that keep misrule'.

That might mean frequenting 'blind' or secret inns, where who-knows-what went on, or indulging in unlawful pursuits like 'roving'. The Leet was uncompromising about this. Roving meant firing arrows at targets on the move and in 1468 it outlawed the sport (perhaps because it was dangerous), ordering instead that butts should be set up at which citizens could practise their skills in archery, in line with a command from the king, Edward IV.

Brawling was expressly forbidden and there were severe doubts about the rowdiness of the celebrations that attended Coventry's festive calendar, notably the feasts of Midsummer eve and St Peter's eve in the autumn, when houses were decorated with greenery, neighbours caroused in the streets and bonfires were lit in every area.

An unprecedented snapshot of those living in Coventry at the time comes from a remarkable document, the earliest surviving census of a town in England. It was commissioned by the mayor, John Bond, in the autumn of 1520, and included population figures for each of the city's ten wards as well as information about stocks of corn held in what was still England's ninth largest town. The total population reckoning of around 6,600 might be a little on the low side, but it also included a breakdown of occupations, recording, for example, that there were sixty-eight brewers and forty-three bakers at work in the city.

By that time, the bloom on the new trade in caps had faded and Coventry was experiencing severe economic hardship. Poor harvests in 1518 and 1519 had been followed by the 'year of dearth' in 1520, when disease and even starvation threatened.

In 1518, 'about the feast of Lammas' an outbreak of the 'sweating sickness', believed by some historians of medicine to have been influenza, led to significant fatalities. On top of that, a slump in the cloth trade and steep rises in the price of wool led to looms falling silent and had encouraged some to believe that Coventry's fortunes had taken a blow from which they would never recover. The city was swollen with beggars from the countryside, fleeing abject poverty and even starvation, and the ruling elite proved somewhat short on sympathy, ordering that 'those lying in the fields, breaking hedges and stealing fruit' should be expelled forthwith.

Even so, such hard times also prompted a string of charitable acts from those years, as well-to-do members of Coventry's oligarchy, with one eye no doubt on their own personal legacy, made a series of philanthropic bequests.

Ford's Hospital, still in use as a home for the elderly. (CV One/Coventry City Council)

The merchant William Ford, mayor in 1497, died in 1509 and left money in his will to build an almshouse on monastery ground close to Greyfriars Gate that would house six elderly couples, with a woman to look after them and a stipend of five pence a week. Eight years later, the capper William Pisford added to his bequest and introduced another of his own, leaving money to give thirteen poor maidens twenty shillings each when they married.

Thomas Bond, a wealthy draper and Mayor of Coventry in 1498, had in 1506 bequeathed money to found another almshouse for ten elderly men, with a woman to look after them, close to the collegiate church of Bablake.

Draper John Haddon, by his will dated 1518, left £100 to be divided into loans for young cloth-makers pursuing his own trade, and a further £100 in loans for the use of struggling craftsmen in other trades.

That these powerful men might have harboured feelings of support for their fellow citizenry that went beyond mere sympathy cannot be proved, but it is true that even among the elite the Lollard creed was very much alive in Coventry.

The Martyrs' Mosaic, a modern tribute to those who went to the stake in Coventry. (Coventry City Council)

In 1491, it was reported that the mayor, John Wigston, 'did strive against Our Lady place of the Whitefriars' in what seems to be a clear repudiation of the cult of the Virgin.

The first Coventry follower to suffer the ultimate penalty for her faith was Joan Ward, who had admitted being a Lollard back in the 1490s, recanted and moved away from the city, but had returned in 1511 and re-adopted her old beliefs. She was condemned as a relapsed heretic and was burned at the stake on 12 March 1512.

Eight years later, on 4 April 1520, seven further Lollards followed her to the execution ground, in a hollow in what had been Richard II's old quarry in the park at Cheylesmore. Thomas Bond, Hosea Hawkins, Robert Hachett and John Archer were shoemakers, Thomas Landesdale was a hosier and Thomas Wrigsham a glover. The seventh, the widow Joan Smith, was simply unlucky. Initially discharged, she was brought back to trial when the official escorting her home discovered an English translation of the Lord's Prayer and the Ten Commandments hidden in her sleeve. She went to the fire with the others.

An eighth Coventry Lollard, the sect's librarian Robert Silkeby, had also been arrested but escaped. He was captured some eighteen months later and on 13 January 1522 he too paid the horrifying price for his heresy.

The executions of these so-called 'Coventry martyrs' cannot have helped calm the mood of a public struggling to stem a worrying decline in prosperity. Confidence in Coventry's stability must have been further weakened in 1523 by the discovery of a bizarre plot to kill the mayor, wealthy draper Julian Nethermill, and his brethren, rob St Mary's Hall and storm Kenilworth Castle. The plotters, two men named Pratt and Slouth, thought to be Thomas Slouth who was a scrivener, were hanged, drawn and quartered and their body parts liberally spread among the spikes on Bablake Gate, New Gate and Greyfriars Gate on the town wall.

During the summer of that year, Nethermill ordered a further census to be taken of Coventry's inhabitants. In its register of occupations, cappers were still prominent at eighty-four, second only to widows, who numbered 151. Worryingly, there were 565 houses empty in the city and the population had fallen by 900 since 1520, an alarming dip in just three years.

The census may have been prompted by new tax demands imposed on England by Henry VIII's formidable Chancellor, Thomas Wolsey, to pay for the king's vainglorious sabre-rattling on the Continent. Coventry's contribution to this over three years, Wolsey estimated, should be £2,044. Even though he later moderated his demands, it was a burden the city, used to the Crown taking barely £50 a year from it in tax, could hardly bear.

In the event, a quarter of Coventry's tax was paid by just three men, including Nethermill and the fabulously wealthy mercer Richard Marler, who owned fifty houses in the city and possessed a fortune that made him the third wealthiest provincial merchant in England. Marler came from a family who had moved to Coventry as little more than peasants a century before, and had ridden to prosperity on the back of the city's fourteenth-century boom. He was content to remain a resident and the chantry chapel he built for himself still survives in Holy Trinity Church, but other members of well-to-do city families had begun to see greater opportunities elsewhere. Coventry could no longer encompass their ambitions.

One such was John Rastell, the son of a magistrate, born around 1475 into a prominent Coventry family who had long been active in city affairs. Lawyer, printer, dramatist, designer, reformer and cosmographer, Rastell was perhaps the closest a native Coventrian has ever come to being a truly renaissance man. Although much of this extraordinary career was achieved in London, its roots lay in Coventry.

Sworn into the Corpus Christi Guild while still in his teenage years, John trained as a lawyer and in 1507 was appointed coroner of Coventry.

The Marler chapel in Holy Trinity Church. (Holy Trinity)

His horizons had already extended beyond the city with his marriage, sometime before 1504, to Elizabeth More, sister of Thomas More, Henry VIII's future Lord Chancellor and notable victim. But there's evidence that he retained close connections with his birthplace, acting as a paid adviser to his guild and helping to stage pageants performed in Coventry as late as 1510.

From 1508 Rastell appears as a printer in London, one of a handful of pioneers in the art, as well as a lawyer of the Middle Temple, his position there possibly brokered by More. Four years later, when war broke out with France, he was working for Sir Edward Belknap, brother of Henry VIII's Clerk of Works. He played a role in the conduct of the war, overseeing the transport of guns.

Rastell was profoundly influenced by the utopian ideas of his brilliant brother-in-law and, in search of a living embodiment of More's utopia, he joined an expedition to the New World in the summer of 1517. Once afloat, the ship's master declared that they intended 'to go robbing on the seas' and put Rastell ashore in Ireland, where he may have remained for two years.

In 1520, back in London, he was tasked with designing the lavishly decorative temporary buildings for Henry VIII's celebrated meeting with the

King of France at the Field of Cloth of Gold. And that artistic flair remained a key element in pageants he devised for Henry in the years that followed. In 1524, he built himself a house in Finsbury Fields in London, complete with its own theatre, the earliest recorded Tudor stage. Even though it was for his own use, as he was an enthusiastic writer and director of plays and masques, fifty years later the first public theatre in England was built on the site.

In the last decade of his life, Rastell emerged as a prolific writer and publisher on law; at least one of his works is still in use. Radicalised by his early life in the Lollard atmosphere of Coventry, he also became a highly vocal exponent of religious reform, and it was that which led to his downfall. After calling for an end to the clergy's right to tithes, very much part of the Lollard creed, he was hauled before Thomas Cranmer, Archbishop of Canterbury, and then flung into jail. He died there in June 1536, leaving a final letter in which he bitterly reflected on his fall after such a life of achievement. He was, he wrote, 'now by long imprisonment brought to extreme misery, forsaken by his kinsmen, destitute of his friends, comfortless and succourless.'

Back in Rastell's home town, it had been a riotous ten years, with public disorder sparked off by that old powder keg, the use of common lands, making the city almost ungovernable. The trigger was an order of the Leet in 1522 that at least half of the recently enclosed common lands should be ploughed and sown. That meant they would still be under crop on Lammas Day, 1 August, the traditional date for opening them up to general use as pasture, and so would not be available until after the harvest.

Acts of vandalism in 1524 were followed by serious trouble on Lammas Day 1525, when the annual ceremonial ride by the city Chamberlains to formally open up the commons was accompanied by a large, rowdy crowd, who tore up hedges, battered down fences and even filled in a ditch.

Meanwhile, another angry crowd gathered in the streets, and as the Chamberlains rode towards the walls they closed the New Gate, shutting them out. At the same time another group broke into the city treasury in St Mary's Hall and seized the box containing rents for the common lands.

In the confusion that followed, the mayor, capper Nicholas Heynes, sided with the common people, and Thomas Grey, 2nd Marquess of Dorset, was ordered by the king to regain control of the city with the force of 2,000 men at his disposal.

On 11 August, Dorset summoned the mayor and council to his headquarters on his estate at Astley, just over the County of Coventry border, and demanded

Riding the bounds on Lammas Day, always a potential flashpoint. (Herbert Art Gallery)

the surrender of four ringleaders, whose names remain unknown. They duly handed over the men but informed him that they could not rule the city without his help. By 19 August, Heynes had been relieved of his mayoralty and sent under guard to London for questioning. A new mayor, John Humphrey, was installed by Dorset to act as governor of the city.

A total of thirty-seven rioters were committed to the castles of Warwick and Kenilworth and another seven to the Marshelsea prison in London, five of whom later had their ears nailed to the pillory back in Coventry.

Heynes was treated more leniently, returning to the city a free man, to the acclamation of his fellow cappers. A special meeting of the forty-eight, the rarely convened full council, actually backed the actions of the rioters. Remarkably, so did Henry VIII, who underlined his forgiving mood by sending his daughter, Princess Mary, to Coventry the following year to see a special performance of the mystery plays.

Encroachment of the common lands had been successfully resisted, yet Coventry was not done with discord. In 1533 Humfrey Reynolds, the younger son of a Coventry family of fullers, made a special supplication to the king on behalf of a small group of shadowy reformers in the city. As a younger son, Reynolds claimed he was being disadvantaged, by lacking the funds to compete for land and property against wealthy merchants or even the financial muscle of the monastic orders, particularly the Black Monks or Benedictines. His solution was to suggest that urban monasteries, such as Coventry's, should have enough money from their estates to keep the brethren in reasonable comfort, but that the rest of their income should go towards establishing a royal military presence in every monastic establishment, with officials and armed men to enforce the law and supervise the local authorities.

Turning his fire on the civic governance of the city, Reynolds claimed that it was leading Coventry towards ruin and warned that there were few magistrates left capable of keeping disorder at bay. It would be the military force, led by a head captain, who would also act as a chief Justice of the Peace that would have the last word in governing the place and its inhabitants.

A flagrant challenge to Coventry's hard-won liberties, Reynolds's proposals were stoutly opposed by the city officials and only found an echo in the strictures of the Puritan Commonwealth, more than a century later. But the impression had been given of a greedy monastic order and a city virtually ungovernable. And that may well have helped to encourage what happened next.

The first sign of the old order beginning to crumble had its roots in the city's recent economic struggles. In late 1534 the membership of the Corpus Christi Guild met to consider their future. Reduced in numbers and unable in many cases to afford even to take office, they decided to merge with the Trinity Guild, at a stroke bringing to an end almost two centuries of political, economic and cultural influence in Coventry.

Another portent can be seen in some unusual activity at the commercial centrepiece of the city's calendar, the Coventry Great Fair, held around the Feast of Corpus Christi in June. At one fair in the mid-1530s, it was reported that the Prior of Selby in Yorkshire sold his cross-staff to the wife of a London goldsmith, while Coventry goldsmith John Calais bought silver religious items worth £14 from the Cistercian monks of Stoneleigh Abbey.

Then, on 1 October 1538 the house of the Carmelites, or Whitefriars, surrendered to Henry VIII's commissioners as the king's attack on the monastic orders gathered pace. Four days later it was the turn of the Greyfriars.

An artist's impression of the scale of the cathedral, dominating the town and other churches around it. (Image courtesy of Continuum Group Ltd)

In vain the mayor, William Coton, petitioned Henry's wily Chief Minister Thomas Cromwell, arguing that the two friary churches were desperately needed as places of refuge and comfort in time of plague. Instead, the friars, fourteen Carmelites and eleven Greyfriars, were summarily turned out without a single pension between them and work began almost immediately to prepare friary buildings for demolition and sale.

As 1539 dawned, events moved with frightening speed. On 15 January, the Benedictine Prior Thomas Camswell and twelve monks formally surrendered the priory and its huge cathedral church to Cromwell's brutal commissioner Dr John London. The following day he accepted the surrender of the twelve remaining Carthusian monks at the Coventry Charterhouse, and the two great Cistercian abbeys at Coombe and Stoneleigh followed within days.

London reported that there had been little trouble from any of them and felt able, in a letter to Cromwell, to crack a joke at the expense of the Benedictines. Amongst the venerated relics of their cathedral church, he wrote, alongside St Osburg's head, part of the Holy Cross, the arm of St Augustine of Hippo and a piece of Our Lady's tomb, was the most holy jawbone of an ass with which Cain had slain Abel. How they must have chuckled at that little jibe.

Essentially, Coventry's misfortune was to be tied into a diocese with Lichfield, a cathedral run by secular canons instead of monks, a definite plus point as far as the monk-hating Henry was concerned. On top of that, successive Bishops of Coventry and Lichfield had long made Lichfield the chief focus of their activities, rarely using their somewhat ruinous palace in Coventry. With two cathedrals in just one diocese, it was always going to be hard to argue for the status quo.

The Chapter House of the cathedral – still a glittering treasure house. (Image courtesy of Continuum Group Ltd)

Even so, Bishop Rowland Lee petitioned Cromwell to spare the cathedral, on the grounds that he needed it to be 'my principal see and head church.' As an alternative, he suggested that it might become a collegiate church or even a kind of retirement home for senior clergy. For a month or two, with the mayor and council adding their own entreaties, it looked as though Lee might have a deal. But in the end all the appeals fell on deaf ears. Although the age of its great wealth had passed, Coventry priory still ranked ninth in the Benedictine rich list, its cathedral a blaze of gold. Henry and his advisers were not about to forego all of those riches. It was the only cathedral in England to be destroyed at the Dissolution.

Questions must remain over the conduct of the final prior, Thomas Camswell, nominated for the job by Thomas Cromwell only ten months before. He walked away with a very generous pension of £133 13s 4d for life, and his brother Michael did rather well in the land and property disposals that followed.

Henry Over, a Sheriff of Coventry in 1538, must have tested his fellow citizens' tolerance too. He was a keen assistant to Dr London, who called him a 'lively, politic man.' He was given the job of guarding the suppressed houses against looters, a role that allowed him to amass a handsome property portfolio out of it all.

By July 1539, royal agents were in Coventry to demolish the great cathedral church and the church of the Whitefriars, although it was to be another six years before much progress was made. Fragments of the great cathedral church were to remain part of Coventry's skyline for many years. William Smyth's sketch of 1576, possibly the earliest surviving image of the city, shows what is

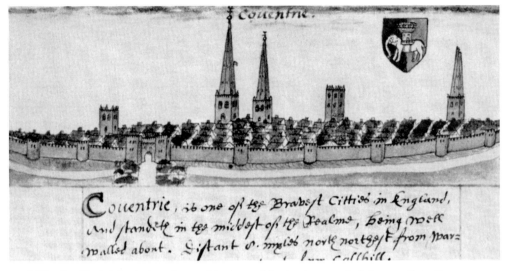

Couentrie.

Couentrie, is one of the Brauest Citties in England, and standeth in the middest of the Realme, being well walled about. Distant o. miles north north est from War = ... Callhill.

William Smyth's 1576 sketch, the earliest surviving image of the city, shows a cathedral tower still standing (centre right). (Coventry City Council)

almost certainly the building's central tower, still standing alongside the three spires and the church of St John's, Bablake.

Other buildings vanished much more quickly. By 1542, the house of the Greyfriars had been dissolved and its buildings soon demolished, while large quantities of stone were already being removed from the Charterhouse site. The following year the church of the Whitefriars passed into the Corporation's hands, and in 1544 royal civil servant John Hales picked up the friary buildings and lands of the Whitefriars for £83 12s 6d.

Hales was again the purchaser the following year when the Hospital of St John the Baptist in the Burges was dissolved, making himself uniquely unpopular in Coventry. In 1547 the Trinity Guild, once one of England's most powerful, was suppressed and its chapel, the collegiate church of St John's Bablake, confiscated. The chapel of St George next to Gosford Bridge was suppressed soon afterwards and all the guild and chantry chapels ripped out of St Michael's and Holy Trinity churches.

The final act of despoliation took place in 1552 when all the wall paintings in these churches were whitewashed and their tools of worship – chalices, pyxes, censers, processional crosses, bells, chasubles, satin and gold copes and gold thread – were loaded onto carts and trundled off to the royal coffers. In little more than a decade, the physical and spiritual heart of the city had been torn out.

Over their long history, the monastic orders in Coventry had produced a number of distinguished divines, from the writer Vincent of Coventry in the early thirteenth century, the first Franciscan to teach at Cambridge, to William Maklesfield, general and theologian of the order of Dominicans, and John Bird, the last provincial head of the Carmelites in England.

The city's economy too had been dealt yet another devastating blow. The monastic houses, with their extensive networks of staff and visitors and their pilgrim-attracting shrines, had been very good for business. And now they were gone.

It was left to two outsiders to provide some small comfort in Coventry's hour of greatest need. In late 1541 the merchant and former

The spire of the Greyfriars. Its church was quickly demolished. (Chris Ross)

Lord Mayor of London Sir William Holles, who was born at Stoke Hall just outside Coventry, bequeathed the city £200 to build a new market cross, replacing a predecessor constructed in Cross Cheaping in 1422.

There had been a market cross in Coventry since before 1300, but Holles's new version was something to behold. Modelled on a cross in the important cloth town of Abingdon in Berkshire and taking two years to build, it was fifty-seven feet high, superbly ornamented with figures of kings, monks and saints, and was invariably picked out for special mention by travellers writing about the city over the next 200 years.

Another London merchant, Sir Thomas White, who had no local family connections but had clearly done a lot of business with Coventry over the years, was even more generous. In 1548, White gave the city the handsome sum of £1,400, with which the council bought property being sold off by the king's commissioners, notably the Trinity Guild's headquarters, St Mary's Hall, which was to become the new Council House, but significantly not the abandoned

Above A fifteenth-century wooden carving of St George fighting his dragon, from the chapel that bore his name. Not valuable enough to be confiscated? (St Mary's Hall/Coventry City Council)

Left Coventry's beautiful new market cross, a landmark admired by travellers for 200 years. (Coventry City Council)

The unveiling of the Martyrs Memorial in 1910. (David Fry)

cathedral church. White, who also founded St John's College, Oxford, fell on hard times in later years and called on the council to ensure his widow benefitted from their support after his death. One hopes they complied because his generosity almost certainly prevented a disaster turning into a real catastrophe.

The speed of the Dissolution's effect on Coventry threw up a curiosity more than 300 years later when in 1852, during dredging work in the River Sherbourne not far from the site of the priory, a bunch of twenty-two huge keys from the period was discovered on the river bed. Had these perhaps been tossed away, in anguish or indifference, as Prior Camswell and his fellow Benedictines made their final departure from a religious house that had helped orchestrate the rise of Coventry for almost half a millennium?

There was to be one further spasm of religious turmoil in Coventry. In February 1555, with the fiercely Catholic Queen Mary on the throne, the prominent Protestant cleric Lawrence Saunders, rector of All Hallows in London, was burned at the stake in the hollow in the Cheylesmore Park.

Saunders had connections with Coventry. He had lived in the city as a child for some years and his brother Edward was its fiercely Catholic recorder in 1553. But for Mary's prosecutors the real point was to make his martyrdom, deliberately prolonged by the use of green wood on the fire, a warning to this rebellious, fanatic town.

In September of the same year, Robert Glover from Mancetter in north Warwickshire, and a Coventry capper named Cornelius Bungey followed him to the pyre, condemned for arguing that a priest had no power to absolve any sinner from his sins. The hollow where they died was levelled early in the nineteenth century, but there was to be a postscript. In 1854 the Park keeper William Mansfield made a grim discovery while digging in the area:

> When I had dug down about six feet from the surface I came to some very black soil, different from that which I had dug through. I also found some charred or burnt wood, some cinders and pieces of bright coal. I also found a number of bones, and a piece of silk, which might have been part of a dress, close by the bones. I had got down to a rock in which was what appeared to be a grave, and the bones and piece of silk were in this grave.

It was a pitiful reminder of the brave men and women who had submitted themselves to unspeakable agony for their faith. But it did provide an accurate location for the memorial cross that in 1910 was erected close to the spot.

COVENTRY'S TOWN WALL

Writing in 1639 on the eve of the English Civil War, John Taylor the Water Poet offered an enthusiastic first impression of Coventry: 'A fair, famous, sweet and ancient city so walled about with such strength and neatnesse as no city in England may compare with it.'

The walls he was so enthusiastically describing had little more than twenty years left to stand. In the summer of 1662, by order of Charles II, the Earl of Northampton set about demolishing them, destroying in three weeks what had taken 180 years to build. One of the sights of provincial England and commented upon by many travellers, Coventry's red Warwickshire sandstone walls had protected the city from the worst depredations of the Wars of the Roses and allowed it to defy King Charles I, yet its construction was dogged by what looks like a surprising lack of urgency.

An alarming outbreak of lawlessness, with organised criminal gangs roaming the Midlands countryside, may have been the spur in 1329 for Coventry's prosperous ruling class to seek royal consent to build a wall, but it was decades before real progress was made.

In 1365, ten years after work had begun at a site near the new friary of the Carmelites, or Whitefriars, an agreement was still being thrashed out over how to protect the order's Chapel of the Blessed Mary within the walls, an important site for pilgrimage.

The following year, Edward III's grant of a tax on victuallers to help pay for the wall was greeted with howls of anguish that the charges (for example 2s for every cask of wine brought into Coventry and 4d for every ox) would bankrupt those victuallers. So vociferous was the opposition that the tax was soon widened to include wealthy citizens of all stripes and even the monastic orders.

The quality of the stonework varied considerably but perhaps reached its high point in the 1380s when Richard II decreed that, in return for stone from his quarries, the wall should encompass his manor house at Cheylesmore. During archaeological excavations in this area in the 1990s, the base of a mortar mixer's barrel was found next to the wall, with its putty still malleable after 600 years. The stonework was so neat and precise that it might have been finished the day before.

By the turn of the fifteenth century the wall had reached the Benedictine prior's half of the town. In 1410 priory records show that thirteen houses had been destroyed in the Spon Street and Well Street areas to facilitate the building of the wall and its accompanying ditch. The Benedictines clearly wanted their lands and property to be included within the wall's defensive embrace, but were often at odds with the townsfolk over the access it gave to them.

In 1480, Prior Thomas Deram complained bitterly that the building of it had cost him financially. While townsfolk trampled down fences, stopped up the river with rubbish, trespassed in his orchard, damaged his grass, shot his game and spoiled the fish in his pools by washing there, he had to pay £10 a year 'murage' for the privilege.

The longest surviving stretch of Coventry's famous town wall, with the Swanswell Gate on the right. (CV One/Coventry City Council)

The mayor's angry response pointed out that St Osburg's pool and other priory land-holdings had enjoyed protection since the early 1460s, and anyway, washing in the fish pools made the fish fatter. Deram went to court, and although he died the following year it was to be 1498 before the priory resumed its annual payments.

Begun at the height of Coventry's prosperity in the 1350s, the wall finally inched towards completion in 1538–39, with the city already deep in decline and about to experience the devastation caused by the dissolution of the monasteries.

A century later, in 1642, as Civil War loomed, the wall was to undergo its severest test. Charles I, looking for a fortified city in which to establish his military headquarters, found the gates barred against him and ordered his cannons to fire on the New Gate. They did little damage, and Coventry sat out the war behind its sandstone ramparts, relatively safe. Its defiance would, however, be remembered.

six

'WHAT FOOLS YE BE'

ealthy cardmaker Thomas Wheatley was quick to recall his own impoverished start in life when an unexpected stroke of luck thrust a small fortune into his hands.

Wheatley, who had risen to Mayor of Coventry after arriving in the city as a servant or 'poor boy in white', had ordered from his agent in Spain a consignment of steel wedges. But when silver ingots turned up instead and nobody claimed them, he used part of the windfall to endow a hospital and school for poor boys at Bablake. His will, dated 17 April 1563, gave enough money to set up twenty-one boys, with a nurse to look after them, in a building alongside Bond's Hospital on Hill Street.

It is probable that a school had been operating at Bablake since the foundation of the collegiate church in the mid-fourteenth century, but Wheatley's gift was timely as the educational establishments run by the Benedictines and the Carthusians in Coventry had been swept away in the Dissolution.

This was just one example of the effect that the malignant Dr London and his eager suppressors had on the city. And for all the widespread disenchantment with the monastic orders (it was said at the time that only the Carthusians remained true to their founding code of abstinence) there must have been many adherents to the old faith in Coventry.

That may explain why, in 1536, the city had found itself playing a walk-on role in the Pilgrimage of Grace, the rebellion in the north against Henry VIII's attack on the monasteries.

In October of that year, Thomas Kendall, vicar of St James's, Louth and one of the ringleaders of the Lincolnshire Rising, the precursor to the full-blown rebellion, had sought sanctuary in Coventry when the rising was put down. It didn't save him. He was later arrested and taken to London, where on 25 March 1537 he was hanged, drawn and quartered at Tyburn.

Bond's Hospital (left) and Bablake old school (right). (Andrew Paterson)

The polarisation between Catholic traditionalist and emerging Protestantism in Coventry sharpened during the reign of Henry's eldest daughter, the fiercely Catholic Mary.

In January 1554, during the Wyatt Rebellion against Mary's proposed marriage to Philip II of Spain, Henry Grey, father of the Protestant claimant to the throne, Lady Jane Grey, arrived at the gates of what was still the Midlands' most important city asking for support. But those gates remained firmly shut, for although many of the city's population would count themselves Protestant, the ruling elite still held to Catholic Mary, either out of conviction, or fear.

In 1555, the year that the Protestant martyr Lawrence Saunders went to the stake in Coventry, one of the city's sheriffs, Richard Hopkins, was 'put out for religion' and thrown into the Fleet prison in London. Hopkins, it was said, had been ordered to torture Saunders and had refused. On his release he gathered up his wife and eight children and fled to Basle in what is now Switzerland, where as a Protestant he felt safer.

The death of Mary, in late 1558, brought to an end the horrors of the stake, but as the Protestant ascendancy that followed her tightened its grip, Coventry found its old ways increasingly challenged.

The cold winds of economic decline now buffeting the city had blown in a new Puritanism, advocated by clergy and prominent citizens, whose beliefs about how their fellow Coventrians should live went far beyond a simple work ethic.

A sustained attack on a culture of drinking and ale houses, aimed particularly at the idle poor, had been given moralising voice in a Leet Book entry from 1547, 'Those that be of the poorest sort do sit all day in the alehouse drinking and playing cards at tables and spend all they get prodigally on themselves, to the high displeasure of God. Whereas, if it were spent at home in their own houses, their wives and children would get a part of it.'

In 1559, 'good ministers' were sent to Coventry to sort this out, and the mayor and aldermen decreed that there would be a levy on every household in the city to pay for them. Before long, images and relics from city churches were being destroyed and their colourful wall paintings whitewashed.

Even the registers of St Michael's church were burned as they were thought to contain 'some marks of Popery' and in their zeal, Puritan supporters set out to demolish Coventry's new and elaborately decorated market cross – until a large crowd of butchers, armed with cleavers, stopped them in their tracks.

In 1561 the clergy moved against Coventry's Hock Tuesday play, which took the defeat of the Danes in 1002 as its theme and had been performed for at least 150 years. Complete with a crowd-pleasing final scene of the women of Coventry dragging the defeated raiders off to prison, the play had become a symbol of civic pride and there was outrage when it was suppressed.

The townsfolk blamed the clergy, 'men very commendable for their behaviour and learning and sweet in their sermons, but somewhat too sour in preaching away their pastime'. And in time they were to find a somewhat unlikely ally in their cause.

On Saturday 17 August 1565, the mayor, Edmund Brownell, and the recorder, John Throckmorton, led a civic party arrayed in their scarlet to the Bishop Gate in the town wall, where they awaited the arrival of Queen Elizabeth I on royal progress. It was the Queen's first visit to Coventry. She stayed two days, took in special performances of mystery plays presented by the drapers, tanners, smiths and weavers companies, and was given the obligatory £100 in gold, at which she exclaimed, 'It is a good gift of gold. I have few such gifts.'

Throckmorton's speech of welcome, reeking of sycophancy, steered fairly close to embarrassment too. He heaped lavish praises on the queen's father, skirting around the damage that Henry VIII's pursuit of the monasteries had inflicted on Coventry. And he took the opportunity to complain to the queen about the 'sinister, underhand, unjust means' by which the council were being prevented from funding a new free grammar school in the city by her father's former Clerk to the Hanaper, the hated John Hales.

Hales was actually Elizabeth's host for the weekend at his home in the friary building at Whitefriars, now re-named Hales Place, and may well have been present. In the event, the queen's first stop, on entering the city, was to visit the new grammar school, housed in the former Hospital of St John, and make a small gift of money to its library.

John Hales, a villain to many in Coventry. (St Mary's Hall/Coventry City Council)

Hales's battle with the council stemmed from his seemingly effortless acquisition of Whitefriars, much of the priory site and the Hospital of St John at the Dissolution, by virtue of his position as a royal civil servant. In the words of the writer and traveller, John Leland, who passed through Coventry in 1543, 'Hales with the club-foot has gotten interest in this college [the Hospital] and none but the devil can get him out of it'.

The club-foot reference was a jibe at Hales, who limped because of a youthful injury suffered when he stood on his own dagger. But the council's more serious accusation was that Hales had agreed with Henry VIII to found a free school in the king's name and then reneged on funding it.

The queen had the council's complaints against Hales investigated, but no real evidence of wrong-doing was found. The campaign against him, which lasted until his death in December 1572, may have been a bit unfair on Hales who, all the evidence suggests, was fond of Coventry and tried in his years of power and influence to support the city where he could. But it is true that the free King Henry VIII grammar school did not secure stable roots until after he had died.

A cultured man, with several pamphlets on education and administration to his credit, Hales had faced prison briefly after writing a tract on the succession to the throne, if Elizabeth should fail to have children. And some fifteen years after his death, his home in Coventry, Hales Place, would be used as the secret printing centre for one of the anonymous Martin Marprelate tracts, which attacked the bishops in the Anglican Church.

The 1565 royal progress was the queen's sole visit to Coventry but, certainly on the city's side, the feeling was that Elizabeth viewed the place with some affection. It is said that she addressed the citizens from an oriel window at Whitefriars, admonishing them with a fond, 'Ah, men of Coventry. What fools ye be,' when the flattery became somewhat cloying.

In 1568 she gave Coventry the sole right to manufacture some new kinds of cloth, formerly imported from Armentieres in Flanders – utterfynes and crompstyles. Within two years there was a Dutch chapel in the city, used by those specialist weavers brought in to teach Coventry folk the mysteries of this new manufacturing. They brought with them a modest recovery in the economy too.

In the same year, the council sought advice from the queen on how to deal with the mayor, John Harford, a tanner, who while walking his grey-hounds in the park, had fought with an embroiderer, William Heley, who was trying to save his own spaniel from their attack. Heley died and the queen took a close interest in the case. Harford was stripped of office and tried for manslaughter, eventually escaping execution by paying hefty compensation to the embroiderer's widow.

In November 1569, it was to Coventry that Elizabeth turned when rebellion broke out among the Catholic earls in the north and she needed to move the focus of their revolt, her cousin and prisoner, Mary, Queen of Scots, from Tutbury Castle near Burton-on-Trent to a more secure confinement further south.

The letter that she sent to the mayor survives and is a model of brevity and directness. The good people of Coventry were, she wrote, to keep the Scottish

A brooding Elizabeth, agonising, perhaps, over what to do about Mary, Queen of Scots. (Herbert Art Gallery)

Queen 'safely kept and guarded' and were to obey her jailers' instructions to the letter.

Mary was moved to Coventry on 25 November, in the custody of the Earls of Shrewsbury and Huntingdon, and was initially housed at the Bull Inn in Smithford Street, formerly the home of the prominent Onley family and where Henry VII had lodged after the Battle of Bosworth.

In a letter to William Cecil, Elizabeth's formidable Secretary of State, Shrewsbury expressed his nervousness at the lack of security, despite having 400 soldiers with him and the gates on the walls being double-manned. Mary was moved to St Mary's Hall, better protected but a miserably cramped confinement for someone who brought a sizeable retinue of Scottish and French servants with her.

There, in a story that has apocryphal written all over it, it was said that Mary's jailers devised an extra humiliation for her by positioning a portrait of Elizabeth in front of a low and narrow doorway, through which the six-feet tall Queen of Scots would have to bow as she entered. Mary, the tale went, simply turned her back and reversed through the doorway, thus delivering one of the Elizabethan age's most forthright insults to her captor. Whatever the truth of it, Elizabeth's trust in her 'fools' in Coventry must have frightened the life out of them, and they were no doubt thoroughly relieved when, early in the new year, Mary was moved back to Tutbury.

They could feel rather more at ease in their next encounter with Elizabeth, during her eighteen-day stay with Robert Dudley, Earl of Leicester, at Kenilworth Castle in July 1575. One Captain Cox from Coventry, described as a skilled fencer and knowledgeable in stories, poetry, ancient plays, ballads and songs, led the revels, while the queen was treated to a special command performance of the Hock Tuesday play.

Elizabeth, it was reported, laughed heartily as the women of Coventry dragged away their Danish captives in the final scene, and showed her appreciation by giving the performers five marks in money and two bucks (deer). Such royal enthusiasm must have given supporters of Coventry's Hock Tuesday play, and indeed its beleaguered cycle of mystery plays, hope that the tide of Puritan disapproval could be rolled back. Yet it was not to be.

Despite last-ditch efforts by supporters like the general contractor Thomas Massey, the last complete cycle of the old mystery plays was staged in 1579. By the early 1580s pageant houses, used by the craft companies to store equipment, were starting to be sold off.

In 1584, a new play dealing with the destruction of Jerusalem was commissioned from Oxford writer John Smythe, but it involved all the crafts and its subject matter was bland and designed not to offend reformist sensibilities. Seven years later the council reluctantly gave permission for the Jerusalem play, and the Hock Tuesday play, to be given a final performance together on Midsummer's day and St Peter's day.

The authorities' displeasure with 'papist' pastimes did not end at traditional mystery plays. Coventry's festive processions, a colourful feature of the city's life that for nigh on 200 years had drawn gawping crowds from far afield, were banned; the Midsummer Eve procession, for example, was suppressed in 1563. It would be another century before they were revived.

Coventry's ten-foot-high maypole, the focus of many a summer celebration, was taken down in 1591, not to be raised again until the Restoration. From 1595 anybody caught playing football in the street could be taken to the common gaol and kept there as long as the mayor chose.

The men in power were busy making sure that their fellow citizens observed the proper proprieties, particularly on the day of rest. An order from 1588 had decreed that opening shops, playing games and even idly walking about were forbidden during Sunday services, and that was to be followed up by further bans on the playing of indoor games and even sitting around in the streets.

They weren't slow, either, to move against any dissenting voice. In November 1592, John Boothe, a glover, was brought before the council, accused of being a 'very babbling, disordered person', especially against the mayor and other important citizens. He was committed to jail but was released on making an abject apology.

The following year, Coventry's still fragile economy prompted the authorities to toughen up the penalties for those found selling Coventry blue thread of inferior quality, and in such uncertain times suspicions that immigrants to the city were taking jobs from locals predictably began to surface.

Forty years earlier, no stranger had been allowed to settle in Coventry without a job to go to and without the express approval of the mayor and aldermen. Now strangers who were unemployed and unable to support themselves had to leave the city and this was followed, in 1598, by an order that a stranger who had married a Coventry woman had to take her to his birthplace for a year before being allowed to settle back in Coventry.

In this highly charged atmosphere, it wasn't difficult to get on the wrong side of the authorities. In 1600, actors from the visiting Lord Chandos' Men, performing at the Angel Inn on Smithford Street, were arrested for contempt against 'master mayor's pleasure' and were not released from jail until they had made a full apology. The Chandos company did not include William Shakespeare, already the rising star in London's theatrical firmament. But in his earlier days as an actor it is almost certain that the Bard played Coventry more than once, with St Mary's Hall the likely venue.

St Mary's Hall. Shakespeare almost certainly performed on the stage beneath the far window. (CV One/Coventry City Council)

What Chandos's men had done to upset the mayor wasn't recorded, but if the authorities were looking for an excuse for what appeared to be paranoid and over-bearing behaviour, they would no doubt have found it in the events of November 1605.

Against expectations, Elizabeth I's successor, James I, had not tempered her harsh policies towards Catholics and in early 1605, Warwickshire landowner Robert Catesby, whose principal estate was at Lapworth, decided the time had come to hit back.

At thirty-two, the charismatic Catesby came from a noted Catholic family. His father had even been imprisoned for harbouring a priest, and he himself had failed to complete his university degree because he refused to sign the obligatory Protestant Oath of Supremacy.

The Catesbys had a history in Coventry. William de Catesby had risen from Warwickshire peasant roots to become a knight in 1339 and had later purchased a substantial house and up to forty tenements in the town. For nearly 150 years his descendants had been among Coventry's most powerful landlords, with property in Bishop Street, West Orchard and Earl Street, but perhaps surprisingly, had never sought public office, the traditional route to power and influence. There had been a Catesby Lane in Coventry, but it does not appear on John Speed's map of 1610. It had been written out of history, possibly by an earlier Catesby's ill-advised support for Richard III, or by the events of 1605.

Robert Catesby's plan was to blow up the King, along with the House of Lords and House of Commons, using gunpowder stockpiled in the cellars below where they met for the State Opening of Parliament. Then he would place James I's eldest daughter, Princess Elizabeth, on the throne and marry her to a prominent Catholic to seal the succession.

Elizabeth, then aged nine, was living at Coombe Abbey under the care and protection of Sir John Harrington and his wife, old friends to whom James had entrusted her education. Two years earlier, she had been formally presented to the mayor and council in Coventry, receiving a silver gilt cup three-quarters of a yard high that was much too heavy for her to pick up. Now, she was to be the unwitting instrument of rebellion.

Catesby gathered together a group of conspirators that included several more Warwickshire gentlemen: his cousins, Thomas and Robert Wintour, and John Grant. Thomas Wintour recruited Guy Fawkes, a Yorkshire-born soldier who had been fighting Protestants in the service of the King of Spain, and the plotters began stockpiling barrels of gunpowder in little-used vaults. Fearing that Catholic Lords and MPs would be killed by the explosion too, they decided to warn a number of them to stay away on the date of the State Opening, 5 November. And that was a fatal mistake.

Robert Catesby (second from the right), chief conspirator and a man with Coventry connections. (THP)

Palace Yard, where Princess Elizabeth was safely lodged. (David Fry)

The government was tipped off and Fawkes was arrested on 4 November as he guarded the thirty-six barrels of gunpowder. Catesby and his fellow conspirators fled back to the Midlands, hoping to raise Catholic support and seize the nine-year-old princess. They were too late. Word of the plot had reached Coombe and on the same day Elizabeth was moved, in the custody of Sir Thomas Holcroft, into Coventry. Here she was lodged at Palace Yard, the substantial mansion owned by the staunchly Protestant Hopkins family in Earl Street.

The Gunpowder Plot ended with a siege at Holbeche House in Staffordshire, in which Catesby was killed, and in a string of grisly executions in London the following January. But might it have had a different outcome?

On the night of 4 November, no more than a couple of hundred yards from Palace Yard, Robert Wintour and another of the plotters, Stephen Littleton, were staying at the Bull Inn, before heading out to the plotters' rendezvous at Dunchurch the following day. Had they known Elizabeth was so close an opportunity might have presented itself to spirit her away from her escort, who presumably believed they were secure in Puritan Coventry.

Gunpowder Treason Day, as it became known, was added to the list of feast and holy days that could be celebrated in Coventry, but the authorities showed no signs of easing up in their sabbatarianism – the fanatical veneration of Sundays.

In the year of the Gunpowder Plot, attending church on Sunday was made compulsory in Coventry, and before long a weekly lecture had been introduced to combat what was called 'disreputable pursuits'. This was a habit large numbers of Coventrians had acquired, of either spending Sunday in bed or leaving the city for nearby villages, where they spent the day swearing, drinking and enjoying themselves 'to the great dishonour of God and the offence of others.'

Repeated attempts to tackle the drinking culture were to lead to an order in 1622, prohibiting strangers from becoming brewers, maltsters and victuallers in Coventry – without much success, it would seem. A survey of the city at the Restoration counted 137 inns and alehouses in its narrow and crowded streets.

Those streets were also the focus of the authorities' pursuit of cleanliness and sobriety. In 1611 the Chamberlains had been ordered to erect a pair of stocks in Vicar Lane, close to the River Sherbourne, to punish 'divers persons who have heretofore laid muck, ashes and filth, to the great annoyance of their neighbours.'

They were tough on anti-social behaviour too. A few months before, a woman named Ann Prinn had been brought before the mayor and brethren, charged with being 'a common swearer and a disturber of the peace among her neighbours.'

An attack on the dour and unbending Puritan worthies of Coventry came, some years later, from a surprising quarter. In verses published in 1625, the playwright, poet and controversialist Ben Jonson laid into the breed:

A pure native bird
This: and tho' his hue
Be Coventry Blue
Yet is he undone
By the thread he has spun
For since the wise town
Has let the sports down
Of May games and morris
For which he right sorr' is.
Where their maids and their mates
At dancing and Wakes
Had their napkins and posies ...

Jonson, who had dabbled with Catholicism throughout his life, goes on to suggest that the only proper use for the Puritan's thread is to hang or choke him.

Yet alongside this priggish Puritanism, Coventry in the early years of the seventeenth century was, perhaps surprisingly, developing a modest intellectual reputation.

In 1601, John Tovey, headmaster of King Henry VIII grammar school, appealed for books to supplement his scholars' meagre supply, and before long there was an annual stipend of 13s 4d from the will of the merchant William Wheate for someone to look after them. This library was to become sadly neglected – by the 1830s it was found that some of its volumes, largely religious works, had been used to light fires. But from the start it was open to scholars of the city, not just of the school, ensuring that Coventry vies with Norwich in being home to the first public library in England.

The embodiment of this new intellectualism must undoubtedly have been Philemon Holland, doctor, teacher and the greatest classical translator of his age. Born in Essex in 1552, Holland made Coventry his home in the 1590s, where he worked as a doctor, ministering to the poor, and developed his prodigious talent for translation. His work on classical authors like Pliny, Plutarch and Suetonius is still held in high regard.

He taught at the free school from 1608 and became its headmaster in 1628, retiring just eleven months later. After living in poverty for some years he was given a pension of £3 6s 8d a year by the council and died, aged 85, in February 1637. His tomb, with the epitaph he composed, 'I was all earth [Holland] and all earth shall I be', can still be seen in Holy Trinity Church.

One of Holland's pupils at the free grammar school was the remarkable James Illedge, born blind in 1596 into a poor family in the city. Despite his disability, an almost unconquerable disadvantage at the time, young Illedge showed such an aptitude for learning that he was sent to the grammar school and in 1612 was presented to James I's ill-fated eldest son Henry, Prince of Wales, when he visited Coventry.

The highly intelligent and serious-minded Henry, who was to succumb within months to typhoid fever, recognised James Illedge's promise and arranged for him to go to Exeter College, Oxford. He was given a grant of £4 a year by the council to do so. Graduating in 1616, Illedge returned to Coventry to become a lecturer or preacher at Holy Trinity Church and in 1632 became vicar of Ansty and Shilton, where he died twelve years later.

It was Philemon Holland, dubbed Translator General in England, who on 2 September 1617 gave the oration, dressed in a suit of black satin, to mark the visit of James I to Coventry. The king was greeted at the Bishop Gate by a council delegation led by the mayor, Samuel Miles, and put up overnight at Whitefriars. At a huge banquet in St Mary's Hall, which itself cost a frightening £147, he was given a golden cup valued at more than £200.

James was suitably gracious, promising that wherever he went he would drink out of his Coventry cup. But in truth he had his suspicions of the Puritans of Coventry and was always wary of them. In 1611, he had commanded that they should kneel while taking Holy Sacrament,

Philemon Holland as Translator General. (Coventry City Council)

something that a number of them found hard to stomach, and in 1621 he demanded assurances from the Bishop of Coventry and Lichfield that they were obeying the rules of the church before he would grant the city a new Governing Charter.

Granted by royal assent on 18 July 1621, the new charter established two new three-day fairs in the city in April and August, set up a Court of Orphans to adjudicate on the city's care of bereaved children and established the 'close corporation' that was to rule Coventry, sadly at times making the city a byword for civic corruption, until the municipal reform legislation of 1835. The Governing Charter, so called because the Corporation later decided it superseded all other charters, either before or after, instituted a new system of government, with the mayor and ten aldermen (one for each ward) sitting with a permanent Grand Council of up to twenty more councillors. They were self-selecting and their appointment would be for life.

A second Common Council of twenty-five was nominated by the mayor and aldermen, but was only convened when the Grand Council wished for a second opinion – and that was pretty rare.

To its promoters, the new charter seemed a sensible way forward in unsettled times. It was only much later that the 'close corporation' would descend into internecine conflicts of staggering longevity, its members being unable to resist embezzling the revenues of Coventry charities and landholdings in their care.

The new way of doing things owed much to Coventry's able and well-connected town clerk, Humphrey Burton, who codified Coventry's liberties as an independent and equal-ranking county to Warwickshire, and was rewarded with a handsome gift of £50 from a grateful corporation.

The city's relationship with the county that surrounded it had always been distant at best. The trading oligarchy that ruled Coventry kept themselves aloof from the landed gentry who governed Warwickshire, while they in turn made Warwick, not Coventry, the focus of their interest and patronage. They borrowed money from Coventry's merchants but did not marry their daughters. They frequented the city's markets but not its social circles.

The divide between these two power cliques deepened dramatically in 1635, when the imperious Charles I ill-advisedly decided to raise revenues for foreign military adventures by imposing on his subjects a tax known as Ship Money, as it was closely related to Charles's ambitions for his navy.

Coventry's economy had made something of a recovery from the depths of recession in the 1550s, but the city rightly still felt its prosperity to be fragile and among its population of around 7,000, there were still many struggling in poverty.

An outbreak of plague in 1626 had taken a shocking toll in some of the city's poorest streets, and in 1631 the high price of corn had prompted the Corporation to buy up stocks and sell them cheaply to the poor. When news of the king's high-handed taxation plans broke, Coventry complained that 'trading was greatly decayed, by reason whereof a number of shops were shut up and houses stood empty, while the number of poor had considerably increased.'

Ship Money was resented because of its unconstitutional nature, but what really riled the men who ruled Coventry was that it was to be administered by the Sheriff of Warwickshire, who would decide what proportion of Warwickshire's burden would fall on the city. Traditionally, it had been one-fifteenth, but when he assessed it at one-eighth, asking Coventry to pay £500 out of the Warwickshire total of £4000, there was uproar. 'No man alive ever knew or heard the like' was the city's blunt reaction and appeal was immediately made direct to the Privy Council, demonstrating Coventry's well-practised ability to find routes of appeal into government at the highest level.

It was decided that the Bishop of Coventry and Lichfield, the greedy and acquisitive Robert Wright, would arbitrate. On finding in favour of Coventry he was duly rewarded with a silver gilt bowl worth £19 10s by a grateful corporation. In the end Coventry had to find something over £200, but even then it shunned Warwickshire, paying what it owed directly to the King's Treasury.

Four years later, when Charles wanted more money, for the so-called Coat and Conduct tax to pay for a campaign against the Scots, Coventry argued that the remit of the Sheriff of Warwickshire did not run to the city.

Chief among the king's opponents this time was a wealthy dyer and landowner, William Jesson, who had been mayor in 1631 and was to become one of the city's two MPs in 1640. Jesson was typical of the oligarchy, related through kinship and marriage to many of the other prominent families in Coventry, public-spirited to an extent but mindful of his own interests. His brother Thomas, who died in 1634, had made a fortune in London and left the city the huge sum of £2,000 in his will to be invested in land.

William Jesson and his uncle, and fellow dyer, Simon Norton, represented Coventry at the Short Parliament, a failed attempt to repair the king's worsening relationship with his subjects in early 1640. But both found themselves having to defend their own business practices from criticism much closer to home.

For some years, when it suited them, Coventry's powerful clothiers and dyers had been importing cloth from Gloucestershire, arguing that in hard times it was cheaper to do that than to use local weavers, spinners and fullers to produce cloth from Warwickshire wool. Naturally resentful of this, their fellow tradesmen had appealed to the Privy Council, whose compromise solution was blithely ignored by the likes of Jesson. But in April 1640, a Coventry weaver, Anthony Ashmore, petitioned parliament over the heads of the city's MPs to try to stop the import of cloth.

A counter petition raised by Jesson and Norton and presented to parliament, described him as a 'contentious fellow and idle person, much given to drink and at times quite distracted'. And that view prevailed. Ashmore was promptly committed to prison for what was described as misdemeanours.

His mistake had been to directly confront those who still represented the city's most influential trading clique. Of Coventry's twenty-three mayors between 1620 and 1642, almost two-thirds were drapers, clothiers or dyers. None were weavers, spinners or fullers. But while the production of cloth, now in many different varieties, still represented the core of the local economy, other ways of making money were beginning to make their presence felt.

Silk weaving was to become Coventry's great industry of rescue at the turn of the eighteenth century, but in 1627 a silk weavers' company was established in the city, indicating that there were already a number of craftsmen at work in that field. Even though its time as the Midlands' most important city was beginning to run out, in 1635 Coventry was still being described as a 'great thoroughfare town', on the main road that led from London to Chester and then on to Ireland, and at the heart of England's north-south trading web. Goods bought and sold, or just passing through, all earned an income for Coventrians.

Just north of the city, the old craft of mining coal from shallow diggings or coal pits was beginning to turn into an industry. Coal mining in the area went back hundreds of years, and in 1578 the city had given a licence to a local landowner to dig a pit on land in Hawkesbury, which had once belonged to the Cheylesmore Manor estate. In 1622, Matthew Collins, a Coventry merchant, and John Potter, whose line of work was almost certainly in mining, obtained a lease to extract coal on the Griff estate, owned by Sir Thomas Beaumont. Their avowed intention was to undercut Warwickshire miners already supplying fuel to the city, a move that was bitterly opposed in communities like Bedworth, which relied on the coal trade for its very existence.

A year or two before, the two Bedworth miners John Bugges and Thomas Robinson had been given a monopoly on coal production after rescuing local pits from flooding, the constant menace that faced all coal miners. In November 1631 a vengeful Robinson was accused of damming an old watercourse to deliberately flood the Coventry men's workings, causing them at one point to flee for their lives, leaving some of their clothes behind.

It hadn't deterred Collins and Potter, who were soon making handsome profits in a new trade for which Coventry was to become the access point to a much wider market.

Despite its somewhat reduced circumstances, visitors to the city could still be favourably impressed by its air of imposing antiquity, a place, as one commented, 'mostly built in the old wooden way.'

A Lieutenant Hammond from East Anglia, passing through in 1634, praised its many fair streets and buildings and its market cross and was struck, most of all by St Mary's Hall, a building, he said, 'with a stately ascending entrance, the upper end adorned with rich hangings, and all about with fayre pictures, one more especially of a noble lady, whose memory they have cause not to forget.'

Godiva's legendary support for the put-upon townsfolk had indeed not been forgotten, as tensions still flared around that perennial flashpoint, the use of common lands by private landowners in defiance of age-old liberties. On Lammas Day 1639, an angry crowd had marched out to spoil a field of oats and throw down a wall erected on common land. Five ringleaders were arrested and hustled off to the city's jail, but that night more than 300 supporters, armed with clubs and iron crow bars, gathered outside to batter down the doors, and they were hastily released.

After poor freemen of the city complained to the Privy Council that common land was being ploughed up, the Leet ruled, probably reluctantly, that no ploughing should take place for two years. Real power may have already passed to the mayor and council, but its ruling was still adhered to.

As England slipped steadily towards Civil War, it didn't take much to set the nerves of Coventrians on edge. Their city's central location and nationally renowned defensive wall would, they knew, make it a prized possession in the event of hostilities breaking out, and they must have been further unnerved by news of ghastly occurrences that could easily be seen as portents.

In Coventry there was the shock of mass murder at Bond's Hospital, when an elderly resident, named John Johnson, used the poison ratsbane to kill himself and five of his fellow pensioners who had upset him. Then came news of appalling massacres, later shown to be wild exaggerations, perpetrated by Catholics on Protestants in Ireland.

The combination of bad news, near and far, was perhaps the spur for the biggest review of the city's defences since the general alarm sounded at the time of the Armada, back in 1588. In December 1641, the council ordered the purchase of new cannons, having found the existing weapons defective when it came to trials. Alongside a significant stockpiling of arms and ammunition, most of it in St Mary's Hall, the council also ordered that every householder 'of abilitie' was to provide at least one musket, 'so that this citie maie have in readiness up on any sudden occasion at least 500 muskets for its defence and safeguard'.

Little did they know that within months, those defences would be severely tested.

In the religious and political turmoil of the early seventeenth century, few families can have experienced such divided loyalties as the wealthy and influential Davenports of Coventry.

Born in the late 1590s, John and Christopher Davenport were almost the same age, despite being uncle and nephew, and spent their formative years together in a city where their Protestant and well-connected family had produced mayors since the 1550s.

Yet one was to become one of the Franciscan order's most important divines, chaplain to two Catholic queens, while the other was one of the hard-line founders of a Puritan colony in the New World.

The boys both attended the free grammar school, where Philemon Holland was one of their teachers, and in 1613 both went up to Merton College, Oxford, transferring to Magdalen Hall together the following year. It was at Oxford that their paths were to dramatically diverge.

Christopher was converted to Catholicism by a priest living near Oxford and the following year went to the English College at Douai in Flanders, where he joined a reformist branch of the Franciscan order. Sent to the University of Salamanca in Spain, he studied to become a Doctor of Divinity and later became the first professor of theology at the newly established friary of St Bonaventure in Douai, before returning to England as chaplain to Queen Henrietta Maria, wife of Charles I.

Life was difficult for Davenport after the king's execution, but he did not spend all the years of the Commonwealth in exile, using the name Francis Coventry as cover when he was in England. At the Restoration in 1660, he was appointed chaplain to Queen Catherine of Braganza, wife of Charles II, and spent the remaining years of his life in London, writing influential treatises and reconciling numerous converts to the Catholic Church. He died at Somerset House on 31 May 1680, his intellectual gifts and attractive personality mourned by many, not just within the Church.

Christopher Davenport was not a fanatic. In his *Explanation of the Catholic Belief* (1656) he argued that the difference between the Thirty-Nine Articles, the defining doctrine of the Church of England, and Roman Catholic liturgy was slight. It was a view that did not endear him to the Jesuits, who wanted him burned for it, but he had no hesitation in sending it to Oliver Cromwell, the Lord Protector, although no answer was recorded.

If Christopher was a divine in search of compromise, his uncle, John Davenport, was cut from a very different cloth. After leaving Oxford he became a curate in London and in 1624 was chosen to become vicar of St Stephen's Church in Coleman Street, one of the capital's most influential parish churches.

A fiery speaker and tireless campaigner, increasingly at odds with the mainstream Church, he resigned in 1633 and moved to Holland, where settlements of English Puritans were always ready to welcome new blood.

He became pastor of the English Church in Amsterdam, but his uncompromising nature led to quarrels and four years later he acquired the patent for a colony in Massachusetts and sailed for the New World with most of his congregation. In 1638 he founded the colony of New Haven with his great friend Theophilus Eaton, a wealthy London merchant who became the new colony's first governor.

In 1661 Davenport allowed William Goffe and Edward Whalley, two of King Charles I's judges now on the run as regicides, to take refuge in the New Haven settlement. Seven years later he was installed as Pastor of the First Church in Boston, although even that caused dissension – a third of the congregation promptly left to set up a rival church.

A 1670 painting of the fiery John Davenport. (Yale University)

John Davenport died, appropriately enough, of apoplexy in March 1670 in Boston, half a world away from that old English city where he had spent his childhood alongside his kinsman Christopher. It is tempting to wonder if, as adults, they ever communicated again, or whether all traces of the friendship they had shared as boys had been lost in those bitter times.

seven

A GREAT REBELLION

On 13 August 1642, a royal herald appeared at the gates of Coventry, bearing news that King Charles I was approaching and wanted to enter the city. The king had with him a small force of 800 cavalry and 300 foot soldiers but the response, when it finally came back, was that he was welcome, but only with an escort of 200.

Charles flew into a rage and ordered his herald to declare the mayor and aldermen, and indeed the whole city, traitors to the Crown. For the herald, or to give him his full title, Rouge Croix Pursuivant of Arms, it must have been an uncomfortable task. He was Sir William Dugdale, antiquarian and Warwickshire country gentleman, and he had friends and even kinsmen inside that treasonous city.

Born at Shustoke in north Warwickshire, Dugdale had been sent to King Henry VIII grammar school in Coventry, where he was amongst the pupils of Philemon Holland, who first inspired in him a love of history. Despite this grounding in a city long known for its non-conformity, he was by 1642 an ardent Royalist.

In the eyes of the king, Coventry had plenty of form for this act of defiance. He shared his father's suspicion of the place and must have felt himself vindicated when in 1637 Coventry had given a fulsome welcome to one of Charles's most intractable Puritan critics, the lawyer and polemicist William Prynne, as he passed through on his way to imprisonment in Caernarvon Castle.

Yet Coventry was also a place whose central geographical location and highly defensible town wall made it an ideal headquarters from which Charles could launch the defence of his crown. Militarily, it would be useful in the coming armed confrontation with Parliament.

For months, that confrontation had manifested itself in a quietly ferocious contest for supremacy inside Coventry itself. The struggle centred on two men:

Spencer Compton, Earl of Northampton, Warwickshire's most prominent Royalist and Recorder of Coventry since 1640, and Robert Greville, Lord Brooke of Warwick Castle, a noted Puritan who had taken Parliament's side from the beginning. Each had their supporters among the city aldermen – Henry Million and John Clarke for the king, John Barker and Thomas Basnet for Parliament, who took on the responsibility of distributing among their followers the 'colours' – green ribbons for the king, purple for Parliament.

In June, John Barker defied Northampton when he tried to implement the king's Commission of Array, Charles's attempt to raise troops around the country. The following month when the king summoned Coventry's mayor, Christopher Davenport, and its sheriffs, Nathaniel Barnett and Samuel Wheat, to meet him at Leicester, it was reported that just as they were mounting horse to do so 'some that favoured Parliament forced them to stay at home.'

This may have been an excuse. Studied neutrality was still the favoured stance of many of Coventry's leading citizens at such a time of crisis. Among ordinary folk, the king's supporters were reckoned to be slightly more numerous, but those who took Parliament's side were more active and were reinforced by

The ardent Royalist Sir William Dugdale. (Coventry City Council)

Lord Brooke. (With kind permission of David McGrory)

supporters drafted in from the nearby anti-Royalist stronghold of Birmingham.

Tensions were high in the city as neighbours sported the rival green and purple in their hats. They were ratcheted up on 10 August when, on the instructions of Northampton, aldermen Million and Clarke moved to seize the county magazine stored in the tower of Spon Gate. They were ousted by a force led by Barker and Basnet, who promptly declared that it was now in the possession of that agent of Parliament, Lord Brooke. Realising that Coventry could not be held for the king, Northampton, who was staying at the Bull in Smithford Street, quietly slipped out of the city through a postern gate in the wall and joined Charles at Oxford.

A portrait of Charles I, hastily commissioned after the Restoration, when the city realised it needed to build bridges with the Stuarts. (St Mary's Hall/ Coventry City Council)

All of this Charles now knew, as he contemplated Coventry's defiance from a slight rise to the south, known as Park Hill. Declaring that he would 'lay the city in a ruined heap of rubbish, ere he left it', he ordered his artillery to open fire. On 19 August the siege of Coventry began.

It lasted two days and accounts of it vary wildly. One has the royal artillery inflicting little damage, barring a stray shot that hit the former Whitefriars near New Gate and killed bedridden Lady Hales and an elderly woman attending her. The other version was that a breach in the wall was made, but barricades were thrown up and the citizens spilled out in such fighting array that the king's men were forced to retreat, leaving seventy dead behind them. This came from a report by a fanatical Puritan, John Vicars, and is likely to owe more to wishful thinking than hard fact.

What is true is that Charles and his small force withdrew at news that Brooke and the Parliamentary general John Hampden were approaching from the south with eleven troops on horse and 4,800 foot. The King went to Leicester and then on to Nottingham, where he raised his standard on 22 August, formally declaring war on his enemies in Parliament.

Coventry greeted Lord Brooke's approach with open arms. The city's welcome was equally warm for the Earl of Essex who, at the end of August, arrived with an army that included within its ranks Nehemiah Wharton, sergeant of foot and in a former life apprentice to a London merchant. Writing to his master, Wharton was suitably impressed. He wrote, 'The city has magnificent churches and stately streets; within it there are also several sweete and pleasant springs of water [wells] built of freestone, very large, sufficient to supply many thousand men,' adding that its wall was the equal of London's in breadth and height.

Whether it liked it or not, Coventry was now a stronghold for Parliament. John Barker, its most active supporter in the city, was appointed governor, a garrison was put in place and in the months that followed efforts were made to stiffen the city's already impressive defences, thanks largely to a huge loan of £1,000 from the former mayor and MP William Jesson.

A stone wall dividing the Great Park and the Little Park, which had hidden the king's gunners as they bombarded Coventry, was torn down. Houses that had crept out along every main road beyond the town wall over the past 100 years were demolished to improve the field of fire. Apart from New Gate, Spon Gate, Bishop Gate and Gosford Gate, all the gates in the wall were blocked up and half-moon trenches and extra fortifications were dug to improve the defences. Cannons were mounted at each of the gates remaining open.

It worked. Over the next two years, while Leicester and particularly Birmingham suffered from repeated pillaging as the war swung across the Midlands, Coventry and its garrison appeared too strong a nut to crack, even for such a talented and bull-headed Royalist commander as the king's nephew, Prince Rupert.

Gosford Gate, one of a handful left open as defences were strengthened. (Coventry City Council)

There were plenty of alarms. In 1643 parties of women under the command of a goodwife Adderley were sent out with spades and mattocks to fill in quarries in the Park that might screen another Royalist approach. Their signal to withdraw into the city at the end of their daily labours was a pistol shot fired by a woman named Mary Herbert. The following year it looked as though Coventry might undergo another siege, and the Warwickshire County Committee for Parliament, now based in the city, ordered more arms to be distributed. But the Royalist defeat at the battle of Naseby put an end to that threat.

Coventry had become a refuge for many of those who might face persecution from the king's forces in the Midlands, and houses were thrown up to accommodate them in the yawning open spaces left by the destruction of the monasteries, particularly on the site of the priory and Greyfriars churchyard. The population quickly rose, possibly to around 9,000, but steady support for Parliament in the surrounding farming heartland of Warwickshire ensured that food supplies were still plentiful.

Among those seeking shelter in Coventry were more than thirty Puritan ministers, led by the eminent preacher and theologian Richard Baxter, who preached a weekly sermon to the garrison and another on Sunday to the citizens. Baxter clearly felt at home in the embattled city, among a 'sober, wise, religious company' of fellow refugees: 'We that lived quietly in Coventry did keep to our old principles, and thought all others had done so too, except a few inconsiderable persons.'

Among that sober and wise company were three other notable clerics: Richard Vines, who was offered the living of St Michael's church but whose future lay in London and as Master of a Cambridge college, Obadiah Grew and John Bryan. Grew, formerly headmaster of the grammar school at Atherstone in north Warwickshire, became vicar of St Michael's in 1644 and in the same year, Bryan, a protege of Lord Brooke, accepted the living of Holy Trinity. Both men were moderate Presbyterians who strongly opposed Charles I but when it came to it could not support his execution. They would

The Puritan preacher and theologian Richard Baxter. (Coventry City Council)

go on to be much-loved and influential ministers to their congregations and to the wider city.

Coventry had need of such moderating influences, for the relationship between the garrison, the townsfolk and armies passing through flared into open conflict at the drop of a beribboned hat. When Richard Baxter announced in 1645 that he was joining the New Model Army as a regimental chaplain, desperate, but ultimately unsuccessful, attempts were made to persuade him to stay. It was thought that only he could keep the brutal soldiery in line. Fighting had erupted between the garrison and troops from the Earl of Denbigh's army in the winter of 1643, and in 1646 a Parliamentary army that had been fighting in Scotland was refused entry to the city, bivouacking instead on Gosford Green, from where they sent into Coventry for provisions.

All of this may well have given rise to the expression 'Sent to Coventry', meaning to be cold-shouldered or shunned. It first appeared in the *History of the Great Rebellion*, written by the prominent Royalist Edward Hyde, first Earl of Clarendon, in the 1670s and published in 1702. However, it is more likely that the phrase came from the aftermath of a single event during the Second Civil War, the defeat of the Royalist Duke of Hamilton's Scottish army at the battle of Preston in 1648.

Prisoners were sent in large numbers to Coventry and were lodged in the Leather Hall in West Orchard, the towers of Spon and Greyfriars gates and the bridewell or house of correction that had been established behind Bablake Church in 1571. Their alien Scottishness and Royalist sympathies, as well as the extra pressure they must have put on Coventry's food supplies at a time of poor harvests, undoubtedly caused resentments among the locals whose attitude towards them would certainly have been extremely hostile.

Even after the final defeat of the king and the removal of Coventry's garrison in late 1648, violence between citizens and soldiers still occurred. During a riot on Christmas Eve 1649, a soldier on tax-collection duties was killed by a butcher named Howes, who was prominent in the city's butchers' company. He was put on trial for his life, but in the end was convicted of manslaughter and received a remarkably lenient sentence from a jury of his peers.

Surprisingly, as 1650 dawned, Coventry's Royalist aldermen, Million, Clarke and George Monk, who had been barred from becoming mayor five years earlier, were still on the council. But this changed after an attempt to proclaim Charles II king in the city had prompted the Council of State to send one of its members, Colonel William Purefoy, to Coventry to investigate.

Purefoy's family were Warwickshire landed gentry and he had been MP for Coventry back in the 1620s, by which time he was already a fiercely committed Puritan. He was a regicide, one of the signatories to Charles I's death warrant, but nevertheless aligned himself with Baxter, Grew and Bryan in maintaining discipline in the city. He had a close ally in another commissioned officer in the Parliamentary army, Major Robert Beake.

Beake was a draper and became one of Coventry's sheriffs in 1651, an office that was often a precursor to higher things. Three years later he was elected as MP for Coventry and Warwickshire, alongside Purefoy, and the following year he became Mayor of Coventry. Beake's legacy rests largely on the diary he kept during his year in office, which survives as a quirky and telling picture of life in an English city under Cromwell's protectorate. It is a daily account of Beake's doings as mayor and chief magistrate, his Puritan zeal tempered by a gruff humanity.

Beake's steadiness as a supporter of the protectorate won him the post of Admiralty Commissioner when his mayoral year ended, and the focus of his activities moved to London. But in the confusion that followed the death of Cromwell and the end of the Commonwealth, it was back in Coventry that he made his most decisive intervention.

Conflict within the army prompted fears that, in another outbreak of civil war, Coventry might become the headquarters for the hard-line radical Major-General John Lambert. In late September 1659 the mayor, Richard Hicks, ordered the magazine in St Mary's Hall to be opened and arms distributed to the citizens. More than 150 men commanded by Robert Beake gathered in St Michael's churchyard and marched on a detachment of soldiers helping to guard the city, demanding in the name of Parliament that the responsibility should be handed over to them. Their success – when challenged, the guard simply marched away – demonstrated that Coventry now aligned itself with those who saw the return of the monarchy as inevitable.

As a hotbed of opposition to his father, the city must have realised that it had a lot to do to placate Charles II. On St George's Day 1661, the day of the king's coronation, there were bonfires and feasts in the streets and it was reported that the conduits ran with claret wine, paid for by wealthy alderman Thomas Norton, who later got a knighthood out of it. Coventry sent a delegation with lavish gifts to welcome the new monarch, including silver plate worth £160. New portraits of both Charles I and II were acquired and the royal coat of arms was hastily painted on newly whitewashed walls in St Mary's Hall.

Sadly, it was far too late. In November rumours of plots against Charles II surfaced and Coventry was implicated, probably wrongly, in them. A force was dispatched to the city and its commander, Sir Henry Jones, demanded the keys to the gates. Although no evidence of disloyalty was actually found Charles was determined that Coventry, along with other Parliamentary strongholds like Gloucester and Northampton, would have its walls torn down. In the summer of 1662 he instructed the Earl of Northampton, his Lord Lieutenant in Warwickshire and the son of the man who had fled Coventry in some disarray in the summer of 1642, to do it.

The portrait of Charles II acquired by Coventry – much too late. (St Mary's Hall/ Coventry City Council)

The mayor, Thomas Pidgeon, in a final attempt to curry favour, had closed down the weekly lecture established by his Puritan forebears and erected the city's maypole, ready for the summer celebrations. But on 22 July, Northampton arrived with a large entourage of soldiers and members of the Warwickshire gentry and in three weeks demolished whole sections of the wall, while enjoying liberal hospitality from the council in the form of at least one enormous banquet at St Mary's Hall and copious amounts of alcohol sent nightly to the party's lodgings.

For the county gentry it was sweet revenge for Coventry's refusal to bow the knee over Ship Money, and they fully endorsed Northampton's statement that stone from the wall, that ultimate symbol of civic pride, should be used to help poor men in Coventry make better homes for themselves, at just 12d per cart load. It was said that the election of Pidgeon, a Royalist-supporting apothecary, fulfilled an old prophesy that Coventry's town wall would be finally brought to ground by a pigeon, but no reference to the story pre-dates the wall's destruction.

These events were a serious attempt by the Crown to meddle in Coventry's affairs in a way that would have been unthinkable before the Civil War. Obadiah Grew and John Bryan were booted out of their ministries. Beake, Barker and Basnet resigned before they could be sacked, while Purefoy, who stood to lose most from the return of Charles II – maybe even his head – had mercifully died in 1659. The aldermen who now held sway were, if not Royalists, then moderates to whom no stain of rebellion could be attached. In 1661 the city's choice of the Baptist Thomas Hobson as mayor, a remarkably provocative selection in the circumstances, had been quashed by the Crown on the grounds that he was 'a notorious actor against the king in the late rebellion'.

The Corporation Act of the same year, demanding that all holders of municipal office swear allegiance to the king, and the Act of Uniformity of 1662 which required laymen and clerics to obey the rules of the Church of England, were designed to root out free thinkers and nonconformists. Remarkably, the Dissenters, as they were called, still remained strong in Coventry and by 1670 dominated the council, becoming local prototypes of a new political animal, the Whig.

Coventry in the years that followed the Restoration was a mess. Alongside the shattered remains of its stately wall stood the rubble-strewn sites of its monastic heritage, notably the gaunt ruins of the priory itself, which had been a place where butchers kept their hogs.

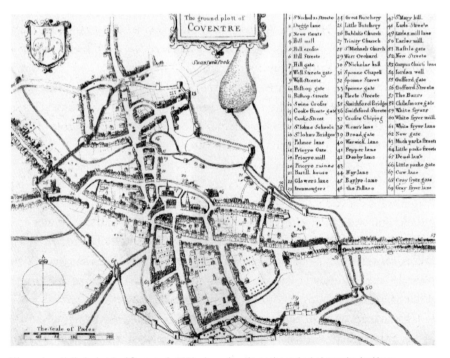

Wenceslaus Hollar's sketch of Coventry in 1656, shows how large the cathedral complex had been. (Coventry City Council)

John Bryan, Holy Trinity's redoubtable vicar, had done what he could to tidy up the priory site, building himself a house at the west end of the great cathedral church and turning other parts of it into gardens. But a lightning strike on St Michael's Church in 1655 had done significant damage to the building, and on 14 January 1665 high winds brought the steeple of neighbouring Holy Trinity crashing to the ground, destroying much of the church and killing a young boy walking through the churchyard.

Economically it was a struggle too. The population of Coventry had sunk back to around 7,000 after the war, and a survey for a hearth tax taken in 1662 showed that the city had slipped to nineteenth on an index of prosperity among English towns, a lowly standing unprecedented in 400 years.

In 1666, Coventry clothiers were said to have lost up to £4,000 worth of cloth, burned or looted during the Great Fire of London. Disasters like that, along with a general decline in trade, contributed to a reluctance among Coventry's more prominent citizens to take on the financial burdens of becoming mayor.

In 1671 an apothecary named Abel Brooksby desperately tried to avoid taking his turn by appealing directly to Charles II, stressing the role he had played in ministering to the wounded after the king's final defeat at Worcester. At first he was successful, but the decision was later reversed and he was forced to take up his year in office.

Yet there were signs that post-war opportunities would still present themselves for Coventry. In 1658 a new stagecoach service had been established between London and Holyhead in north Wales, passing through the city on its

The Godiva procession, brought to life in intricate detail in David Gee's 1867 painting. (Herbert Art Gallery)

way to Lichfield and Chester. The journey to Coventry from the George Inn at Holborn, its promoters announced, would only take three days. Even though it was to be a century before the state of the roads allowed that claim to become at all realistic, it must have looked like real progress.

In 1669, the city's market cross, a feature that had astonished travellers for nearly 150 years, was repaired and re-gilded in a modest reinstatement of civic pride. Shortly afterwards, houses in Bayley Lane that had crowded in St Michael's Church for centuries were demolished to open up the church to view.

In 1678, in an attempt to recover some of the city's once-legendary ability to attract big-spending crowds, the council devised a new procession to accompany the opening of the Great Fair, with a new star, Lady Godiva. For centuries, St George the mythical dragon-slayer had been the key figure in city processions, his association with Coventry so strong that in 1596, Richard Johnson, a writer of romances, had been able to identify the city as the patron saint's birthplace in his *Famous History of the Seven Champions of Christendom*. Now, Coventry's founding mother, allegedly as under-dressed as nature intended, would be used to draw the crowds, with music provided by the city waits who had been re-formed in 1674, exactly forty years after being disbanded for 'being troublesome'. The first Lady Godiva, as it happens, was not a woman but a boy, the young son of one James Swinnerton, and he was fully dressed. There were limits to titillation in seventeenth-century Coventry.

The welcome in the streets for Godiva could scarcely have matched that given on 18 September 1682 to James, Duke of Monmouth, Protestant hero and illegitimate son of Charles II. Monmouth was greeted by hundreds of well-wishers outside the city gates, as bells pealed and bonfires were lit in the streets. He spent a night at the Star Inn in Earl Street, carousing with former Parliamentarians, before making a morning courtesy call on the mayor, Richard Heyward, who had strategically ignored his visit by failing to greet him the night before. A total of eighteen people were arrested for rioting in wild scenes during the night, but in due course were treated with great leniency by the judge, Thomas Burgh, who was Steward of Coventry and had been re-appointed to the job, despite royal disapproval.

The visit highlighted Coventry's instinctive support for opponents of the Stuart kings – Monmouth was to die on the scaffold three years later after a failed uprising against his father's brother, James II. And in 1683 the city was claimed to be one of the crucibles of the Rye House plot, an alleged conspiracy to assassinate Charles II and James, then Duke of York, as they returned from the king's beloved horse races at Newmarket. There was little evidence for Coventry's involvement, or indeed for the plot itself, but that old radical Robert Beake was among those who had his house searched for arms and even poor Obadiah Grew, now elderly and blind, was imprisoned for six months on suspicion of being part of it.

The city was punished by being forced to surrender its governing charter. The replacement, dated 10 October 1683, gave the Crown the right to remove and appoint corporation officers and aldermen, interference of the most direct kind. To add insult to injury, it cost the city £200.

The following year, nearly 200 Coventry nonconformists, or Dissenters, were indicted for failing to attend church and imprisoned for attending conventicles, or assembly meetings, instead. Dissenters were proving remarkably tough to control in the city, despite the authorities' draconian measures to suppress them. In 1668 around 700 had gathered at the Leather Hall in West Orchard for a Great Meeting. By 1703 they had built their own meeting house in Smithford Street and it was estimated that almost a quarter of all Coventry households contained at least one Dissenter, the figure rising to 40 per cent within twenty years. Most were Presbyterians and they were particularly strong in the ranks of the mercers, weavers and clothiers companies.

James II as Duke of York. His 1687 visit was eventful, to say the least. (St Mary's Hall/Coventry City Council)

Oddly enough, it was to these die-hard opponents that the Catholic James II was most anxious to appeal when he came to Coventry on 1 September 1687. A huge number went out to greet him at Meriden as he approached the city and he opted to stay at Palace Yard, home of one of their leaders, Richard Hopkins, rather than at Whitefriars, home to the much more conformist Hales family. Astonishingly he later removed eight city officials and replaced them with Dissenters.

James, quite rightly fearing for his throne, had issued a Declaration of Indulgence back in April that lifted many of the penalties and restrictions on those who did not want to worship in the Anglican way. His attempts to head off opposition looked to be bearing fruit. The city produced its customary gift of a gold cup worth more than £200, although there was some consternation when he promptly gave it to his Master of the Horse, Lord Dartmouth, whose father had been imprisoned in Coventry during the Civil War.

The embarrassment was compounded at a lavish banquet for the king in St Mary's Hall, when a table groaning with good things to eat promptly collapsed, showering the royal guest, according to one version of events, with a local speciality called Coventry custard. The following morning, James was escorted to St Michael's Church, where he touched 300 people suffering from scrofula, or the King's Evil, in a traditional rite that ascribed miracle cures from this form of tuberculosis to a touch from the reigning monarch.

Little more than twelve months later James was deposed by his Protestant son-in-law William of Orange. In the confusion of the Glorious Revolution, James's younger daughter Anne spent the night of 11 December 1688 at Richard Hopkins' house in Coventry after fleeing London and her father's cause with a large entourage of nobles and up to 1,000 horses.

Early the following year, a newly recruited regiment of foot, commanded by the Earl of Kingston, spent three months in the city before joining William's campaign in Ireland. Then on 5 June 1690 William himself passed through on his way to his decisive victory over James's forces at the Battle of the Boyne. He was made welcome but he did not receive the customary gift of a gold cup. After James II's graceless insult in giving his away to a subordinate, Coventry no longer did expensive presents for sovereigns.

The fall of the Stuart kings unleashed an ugly backlash against the old religion and it was reported that in both Coventry and Birmingham 'rude mobs' attacked the properties of known Catholics and hunted down priests.

The usual antipathies had been resumed too over the use of the common lands in Coventry, when in 1689 an angry crowd threw down hedges and spoiled corn planted in the Park. The target of their fury was almost certainly the Townsend family, prominent Royalists who back in 1661 had been given a lease for Cheylesmore Manor and Park by Charles II, despite appeals that up to 1,000 poor families were using it to pasture animals.

It was another example of the way the city's powerful elite had a tendency to set aside the public good in favour of their own interests. And this was something that was beginning to be noticed elsewhere.

As far back as the 1590s there had surfaced the first hints of concern about the mismanagement of income-rich city charities, and in 1641, on the eve of the Civil War, the council had been forced to make good sums of money missing from the accounts of Sir Thomas White's charity. The bitter divisions of the war years, combined with the almost hermetically sealed nature of the 'close corporation' that ran the city, created a climate where naked self-interest and corruption flourished.

In 1695 its stench finally reached the Court of Chancery, where the council was accused of embezzling funds from Sir Thomas White's charity, the first of a series of cases which had resulted in it paying back the huge sum of £2,241 1s 3d by 1720. The revenues were used to line comfortable pockets instead of being spent on the worthy recipients of charity.

While the closed corporation was happily mismanaging the city's extensive property and charity portfolio, the local economy was undergoing another of those seismic upheavals to which it was prone. Traditional cloth-making was being replaced by the production of new types of cloth, notably tammies (striped and glazed worsteds), callimancoes (wool glazed to look like satin) and camblets (a mix of wool and goat's hair).

The weaving of tammies, in particular, was responsible for a small but marked upward swing in Coventry's fortunes. Introduced by the mercer Samuel Smith in 1696, they quickly attracted other manufacturers and the trade was soon worth £20,000 a year.

The famous Coventry blue thread was still in circulation, but its provenance was increasingly hard to defend and its use was declining. As an illustration of that, perhaps, its reputation had already passed into the English language as a proverb. The naturalist and writer John Ray included it in the first edition of his *A Compleat Collection of English Proverbs*, published in 1670. 'Coventry,' he wrote, 'had formerly the reputation for dying of blues; insomuch that true blue became a proverb to signify one that was always the same and like himself.'

Silk weavers had been working in Coventry for at least sixty years and would shortly develop their trade into the city's next staple industry – the manufacture of ribbons. But there were also the first glimmerings of another new industry that would one day carry Coventry's name around the world.

In 1682, a Coventry craftsman named Samuel Watson made a clock for Charles II. The king was so impressed that he invited him to become his mathematician; however, it was the next product of Samuel's Coventry workshop that would really make his name.

It survives still in the royal collections at Windsor Castle, an astronomical clock, complete with planets and signs of the zodiac, that took him seven years to make and remains one of the most extraordinary achievements of clock-making in England. On the strength of it, Watson, who had held the office of sheriff of Coventry in 1686, moved to London and quickly became one of the most celebrated clockmakers of the age. It would be another fifty years before the industry that he helped pioneer truly established itself in his home city.

To the traveller Celia Fiennes, Coventry at the turn of the eighteenth century seemed to be a 'thriving, good trading town', full of Presbyterians, fine buildings and broad streets. The daughter of a colonel who had fought for Parliament in the Civil War, Fiennes visited Coventry in 1697 as part of a twenty-year journey of discovery around England, riding side-saddle with just two servants for company. One of this country's first female travellers, she left a picture of the city in her memoirs that lingered on its fine towers and steeples and, of course, its cross, 'the finest building in England for such a thing.'

If Fiennes found Coventry beguiling, the novelist, journalist and secret agent Daniel Defoe took a much more jaundiced view, some eight years later. His impressions, set out in his magisterial work of travel writing *Tour Through The Whole Island of Great Britain*, were shaped by the city's recent electoral history:

> The mob of Coventry having at the last election beaten the magistrates, wounded the mayor, disarmed the watchmen and taken away their halberds, so carried on the most violent tumult that has been seen in this nation for many years ... Here's a comedy fit for Bartholomew Fair, Mob-a-la-mode or the Coventry election: Walk in, Gentlemen, and take your places, here's the rabble uppermost and the magistrates under their feet.

Defoe was reflecting the reality, for Coventry was headed down a road that would make it a byword for electoral fraud and municipal corruption over the next century or so. It was to become, in short, the classic rotten borough.

The first of many electoral disputes needed to be sorted out by the Court of King's Bench as early as May 1697, when it ruled that Edward Owen had been rightfully chosen as mayor the previous year. Owen, a feltmaker, was the candidate of the Dissenters, or nonconformists, but he had a rival, the butcher John Bennett, who was favoured by aldermen of a Tory persuasion.

After a protracted war of words, parallel mayor-making ceremonies were staged for both men and there was even a struggle in the street between their supporters over the city's ceremonial sword and mace. Among those who must have witnessed this faction-fighting at close hand was the silkman William Bird, a member of the council in 1696, who went on to become mayor ten years later. It is believed to have been Bird who set up Coventry's first ribbon factory in 1703.

He employed Huguenot refugees, newly fled from France after Louis XIV's 1685 revocation of the Edict of Nantes, which gave Protestants equal rights in France. Their skills in weaving silk ribbons were unsurpassed, and William's business acumen brought huge wealth for the Bird family. By the time his son Thomas died in 1746, the family firm employed 2,000 people and had laid the foundations of Coventry's new staple industry. Within a century, ribbon manufacturing was employing a staggering 10,000 people in the city. Daniel Defoe's comment on the ribbons produced by Coventry's new ribbon masters was predictably dismissive. They were, he wrote, 'of the meanest kind, chiefly black.'

Greyfriars Gate. (Herbert Art Gallery)

Another regular visitor to Coventry at this time found rather more to admire. In 1713, the great architect Sir Christopher Wren bought the Wroxall Abbey estate near Warwick as a country bolt-hole, and spent quite a bit of time there over the last ten years of his life. During his visits he liked nothing better than to have himself conveyed into Coventry so that he could spend some time gazing upon St Michael's Church, a building he described as a 'masterpiece of architecture'.

Other old buildings were not faring as well. In 1728 the Old Drapery in Bayley Lane, dating from the time of William Walshman in the fourteenth century, was pulled down and the Half Moon Inn built on its site.

All twelve city gates had survived the Earl of Northampton's demolition crews, but without a complete wall to guard several were being used as tenement housing by 1700, among them New Gate, Greyfriars Gate and Bishop Gate.

In 1733, five years after the demolition of the Old Drapery, another great Coventry institution was laid to rest in the churchyard of St Michael's.

John Parkes had lived his final years in the city of his birth, a well-known character around town, battered and lame no doubt and maybe even disfigured, but once as famous a sporting hero as the legendary Lester Piggott was to be, more than 200 years later.

Parkes was a gladiator, or professional sword fighter, who fought 350 battles across Europe against heavily armed opponents in the feverish atmosphere of the prize ring. A 'man of mild disposition', sometimes regarded as slow and even ponderous, he was also strong and clever, the undisputed master of a dangerous game, in which bouts were not stopped until blood was drawn.

Parkes's brutal thirty-year career was fought far from home, but the clash of swords and the sounds of war were suddenly very close in the autumn of 1745, when the Jacobite Pretender Charles Edward Stuart reached Derby with his invading Scottish army. In Coventry, the alarms were sounding. Wealthy citizens offered considerable donations to pay for extra arms and munitions, a company of foot was raised to defend the city and in November the advance guard of a royal army marched through Coventry heading north. Its artillery train, with sixteen cannon and more than 250 horses, was quartered in the Park before moving on.

On 6 December, six regiments of foot and horse arrived in the city and were billeted on almost every household, to be joined by their commander William, Duke of Cumberland, riding in a post-chaise, the first ever seen in the city.

Oddly enough, Coventry's town clerk Joseph Hewitt was at that moment in Derby on council business. He found himself taken into custody by the Jacobites, drank a cup of wine with Bonnie Prince Charlie himself and claimed that he had actually overheard the order being given to sound the retreat from Derby. On his release, he hurried back to Packington Hall, some five miles from Coventry, to report to the Duke of Cumberland, who was in quarters there. As it happened, intelligence had already been received of the retreat and the royal army moved north, finally bringing the Jacobite rebellion to an end at the battle of Culloden, near Inverness, in April 1746.

Coventry had escaped scot-free, and it was to be the last time in its history that the city felt physically threatened by great events within what had been, since the Act of Union in 1707, the United Kingdom. In future, that threat would come from overseas.

In his diary for 25 April 1656, the Mayor of Coventry meticulously recorded the chief event of what must have been a pretty dull Sunday. 'Being Lord's Day,' he wrote, 'I went to the park and observed who idly walked there.'

In Mayor Robert Beake's book, idly walking anywhere was a punishable offence. Doing it on a Sunday came within a whisker of mortal sin.

Beake's diary survives for only six months of his mayoral year, but it is an illuminating account of life under Cromwell's Protectorate and the character of a man on whose shoulders the governance of his native city rested in turbulent times. A draper by trade, conservative by inclination and Puritan by conviction, Robert Beake was a stickler for rules and an ardent supporter of Sabbatarianism – the idea that Sunday was purely for religion and quiet contemplation.

Yet to dismiss him as merely an officious and interfering busybody, out to stop everybody else having fun, is to miss the essence of the man. He was stiff-necked and lacking humour, it's true, but conscientious and humane too. As mayor, Beake was responsible for ensuring that the city's streets were kept in good order, that its tradesman obeyed rules on prices and quality and that those who looked after the vulnerable and the needy fulfilled their duties. He accomplished all of this, and more, with a commendable incorruptibility, refusing gifts that were clearly meant to influence him.

He won no popularity awards for his unbending enforcement of the rules. In January 1656, an unlicensed innkeeper called Bretford tried to raise a whole street against Beake when his business was closed down, but the mayor prevailed and he ended up in jail. In fact, a sympathetic Beake had released Bretford from an earlier prison sentence for the same offence on the grounds that he had the 'falling-down sickness', or epilepsy.

In his diary for 19 November 1655 the mayor expressed his regret at having to place three Quakers in the cage for travelling on the Lord's Day, 'It grieved me that this poor deluded people should undergo punishment of such a nature'. He released one Goody Pywell from jail because her legs had swollen, attempted conciliation between neighbours who had come to blows and intervened to prevent stocks of corn being hoarded to force up the price.

Beake's political affiliations meant that his active role in city life could not survive the Restoration, even though he did more than anyone to persuade Coventry that the return of Charles II was the right course of action. In 1679 he was briefly re-elected as one of the city's MPs but four years later, somewhat incredibly, was suspected of involvement with the alleged Rye House plot to assassinate Charles and had his house searched.

Beake lived on into the new century, his reputation as an old Puritan undiminished. In 1701, as he went to the polls, Tory supporters pelted him with stones and turnips. The old man deserved better than that.

eight

AN INDUSTRIOUS REVOLUTION

On a wet morning in April 1765, an excited crowd gathered at a lonely spot two miles south of Coventry, on the old road to Kenilworth. They were there to witness the public execution of troopers Edward Drury and Robert Leslie, from Lord Pembroke's Regiment of Dragoons, and a Coventry ribbon weaver, Moses Baker, for the murder of local farmer Thomas Edwards, during a bungled robbery close to the spot.

The execution was notable for two reasons. The bodies of the three men would hang in chains for more than forty years, giving the place the name by which it is still known, Gibbet Hill. And before going to the gallows all three had stated that they would have died in peace had they been able to blow out the brains of the man who brought them to their end – Alderman John Hewitt.

Hewitt was used to being loathed. A self-appointed guardian of public morals, he was an authoritarian braggart, supine in the face of those he considered his superiors, but unforgiving to the poor and the lawbreakers who crossed his path.

Born in 1719, the son of a draper, Hewitt came from an old Coventry family of some influence and was only in his mid-thirties when he became mayor for the first time in late 1755. His first action was to lay on the most extravagant inauguration ball ever seen in the city, inviting nearly 600 guests from the gentry of several counties to a feast that included flocks of geese and turkeys, barrels of oysters, pickled sturgeon, six dozen bottles of claret and gallons of rum and brandy. To make St Mary's Hall better for dancing, he had its historic brick floor ripped up and replaced with floorboards.

But Hewitt's real ambition was to become a noted thief-taker, like his friend the blind London magistrate Sir John Fielding, half-brother to the novelist and magistrate Henry. In 1756 he petitioned the government to allow him to press petty criminals and the idle poor into the army and navy as the Seven Years War loomed. It wasn't to be the first appearance of the press-gang in Coventry. As far back as 1625, twenty men, all individuals the city fathers wanted rid of, had been sent to the Duke of Buckingham for pressing into the king's army.

Scouring the taverns and flop-houses of Coventry for suitable 'recruits', Hewitt's ruthless pursuit of them made him deeply unpopular. Even army units billeted locally refused to help him, fearing a stain upon their reputation.

As a thief-taker, though, Hewitt had his successes. At the Coventry Fair in 1763 he managed to collar William Fall, leader of the so-called Coventry gang, a loose confederation of criminals, actually based in Northumberland, who had been responsible for many robberies all over the country.

While the establishment of a dedicated police force for Coventry was still almost seventy-five years away, Hewitt's activities, set out in his journals published in 1790, did a good deal to galvanise the administration of law and order in the city. The building of County Hall, opened in March 1785 as part of improved court and custodial facilities for the city (and county) of Coventry, may well have been a consequence of that. But it also reflected a time when the appearance of the city was undergoing dramatic change.

In 1762 New Gate, the old medieval gate covering the road to London, was pulled down. There were probably good practical reasons for what looks like an act of civic vandalism. For many years, drivers on the London to Holyhead coaching road had been complaining about how difficult it was to get into Coventry, with its narrow streets and sharp corners, and the old gate cannot have been easy to negotiate. Within twenty years, four more of the city's historic gates, Spon Gate, said to be the most beautiful of them all, Bishop Gate, Gosford Gate and Greyfriars Gate, had been demolished.

After decades of neglect, Coventry's once awe-inspiring market cross was a casualty too, its upper half removed for being dangerous in 1753, the remainder following in 1771. Some of its stone was said to have been used in a new bridge across the River Sherbourne at Spon End. The more decorative features ended up in private hands.

A smaller Swine's Cross, marking the site of traditional livestock markets at the junction of Bishop Street and Silver Street, was removed in 1763, while the Drapers' Hall in Bayley Lane, a 'dark, gloomy edifice' built just before the Civil War, was replaced by a new building in 1775.

But the most radical change to the old city's streetscape was happening because of the success of Coventry's new staple industry – ribbon-weaving. The Great Masters, as local people called them, were few in number, but with their trade protected by a 1766 embargo on imported silk goods, they were enjoying an unprecedented boom. By the 1780s, it was reckoned that the trade employed up to 10,000 weavers, many of them incomers. Accommodation had to be found for them, and from the middle of the century, modest terraces of houses and courts were being crammed into the gardens and orchards that lay behind the old timber-framed houses lining the streets.

A rise in population had other consequences too. By the 1720s, inhabitants of three city centre wards – Cross Cheaping, Smithford Street and Broadgate – were complaining about water shortages; the 100-year-old Swanswell water works and the ancient

Spon Gate, said to be the most beautiful of them all. (Herbert Art Gallery)

systems of wells and conduits were proving inadequate. And in 1734 the old collegiate church of St John's Bablake had been consecrated as a parish church to cater for a new population of worshippers settled around Spon Street.

Even so, Coventry had already surrendered its position as the Midlands' biggest and most important city. Birmingham had overtaken it in population around the turn of the century, and although Coventry had grown steadily to just over 12,000 in 1748, Birmingham was already twice the size, its dramatic expansion fuelled by the metal trades that were feeding off the beginnings of the Industrial Revolution.

The contrast between the rapid industrialisation of Birmingham and a craft-based economy like Coventry was stark, yet there was one major local development from this period that did embrace that rush to new technology. In May 1768 curious crowds gathered in the parish of Foleshill to the north of Coventry to watch a 'porcupine', a giant roller with spikes on it, carving out a huge trench in the ground. They were witnessing the beginnings of the Coventry Canal, a waterway that would eventually link the Warwickshire coalfields with the rapidly growing markets they could service and give Coventry's industries their first truly modern route out into the wider world of commerce.

Coventry's impressive canal basin. (CV One/Coventry City Council)

The man with the vision and engineering ability to make it happen was the great canal engineer James Brindley, hired by the Coventry Canal Company in February 1768. It was Brindley's vision of connecting up the fledgling canal network in a Midlands Cross, with the Coventry Canal at the heart of it, which opened up the commercial opportunities of waterborne transport. But the driving spirits were coal owners like Sir Roger Newdigate of Arbury and Richard Parrott of Hawkesbury, who had actually introduced Brindley to fellow shareholders in the company. Hardly a coincidence, then, that on 10 August 1769 the first two boats making the inaugural journey from Bedworth to the new Bishop Street Basin in Coventry should be loaded with coal.

It was to be another eight years before the connection was made with the Oxford Canal and twenty years before the full thirty-eight-mile length of the Coventry Canal would be completed, from the basin to Fradley Junction on the Trent and Mersey Canal. But the new waterway was immediately profitable and was to remain so for many decades, even after the coming of the railways gave industrialists an even more versatile means of transport to work with.

News of the canal's coming, if not its vital importance to the economy of the city, was announced in Coventry's first newspaper, *Jopson's Coventry Mercury*, launched as a weekly in July 1741 by printer James Jopson from premises in Hay Lane. From the start Jopson's paper accepted Coventry adverts, but for news preferred to give its local readers breathless accounts of foreign diplomacy or the latest doings of London Society.

In the early years, local news was confined to formal notices announcing rewards for the apprehension of runaway apprentices or the return of chestnut mares stolen from the Park. But by the 1760s, the paper had been taken over by Jopson's widow Elizabeth and was beginning to raise its sights a little.

Elizabeth was one of eleven women operating as printers in Coventry in the second half of the eighteenth century, a remarkably high figure for the time, attributed to the city's nonconformist tolerance towards the female sex. Yet women, so active in Coventry's commercial and social life before the Civil War, had been forced to take a back seat as political divisions came to dominate the city's life. Only those who were freemen of the city (either serving a full apprenticeship or paying a fee to become a freeman) could vote and women were excluded from that, as they were from so much else.

For every Sarah Kemble, married to actor William Siddons in Holy Trinity Church on 25 November 1773 and later to become the doyenne of the English stage, there were many more like Mary Clues, living in destitution in a mean hovel in Gosford Street. Poor Mary's claim to fame is a gruesome one. Confined to bed by an illness brought on by excessive drinking, her daily tipple was said to be at least a quart of rum, she had so much alcohol in her body that she became, in the words of an inquest held in March 1772, as flammable as a lamp. While sleeping off her final drunken binge, she caught fire, probably from a candle. Her body, almost completely consumed by the flames, was discovered next morning in a room otherwise virtually untouched.

The actress Sarah Siddons may well have made her stage debut as a child in Coventry, appearing at a theatre converted by her grandfather, John Ward, from his riding school in the Burges in 1752. And she was to return in May 1797, at the height of her fame, to appear for a week in four plays at St Mary's Hall.

Ward's was probably Coventry's first dedicated theatre space, and although the city had to wait almost another seventy years for its first permanent theatre, there is evidence of a modest but growing interest in the arts among Coventrians from the mid-eighteenth century.

Elizabeth Jopson, the newspaper proprietor, was advertising her own circulation library in 1764. From the 1750s, the organist and composer Capel Bond was staging concerts in St Mary's Hall for a new musical society, and in 1746 a new society for gentlemen, 'for the improvement of learning and natural knowledge' started meeting at the Mermaid Tavern. It wasn't exactly

The actress Sarah Siddons, doyenne of the eighteenth-century English stage. (Library of Congress LC-USZC4-6459)

Birmingham's Lunar Society but it was evidence that there were Coventry folk prepared to broaden their horizons.

Some old habits, however, die hard. In the second week of September 1780, hundreds fought in the street in what became known as the Bludgeon Fight, the most violent election in Coventry's bloody and infamous polling history. Between 1689 and the municipal reform legislation of 1835, there were forty-eight Parliamentary elections in Coventry and the closed council wished to take a controlling hand in every one. This time, it was supporting Sir Thomas Fairfax and Thomas Rogers, two London bankers standing as Whig candidates against the sitting Tory MPs, landowner Edward Yeo and John Baker Holroyd, colonel of a regiment of light dragoons billeted locally.

Within half an hour of the polls opening on 9 September, 500 Tory supporters had moved to take possession of the polling booth next to the Mayor's Parlour in Cross Cheaping. Over the coming days an army of colliers, roughs and prize-fighters, recruited by the Corporation as 'constables', fought running skirmishes with them in the streets that culminated in a pitched battle over possession of that polling booth. The Corporation's men were routed. They sought shelter in St Mary's Hall and the medieval stained glass was smashed to fragments as volleys of bricks rained in through the windows.

After eight days polling only ninety-six of nearly 3,000 votes open to city freemen had been cast, and when Parliament re-assembled Coventry was not represented. Another election was called for 29 November, again triggering chaotic and violent scenes in which rival armies marched six abreast through the streets and one man was seen to brandish a sword.

In the uneasy truce that followed, the Corporation, knowing that it had lost, secretly enrolled 150 new freemen, total strangers to the city who came from as far away as London and Portsmouth. They were later to be dubbed the 'mushroom' voters as they popped up overnight. But the game was up. A Parliamentary Commission stepped in, jailed the city's two sheriffs, Thomas Noxon and Thomas Butler, for ten days for gross dereliction of their duty to see elections fairly contested, and forced through a special Coventry Election Act to tighten up on the enrolment of freemen.

The Bludgeon Fight was the most lurid of Coventry's shamefully corrupt elections, but it wasn't to be the last. In the reforming municipal legislation of the 1830s, a special place would be reserved for the city as a continuing sore on the nation's body politics.

Polling day battles in the streets had clearly caused some unease nationally, but it was pure coincidence that in 1793 the government decided to build a barracks in Coventry, bringing a garrison right into the heart of the city.

Election riot at Coventry. Chaotic and violent scenes were commonplace. (Herbert Art Gallery)

SMITH & JABET, COVENTRY

The Bull Inn, Smithford Street.

The historic Bull Inn, the bulk of it swept away for the new barracks. (Coventry City Council)

Coventry had had a long and not always harmonious relationship with the military. For 150 years, soldiers had been billeted for long periods in the city, often making the local headlines in ways that were less than positive. The city records featured a number of cases in which soldiers had committed serious crimes, including murder, against local people, while breaches of military discipline regularly led to very public punishments, floggings or even worse. In April 1757 and June 1758, for example, two soldiers from Colonel Stewart's Regiment of Foot were reported to have been put up against a wall in the Park and shot for desertion.

Now, with war against France looming, the government decided it was time to regularise the stationing of army units throughout the country and determined that Coventry should have a new cavalry barracks.

It was built on the site of the Black Bull, the timber-framed medieval inn on Smithford Street that had once played host to Henry VII and Mary, Queen of Scots. Parts of the old building may have been incorporated into the new barracks, but its disappearance from the street scene represented another grievous loss to the city's already diminishing stock of historic buildings.

For the next 120 years the barracks, with its imposing Georgian frontage, would be an important landmark in the centre of Coventry. It switched in later years from cavalry to the artillery, before succumbing to a more modern way of thinking and eventually becoming a multi-storey car park.

The barracks' first occupants in 1794 were two troops of the 17th Light Dragoons, a regiment that had recently seen service in the American War of Independence. But their stay in Coventry was to be brief. On 8 September 1800, serious riots broke out over food prices, inflamed by the appearance in the city of an armed mob of desperate miners from the Bedworth area, intent on 'liberating' basic food stocks to feed their starving families. There were many in Coventry like them and as trouble spread, the mayor read the Riot Act and called upon the 17th Light Dragoons, aided by volunteers from a newly raised Coventry militia, to clear the streets.

The dragoons, it was claimed afterwards, behaved humanely as they dispersed angry crowds in Bishop Street. But there were many injuries and possibly some fatalities in what in many people's minds came to be seen as a brutal act of repression. Resentment ran high and within weeks the regiment was withdrawn from Coventry and replaced with infantry soldiers from the 18th (Royal) Irish Regiment of Foot, who must have found a cavalry barracks not quite suited to their needs.

The food riots cannot have come as a total surprise, for as the new century dawned, a succession of poor harvests and the war against France had pushed prices for basic foodstuffs too high for many. Two years earlier, a soup kitchen had been established for the poor in Coventry, offering a quart of soup and a slice of bread for a penny.

The Corporation had contributed a paltry £40 a year to support this, but clearly more needed to be done. In the wake of the riots, a Committee for Bettering the Condition of the Poor was set up by the mayor, Samuel Whitwell, to sell food at below cost price and review the provision of accommodation and work for those most vulnerable of Coventry's 16,000 inhabitants.

It successfully petitioned parliament for an Act that would create Guardians of the Poor, effectively every ratepayer in the city who paid more than £20 a year, who would elect eighteen Directors of the Poor to raise money and establish a new House of Industry, or workhouse. What remained of the old Carmelite friary was purchased from its private owners and by 1804 the Directors had brought the inmates of two earlier Houses of Industry, overcrowded and hopelessly inadequate, together under one roof. This was a pioneering move. It was to be sixty years before most towns in England had devised a comparable structure of guardians for the relief of the poor.

THE UNION QUADRANGLE, COVENTRY.

Whitefriars in its final years as a workhouse. (Author's Collection)

Coventry was also fairly early in seeking powers to update the provision of essential services like paving, lighting and policing in the city, as well as modernising the water supply. Back in 1762, following in the footsteps of Nottingham, the council had successfully promoted an Act of Parliament setting up a body of twenty-two Street Commissioners with the power to levy a rate for those essential services.

A second piece of legislation, the Coventry Street Act, extended its scope in 1790 and in 1812 a further street act was secured, authorising the widening of streets and the creation of new thoroughfares, an improvement desperately needed in a city already notorious for its cramped and crooked streets.

In the years that followed, houses were taken down in Broadgate to widen the market area, and in Much Park Street and Fleet Street, among others, corner buildings were demolished to speed up the flow of coaching traffic. But the most important change was the creation of Hertford Street to bypass the old main road in from the south, the bottleneck that was the winding Warwick Lane.

Tolls on traffic were established to help pay for these improvements, but some of the funding for Hertford Street, named after the 2nd Marquess of Hertford who had recently purchased most of Cheylesmore Park from the Crown, came from an unlikely source.

With the ribbon trade see-sawing wildly, the weavers, backed by many of the masters, had formed their own Provident Union to try to stabilise wages. There was criticism of the union's coercive methods and in 1819 it was hauled before the courts and convicted of infringing the Combination Laws, which prohibited collective bargaining. The fines and costs, amounting to around £16,000, were given to the Street Commissioners to spend on their road schemes.

The formation of the union followed an extraordinary boom in the ribbon trade as the Napoleonic Wars reached their climax. Almost overnight, in 1813, Coventry weavers found themselves elbow deep in the 'big purl time', in which a sudden fashion for purl-edged ribbons coincided with shortages in skilled labour, forcing up demand. For a couple of years Coventry ribbon-weavers made the kind of money they had only ever dreamed of before, but then the fashion died equally as suddenly, and they were faced with a half-pay apprenticeship system, introduced by the masters to keep pace with demand in times of plenty. This clearly undermined the journeyman weaver, who had served a seven-year apprenticeship and viewed himself as an independent and superior artisan.

In their desperate attempts to hold prices at a tolerable level, the Coventry weavers often found themselves on the wrong side of the law. At the August

Hertford Street in 1904, opened up as the city's new main route in from the old Warwick road nearly a century before. (Author's Collection)

assizes in 1821, three ribbon weavers, Edward Cave, Joseph Rice and Thomas Smith, were fined and jailed for intent to compel Philip Harrington, a ribbon manufacturer, to ride backwards on an ass through the streets.

The humiliating donkey ride was a traditional punishment levied by the Coventry weavers on people who had incurred their displeasure. The following summer it was in use again, this time employed against Amos Carver, a journeyman weaver who had accepted work at lower rates than those agreed. Twelve weavers, all members of an Aggregate Committee set up to regulate prices, were jailed for riot and assault.

The defiance of authority that these cases highlight was also happening outside the confines of Coventry's biggest industry. On 15 November 1819, radicals staged a public meeting on Greyfriars Green to protest about the recent Peterloo Massacre in Manchester, in which yeomanry cavalry had cut down people attending a huge demonstration calling for Parliamentary reform, killing up to fifteen and wounding hundreds.

As William Greatheed Lewis, editor and proprietor of the *Coventry Recorder*, the city's most radical newspaper, was about to address the crowd, police arrived in large numbers and broke up the meeting. Many were hurt in the melee that followed.

Lewis, a former schoolmaster, had already been charged with sedition, accused of inciting disaffection among the King's subjects at a meeting in Birmingham earlier in 1819. The following year he was jailed at Warwick for that offence and faced a separate charge of undermining the government's lucrative tax levy on coffee by advertising in his newspaper a method of producing an ersatz version from roasted white peas. On this bizarre pretext he was fined a crippling £100 and his newspaper seems to have closed down, presumably as the authorities hoped it would.

The views of seditious radicals like Lewis were at one end of the political spectrum, but a touch of their rebelliousness must have rubbed off on others. In October 1820, the mayor and council sent a formal address of support to Queen Caroline, hapless consort to the newly crowned George IV, who was facing a vicious campaign of smears and allegations orchestrated by her husband.

Coventry's once close relationship with reigning monarchs was now ancient history. It had been more than a century since James II had spent a night or two in the city, and he was the last to do so. True, there had been lavish celebrations in Coventry to mark the coronation of George III, back in September 1761.

And in 1792 wall-space in St Mary's Hall had been found for a new, full-length portrait of George, costing £500, by the royal painter Thomas Lawrence. But that had been a gift to the city from its two sitting MPs, John Wilmot and Samson Gideon, First Baron Eardley.

The nearest Coventry now got to the glamour of a royal visit was welcoming the naval hero, Horatio, Lord Nelson, who stayed overnight at the King's Head Inn in Smithford Street in 1802, accompanied by his paramour, Lady Hamilton, and her cuckold husband, Sir William.

In 1807 when the Prince of Wales, the future George IV, found himself in the district and short of a bed for the night, he preferred to stay with Lord Craven at Coombe Abbey, receiving a civic delegation from Coventry and in somewhat grudging fashion handing over £100 for the relief of the poor.

George III by Thomas Lawrence, a gift to the city from its two MPs. (Herbert Art Gallery)

The money was desperately needed. Between January and April 1809, almost 100,000 gallons of soup and 25,000 six-penny loaves were distributed to the poor of the city. Not all would have been weavers and their dependants. A second trade was becoming more important in the city and that too had its good times and bad.

Watch and clock-making had seemed to make little progress in Coventry in the wake of Samuel Watson's pioneering achievements in the 1680s. But in 1727 a watchmaker, George Porter, was mayor of the city, and exactly fifty years later he was followed in that office by Samuel Vale, who had set up a watchmaking firm in 1747 and is generally regarded as the father of the industry in Coventry.

The watch trade never employed the same numbers as ribbon-weaving, but its highly skilled craftsmen clearly felt a notch above the weavers. A Parliamentary Select Committee, looking into the plight of watchmakers in the city in 1817, was told that they had been harder hit by recession in the trade than others,

A handloom in use. The trade depended on women. (Coventry City Council)

because 'the fraternity thought parish relief dishonourable, since the profession of watchmaker has always been deemed that of a gentlemen and the higher order of mechanics'.

Watchmakers generally had a higher standard of living, could afford better housing and did not need their wives to work, unlike the journeymen weavers who depended on their women folk for help in the complicated and physically demanding business of handloom weaving. Coventry weavers, it was said, preferred to seek a wife from a country area, as she was likely to be bigger and stronger than her city bred sister.

The watchmakers' pretensions to superiority did not always go down well with their fraternal comrades in the ribbon trade. During the prosperous 'big purl time' it was claimed that weavers had taken out a tongue-in-cheek advertisement in a local newspaper, requesting the services of fifty 'distressed' watchmakers to come and shell peas for them on a Saturday night. That said, when the mayor and council decided to follow up their loyal address with a civic gift to Queen Caroline in June 1821, it was a Coventry-made watch that they chose.

The new Christ Church, built around the old spire of Greyfriars. (Chris Ross)

In the same year, the first public gasworks in Coventry was erected at a cost of around £20,000, in Abbotts Lane north of the old city, and all of a sudden, it seemed, the city was embarking upon another period of physical change.

In 1819, William Bunney, a former miller living in Spon Street, had offered to contribute £500 towards the building of a new church to surround the historic spire of Greyfriars, which had stood alone since the Dissolution and at one time had suffered the indignity of being used as a pigsty. At the time, Bunney's

David Gee's painting of haymaking shows how constricted the old city was by common land. (Herbert Art Gallery)

A view of Coventry from Hillfields in 1807, twenty years before work began on the new residential district. (Herbert Art Gallery)

generous gesture was not taken up but by October 1829, a start had been made on a new church, to be known as Christchurch.

The previous year, work had started on another major project, the building of a new Holyhead road, bypassing the narrow and congested old thoroughfare leading out of Coventry along Spon Street.

Impressive though these projects were, there were impediments to growth. Coventry, bound tightly by its ring of common lands, had not increased in size for over 200 years. Small areas of Cheylesmore Park had been enclosed in 1795, but there were still at least 1,000 acres surrounding the city over which the freemen were entitled to graze livestock and which therefore could not be built on.

By the 1820s better-off inhabitants of the city were looking to move out as their comfortable homes and gardens were increasingly hemmed in by the crowded courts and terraced housing of the poor. It was, perhaps, the beginning of a wealth drain that still affects Coventry today.

The first major extension of the city did not turn out to be aimed at the wealthy. In the late 1820s, fields lying between the Swanswell pool and Primrose Hill started to be built on for a new district of sturdy, brick-built homes, with topshops above, to cater for the first-hand journeyman weaver and his family. Initially known simply as New Town, the district was later named Hillfields.

The first-hand weaver was the skilled elite of the ribbon trade, employing others and dealing with the ribbon manufacturers directly as a contractor. He had accommodated himself to new developments in the trade, including the huge Jacquard loom, capable of producing eight ribbons simultaneously and first seen in Coventry around 1823. But in late 1831, a mechanic named Josiah Beck introduced steam-powered looms into his premises in New Buildings. And that lit a spark.

During an angry meeting of weavers in Cross Cheaping on the afternoon of 7 November, a crowd of 200 broke away and attacked Beck's nearby factory, smashing up machines and throwing silk and ribbons out of the windows. Beck himself was roughly handled and the factory set on fire, burning to the ground despite the efforts of the city's primitive fire service to put it out.

In the aftermath, dragoons from the barracks dispersed crowds in the streets; there were a number of arrests and three weavers, including seventeen-year-old Alfred Toogood, were sentenced to death for their part in the riot. Only the intervention of Coventry MP Edward Ellice, a supporter of the weavers and an influential member of the governing Whig Party, commuted the death

Post-war demolition of a building thought to have been part of Josiah Beck's factory. (Coventry City Council)

sentences to transportation for life. Toogood was to return to his native city many years later as a visitor, having become a wealthy man in Australia. Beck's business never prospered again and he died a pauper in the workhouse.

It was the late 1830s before steam power began to get a foothold in the city's ribbon trade, making Coventry one of the last textile manufacturing centres to embrace the new technology. But in the meantime, another kind of revolution was overturning the old certainties at the heart of the city's life.

In June 1832, after a titanic struggle with the House of Lords, the Whig government finally managed to get onto the statute books the Parliamentary Reform Act, in which Edward Ellice was a prime mover. It allowed Coventry to keep its two Members of Parliament, but broadened the franchise beyond the freemen to all householders living in property worth at least £10 a year.

It did nothing, however, to put an immediate end to the way in which Coventry conducted its Parliamentary elections. On Monday 10 December 1832, a date that would be long remembered in the city as The Bloody Tenth, there were pitched battles in the streets as the anti-reform candidates brought in pugilists from Birmingham and hundreds of navvies from Brinklow, where they were working on the Oxford Canal, to disrupt the poll.

The city in due course re-elected its two pro-reform MPs, including Ellice, by substantial majorities, but this latest example of Coventry 'democracy' at work cannot have been overlooked by members of a Royal Commission looking into municipal corporations, sent to Coventry the following June. Their chief opponent in the city was the town clerk, John Carter, who had held the post since 1812 and was also a solicitor who had gained much from his business associations with the old close corporation. Carter claimed that the commissioners were unduly influenced by a former clerk named Marriott, whom he had recently sacked from his office.

Carter spent weeks in London, lobbying the House of Lords, as Coventry, along with Bristol, led the fight against municipal reform. But the Municipal Corporations Act of 1835, which came into force on 1 January 1836, swept away the old corporations with many of the ceremonial jobs and structures that went with them, including the Leet, and the sort of exclusive trading rights that had been enjoyed by Coventry's craft guilds.

Instead, it created new councils with the power to levy a borough rate and create a new police force. In Coventry's case, the city was to have six wards with six new councillors and two aldermen in each, elected by all householders of three years standing. And it would need a new town clerk.

John Carter's revenge was to stir up the communities – Ansty, Exhall, Foleshill, parts of Sowe and the hamlet of Keresley – who had been part of the old county of Coventry, but who had long felt that they paid higher rates to the city than their Warwickshire neighbours and got little for it. With Carter as their legal adviser, they took on the new council in the courts and won. As a result, the Coventry Boundary Act of 1842 returned them to Warwickshire and after 391 years the city no longer had a county to call its own.

Though the reordering of Coventry's administration was momentous, far-reaching change was in the air in other areas of life too. In late 1830, Robert Stephenson, son of the legendary George, was appointed engineer to a new railway company, set up to build the London and Birmingham Railway, at 112 miles and a cost of £5.5 million, the largest engineering project in the country's history. The aim was to link London to the fast-expanding industrial cities of the north and there were two possible routes the railway could take to Birmingham, one through Oxford and Banbury, the other taking a more easterly approach through Watford Gap and Coventry.

Worried about the risk of flooding as the line crossed the River Thames at Oxford, Stephenson favoured the Coventry route and in 1833 the vanguard of a vast workforce of 20,000 men began work at Euston in London and at Curzon Street in Birmingham. Stephenson made Coventry his headquarters during construction of the Midlands section, and the line from Birmingham

Coventry's first railway station, hopelessly unfit for purpose. (Coventry City Council)

through Coventry to Rugby was opened to passengers on 9 April 1838, with a stagecoach shuttle provided for the journey on to Bletchley, where the section heading north from Euston could be picked up.

By September the entire 112 miles was connected and Coventry became the closest city to be linked to the capital by the iron road, a point not lost on the city's manufacturers, but missed somehow by the railway's designers, who gave Coventry a hopelessly inadequate station which had to be entirely rebuilt almost immediately.

On 17 September, the very day that the London and Birmingham Railway formally opened for business, a meeting was held at County Hall in Coventry to discuss proposals for a hospital in the city. It was long overdue. A General Dispensary offering free medical treatment to the respectable poor had opened in rooms in Earl Street as far back as 1793, while a Provident Dispensary, paid for by subscription, was in operation from 1831.

There was even a workhouse infirmary, dating back to 1804, but the medical aid it could give was rudimentary and the standard of care was appalling, judging from a horrific case that came to public attention in the early 1830s.

A resident admitted with a severe wound to his shoulder was refused medical treatment and instead was put to work on a water pump, with instructions to use his other arm. Unable to eat and growing steadily weaker, he complained about the lack of treatment, but when his wife, also a pauper, tried to give him her ration of food and beer, she was prevented from doing so and forced to consume it in the presence of the female warden. Finally discharged as a troublemaker, he died in the Leicester workhouse two days later, a coroner ruling that his death was due to neglect and starvation.

Whether it was this case that demanded a response, the meeting approved the proposal which came from 'an old and influential citizen' called Thomas Wilmot, who said he had £700 available and couldn't think of a better use for it. An old house was purchased in Little Park Street, Edward Bourne was appointed the first Resident Medical Officer and the hospital opened its doors in November 1840, comprising one ward with twelve beds in it. Its services were to be available to all – except those suffering from venereal disease, consumption or any other infectious disease, or women 'big with child'.

Among the worthies appointed to the first Coventry and Warwickshire Hospital Committee was a Quaker stuff-merchant named Joseph Cash, whose two sons, John and Joseph, went on to found the most famous of Coventry's silk ribbon firms, J and J Cash.

Joseph the younger, in particular, was an active promoter of self-help and improvement for the working classes. In 1843, with a friend, Charles Bray, he

Coventry and Warwickshire Hospital, built in the 1860s as the Little Park Street original became overcrowded. (Coventry City Council)

founded the Coventry Labourers' and Artisans' Co-operative Society, which set up 400 allotments around the city, on which working men could grow fruit and vegetables, with a small grocery shop through which they could market the produce their families did not eat.

For Charles Bray, the son of a wealthy ribbon manufacturer who had inherited his father's business in 1835, it was merely the first of a whole host of similar ventures.

Business did not suit Bray. A man of huge enthusiasms and a passionate social reformer, he was much more interested in improving the condition of his fellow men. A committed campaigner for improvements in public health, he was also a prominent

Charles Bray, dilettante and hypocrite, but the man who gave the world George Eliot. (Coventry City Council)

supporter of the city's new Mechanics Institution and started a Working Man's Club for his own weavers, in which reading and smoking rooms, coffee and wholesome meals were meant to fend off the attractions of the public house.

That failed and it is tempting to see the high-minded Bray, for all his reformist zeal, as both a bit of a dilettante and a hypocrite. Almost a century after his death it was revealed he secretly kept a second family in Coventry, fathering six children with a woman who was not his wife, the long-suffering Caroline.

But Charles Bray does have one claim to posterity. It was his charismatic personality and wide-ranging intellectual circle that drew from Mary Ann Evans, the fiercely intelligent but shy daughter of a Warwickshire land agent, the great writer George Eliot.

Mary Ann began attending a school in Coventry run by the Franklin sisters in 1832, the year of the great Reform Act, and she was in her early twenties when in 1841 she moved with her father Robert to a house in Foleshill and was introduced to the captivating brother-in-law of their next door neighbours.

It was for the *Coventry Herald*, purchased by Charles Bray in 1846 to give himself a platform for his ideas, that Mary Ann wrote her first published work, anonymous reviews and satirical pieces, including a hard-hitting attack on the

city's Chief Constable, John Vice, and his alleged connections to a scandal in the butchery trade. Thirty years later, in her great study of provincial life, *Middlemarch*, regarded by some literary critics as the greatest novel ever written in the English language, Mary Ann recalled those Coventry years. It was the silk-weaving city of the reform years, the coming of the railways and the hospital, against which she set her characters. Coventry has rarely had a more intriguing chronicler.

Above The Franklin sisters' school in Warwick Row. (Coventry City Council)

Below Mary Ann Evans, the fiercely intelligent but shy land agent's daughter. (Herbert Art Gallery)

In her 1859 novel *Adam Bede*, George Eliot went back to the Coventry she remembered for the courtroom in which poor Hetty Sorrel goes on trial for her life.

Chapter 43 begins with the words:

> The place fitted up that day as a court of justice was a grand old hall, now destroyed by fire. The mid-day light that fell on the close pavement of human heads was shed through a line of high pointed windows, variegated with the mellow tints of old painted glass. Grim dusty armour hung in high relief in front of the dark oaken gallery at the farther end; and under the broad arch of the great mullioned window opposite was spread a curtain of old tapestry, covered with dim melancholic figures, like a dozing, indistinct dream of the past.

St Mary's Hall, as it happens, was not destroyed by fire although it came very close during the Blitz of November 1940, its roof badly charred in the conflagration that consumed the old cathedral, just feet away across Bayley Lane.

St Mary's Hall in 1873, as George Eliot would have known it. (Herbert Art Gallery)

The description, drawn from the memory of a writer familiar with the hall in the 1840s, is instantly recognisable today, for St Mary's Hall is nothing if not timeless. First constructed by the Guild of St Mary in the early 1340s and extensively remodelled in the first quarter of the fifteenth century, the guildhall has stood at the heart of Coventry life ever since – seat of government, place of refuge, setting for pomp and circumstance.

It has a past packed with incident, from bread riots in the 1380s to service as a military headquarters during the Civil War and a royal banquet at which King James II was showered with Coventry Custard. It has entertained many monarchs and imprisoned one, Mary Queen of Scots, for a short time in 1569. It has been a soup kitchen for starving Victorian weavers, a theatrical

The Guild Chair, made by a craftsman who had never seen an elephant. (Coventry City Council)

stage on which a young William Shakespeare almost certainly performed and an eighteenth-century election day battleground, in which the rival 'armies' smashed many of its medieval stained glass windows with bricks and stones.

Among its surviving treasures is a guild chair, commonly viewed as fifteenth century but which may have been made before that for the city's Benedictine prior. Whatever its origins, the chair bears an early representation of the elephant and castle from Coventry's coat of arms, carved by an unknown local craftsman who had clearly never seen a real elephant.

The chair stands in the old council chamber, alongside an oak table reputed to be the one on which Sir Thomas Lucy of Charlecote signed an arrest warrant for young Will Shakespeare for poaching deer on his estate. On the gallery above hangs seventeenth-century armour worn by the individual playing the role of St George in Coventry processions.

But the greatest glories of one of England's finest medieval guildhalls are reserved for the north wall of the building. Beneath a fifteenth-century traceried window, featuring the images of nine kings in glorious stained glass, is that 'dozing, indistinct dream' of a tapestry, portraying Henry VI and his queen, Margaret of Anjou, with their court.

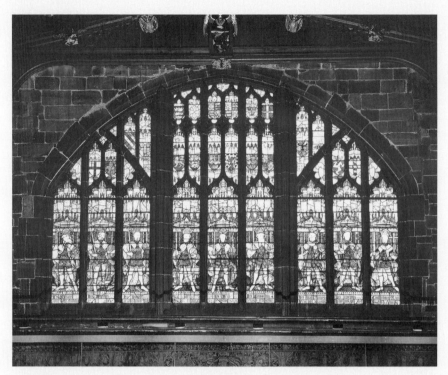

The north window in St Mary's Hall, depicting nine English kings. (Andrew Paterson)

For more than a year in the 1450s the beleaguered royal couple made Coventry, and the hall itself, the seat of their power. The tapestry that commemorates them was designed for the wall where it still hangs and was in place when Henry VII and his wife, Elizabeth of York, visited St Mary's Hall to be sworn into membership of the powerful Trinity Guild in 1500.

It has long been claimed that Hampton Court boasts the earliest tapestries in England still hanging on the wall for which they were made. The tapestry in St Mary's Hall predates them by a generation.

nine

THE AGE OF MACHINES

On the night of 15 July 1849, two next-door neighbours in Harnall Lane, a mean street of crowded dwellings lying close to the old Leicester road in Coventry, were taken ill with violent stomach pains and diarrhoea.

In little more than a week, the sickness claimed ten victims in the street, of whom seven died. Cholera was abroad in Coventry.

Over the next two months, the disease went on to kill 205 people in the city, ranging in age from nine months to eighty-eight years. Among the first victims were Eliza Freeman, mother of four, and her son George, aged five, who lived in a two-room hovel in Harnall Lane, but the infection was already spreading quickly across Coventry's crowded residential districts.

After four deaths at the cavalry barracks in September, its garrison, two troops of the 4th and 5th Dragoon Guards, were sent to Northampton while the whole place was cleaned and fumigated. Others were not so fortunate. Sarah Montgomery of Spon Street died on the 11th of that month, aged forty-nine, and was much mourned in her community as a helper in sickness.

Looking back, the cause of the 1849 cholera outbreak in Coventry is all too clear. The residents of Harnall Lane lived in abject squalor, with a refuse heap blocking most of the road, a stagnant ditch running in front of the houses and two filthy privies shared by dozens – perfect conditions for the waterborne infection.

But at the time, a definitive connection with contaminated water had yet to be made. All that was recognised was that this was another example of a terrible state of affairs that could not be allowed to continue. The Cholera Relief Committee, set up in September 1849, divided the city into three divisions, appointed inspection agents and medical men to each and within two weeks effectively had the outbreak under control.

It could have been worse – it is estimated that 20,000 people died from cholera in England that year – but the warning signs had been around for some time.

Back in 1843, the Commissioners for the State of Large Towns had expressed their unease at the quality of Coventry's water supply, and their findings were echoed two years later in a highly critical special report prepared by civil engineer William Hawkesley. 'Thoroughly bad and utterly incapable of improvement,' was his blunt assessment, and on the strength of that he was commissioned to sink a new well in a corner of Spon End known as Doe Bank and build around it a steam-powered waterworks capable of supplying clean water. It opened in late September 1847, serving some 3,000 of the city's inhabitants, and is rightly regarded as a major step forward in the public health history of Coventry.

The water supply, however, was not the only pressing concern. The appalling state of the city's medieval churchyards, 'crowded pits of putrefaction' as one contemporary called them, had been causing public outrage for many years. In 1844 the council had taken powers, by Act of Parliament, to create a new municipal cemetery on eighteen acres of disused quarries close to the London turnpike. The owners, the city's Freemen's Guild, were paid £900 in compensation and in 1846 the new cemetery was laid out, to a design submitted by a firm of architects led by the landscape designer Joseph Paxton, who went on to create the Crystal Palace and later became Liberal MP for Coventry.

The River Sherbourne, too, had become a serious threat to public health; little more than a foul sump running through a crowded old place in which the population, around 16,000 at the turn of the century, had more than doubled by the late 1840s. As the new waterworks at Spon End was coming on stream, preparations were being made to clear away the ancient priory and Bastille mills on the river, opening up the flow of water for a comprehensive new drainage and sewerage scheme for Coventry, which would take three years to complete.

As an agent of change, William Ranger, a superintending Inspector of the General Board of Health, was appointed in early 1849 to make a comprehensive investigation of Coventry as a place where mortality rates from diseases like scarlet fever and typhus (2.6 per cent) exceeded the national average (2.2 per cent).

Ranger's view was that chronic overcrowding lay at the heart of Coventry's health problems. He pointed to the fact that the city had 164 courts, alleys and yards, with 1,813 houses crammed into them, in which more than 7,400 people had to live. And he laid the blame squarely on the constricting effect of the cherished Lammas and Michaelmas common lands.

His supporters in the city, notably social reformer and now newspaper proprietor Charles Bray, tried hard to persuade the freemen to give up their

Coventry's new landscaped cemetery, with the memorial to Joseph Paxton, erected after his death in 1865. (Author's Collection)

ancient rights, in return for compensation, but it was to be another quarter of a century before the grip of the Lammas and Michaelmas lands would finally be loosened.

In the meantime, Ranger recommended the establishment of a Local Board of Health, sweeping away the old street commissioners and placing the city council at the helm. A new health map of the city, published by the board in 1851, highlighted new streets like Hales Street, designed to open up congested areas around the fringes of the old city core.

There were some modest extensions outside that core, too. An 1846 Act of Parliament had permitted the Sir Thomas White's charity to sell land beyond the old suburb of Spon for the development of a new residential district, aimed at the watchmaking fraternity. It was named Chapelfields, after the medieval leper chapel that had once stood there.

Six years later, the Coventry branch of the Freehold Land Society bought thirty-one acres outside the city in open country to the south-west, divided a framework of eight paved streets into 250 building plots and called it Earlsdon. Again, watchmakers were the chief target.

By that time, the old Bastille Gate on Earl's Mill Lane, one of the last survivors from the medieval wall, had succumbed to the wrecking ball of progress.

Left Beautiful but chaotic. Coventry in the late 1840s. (Herbert Art Gallery)

Below The 1851 Board of Health map for the Hales Street area. (Herbert Collections)

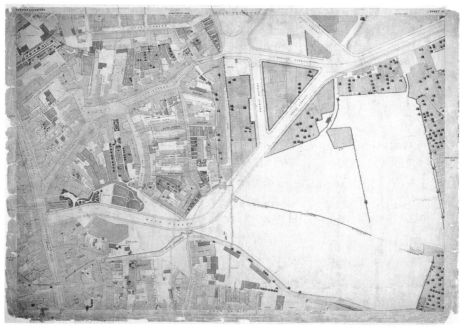

Coventry's new Corn Exchange was a cultural as well as commercial asset to the city. (Coventry City Council)

Time was also running out for the last traces of the medieval bishop's palace, swept away during the construction of Priory Street a year or two later.

Among the new landmarks in the city were the first Public Baths on Hales Street, which, it was claimed, attracted 2,000 bathers on the opening day of 8 July 1852, and a new Corn Exchange on Hertford Street, which opened in 1856.

The exchange was built to house the weekly corn market, held every Friday in the open street in Broadgate. But it also doubled as a 'public room' for concerts, lectures and meetings of all kinds, an indication, perhaps, that with the infrastructure of a modern city came modern cultural aspirations too.

Paganini, the great virtuoso of the violin, had played two nights at St Mary's Hall back in 1833, and Coventry had acquired its first custom-built theatre as long ago as 1819. This was thanks to former mayor Sir Skears Rew, knighted by the Prince Regent at Coombe four years earlier, who built a theatre behind the offices of his plumbing and glazing firm in Smithford Street.

Within a year the Theatre Royal, as it later became known, was attracting the giants of the London stage, including the Shakespearean actor Edmund Kean, who played Richard III to sell-out audiences in September 1820. Among those also entertaining Coventry theatre audiences were Benjamin and

Sarah Terry, members of a Portsmouth-based touring company and the parents of the future star of the English stage, Ellen Terry, who was born in theatrical digs in Market Street, Coventry on 27 February 1847.

By the 1850s, the Theatre Royal was going through something of a purple patch, attracting the gentry from miles around to its Friday night performances of the classics. But not all its audiences from those years were genteel. Police were on regular standby as rowdy drunks in the gallery threatened to disrupt the action on stage.

Sir Skears Rew, glazier and mayor, the builder of Coventry's first custom-built theatre. (Herbert Art Gallery)

Many of those same rowdies, no doubt, had struggled to get a decent vantage point at another spectator event that attracted big crowds in Coventry in the summer of 1849.

On the morning of 9 August, respectably attired and rather more pale than usual, Mary Ball mounted the steps of the scaffold outside the city jail in Cuckoo Lane to hang for poisoning her brutal husband with arsenic. Poor Mary, a weaver from Nuneaton, was the last person to be publicly executed in Coventry and it was reported that nearly 20,000 were there to see it.

Public executions had previously been staged on Whitley Common. The last of them was eighteen years before when nineteen-year-old Mary Ann Higgins had gone to the scaffold for the murder of her uncle, also with arsenic.

The wild expanses of the common were a favoured site for another brutal spectator sport, bare-knuckle prize fighting. In the 1840s Coventry had one of the country's finest exponents of what was then an illegal and less than noble art, a Dublin-born former weaver named William Gill.

Standing just five feet five and weighing little more than eight stone, 'Paddy' Gill was nevertheless a clever, two-handed fighter, deceptively powerful and immensely durable. In 1846 he fought for the unofficial lightweight championship of England, emerging after four gruelling hours as the victor.

Gill was to suffer for his gameness – he ended his days in Hatton asylum near Warwick. But he was only one of many Coventry fighters keen to earn money from their fists. Several city pubs also served as fighting saloons, each with their own stable of pugilists. The most prominent of them all was Paddy Gill's headquarters, the Pitts Head in Far Gosford Street, run by former prize-fighter John 'Fatty' Adrian.

The pub had another claim to sporting fame. From 1830 onwards, its stables were used as temporary accommodation for horses running at the Stoke races, then held on open ground beyond Gosford Green. The first accounts of horseracing in the city went back to August 1755, when races were run over a course carved out of Cheylesmore Park. By the 1780s they were a regular and modestly successful fixture in the English racing calendar.

Rew's theatre, not long before its closure in the 1890s. (Coventry Newspapers)

But on 4 September 1783 a horse competing in a race for a silver cup bolted and being turned away from an open gate leading into Little Park Street, jumped a nearby turnstile, killing a girl of seven standing there. It was to be nearly fifty years before the sport of kings returned to Coventry.

In the meantime the city's Great Fair, held in June, became an important focus for those interested in seeing performing animals at close hand. In 1817, at the fair on Greyfriars Green, the authorities had to shoot a bear that had been shaved and tortured and was being passed off by its owners as the 'Polo Savage'.

In 1848, a live elephant, representing Coventry's medieval coat of arms, took part in that year's Godiva procession. It was a hugely popular addition to the show and looked set to be repeated. But the following year tragedy struck.

The day before the Great Fair, Wombwell's Menagerie, the fair's wild beast contractors, were settling into quarters on Greyfriars Green when a fight erupted between their two elephants. The keeper being dead drunk, twenty-five-year-old William Wombwell, nephew of the proprietor, went into the cage to separate them and was attacked and gored by the animal due to lead the following day's procession. Terribly injured, William died two days later and was buried in Coventry's new municipal cemetery. Six months later he was joined in

Coventry's Great Fair. By the 1920s it had moved to Pool Meadow. (Coventry City Council)

the family grave by his cousin, seventeen-year-old Ellen Bright, known as 'The Lion Queen', who had been mauled to death by a tiger in Chatham.

The principal audience for events like these was the working population of the city, the ribbon weavers and watchmakers, who flocked to public ceremonies like the Great Fair in large numbers.

In 1852, Coventry's artisans themselves came under the national microscope when the magazine *Household Words* published not one but two lengthy accounts of visits to the city.

The first was published anonymously but was attributed to Harriet Martineau, the writer and vivid chronicler of mid-Victorian life. She visited the premises of Messrs Hammerton, a ribbon-weaving firm, and even though that was a picture of modernity, she was forthright in her views of how the trade was still being conducted in Coventry.

No place had made a more desperate resistance to the introduction of steam power, she wrote, and she was highly critical of the way whole families made themselves dependent on the fluctuating fortunes of a single trade:

Prosperous as the working classes of Coventry have been, for considerable time, a season of adversity must be within ken, if the capitalists find the trade a bad one for them.

It might save a repetition of the misery which Coventry people brought upon themselves formerly, by their tenacity about protective duties and their opposition to steam power, if they would, before it is too late, take care that the men of Coventry shall be fit for something else than weaving ribbons.

The second account published in the magazine that year came from its editor, Charles Dickens, after a visit to the leading watchmaking firm of Rotherhams.

Dickens was much impressed by the watches he saw being made, but he too had critical words for some aspects of the Coventry way of doing things, contrasting it unfavourably with what happened in Switzerland, steadily emerging as a major competitor.

One cause of the cheapness of Swiss watches, he wrote, was that women worked in the trade there, 'But the men of Coventry will not allow women to be employed. The employers desire it; the women desire it; but the men will not allow it'.

Hammerton's in Much Park Street, visited by Harriet Martineau. (Coventry City Council)

What both writers were attacking was the innate conservatism of Coventry's staple industries, where the old rules of the craft still held sway while the rest of the world moved on. At the time their warnings must have seemed a shade overwrought. By the early 1850s, Coventry had become the dominant centre for watchmaking in this country, employing around 2,000 people and overshadowing its two chief rivals, Clerkenwell in London and Prescot near Liverpool.

Ribbon-weaving had experienced plenty of bad years, but it still employed half the city's working population, and in 1843 pressure from ribbon manufacturers had led to the creation of a Coventry School of Design in a former warehouse close to the Burges. This new emphasis on innovative design and quality had paid off. At the Great Exhibition of 1851 a piece of broad silk ribbon, known as the Coventry Ribbon, was widely admired, by experts as well as by the public.

The Coventry Ribbon. (Herbert Collections)

Yet Harriet Martineau was to be proved right. Within a decade, ribbon-weaving as an industry of mass employment in the city was dead in the water.

Resentment over the expanding factory system, with its regimented discipline, and strikes over piecework rates weakened the local trade. But the mortal blow was the Cobden Treaty, an agreement between Britain and France, signed in January 1860, that lifted many tariffs on goods imported from France, including ribbons. The treaty had the strong backing of the Chancellor of the Exchequer in Palmerston's government, William Ewart Gladstone, who, when warned of the damage that it might do to industries like ribbon weaving, was reported to have said that the silk trade in Britain didn't matter at all, compared to the prospect of better relations with the French.

In Coventry the trade collapsed, almost overnight. A national appeal was launched on the weavers' behalf and raised £40,000, including contributions from Queen Victoria and Edward, Prince of Wales.

A committee of local industrialists and grandees was convened to look at alternatives that might give the city a replacement for its lost industry, and its most prominent member, Lord Leigh of Stoneleigh Abbey, went on to set up his own worsted and woollen mill in the city to offer employment. As an emergency measure, soup kitchens were set up in St Mary's Hall, among other places, as weaving families literally starved.

Those who could do so, left Coventry. It is estimated that by 1862 up to 4,000 weavers and their dependants had departed for textile towns further north or emigrated to the United States and the Colonies. As a result, the population of the city, 41,000 at the census of 1861, had actually dipped by 3,000 ten years later.

The contrasting fortunes of individuals caught up in this crisis can be illustrated by comparing two men closely involved in it.

William Andrews was an ambitious and clever young ribbon designer who in 1858 had taken on the management of John and Joseph Cash's new cottage factory alongside the Coventry Canal, until his ruthlessness as a boss made him so unpopular with the weavers that he had to be removed.

Joseph Gutteridge, intelligent, well-read and sensitive, remained a weaver all his life, universally respected for his skills but bringing his family almost to starvation at one point as he stubbornly refused to seek help.

Andrews left Coventry for France as the crisis broke, working abroad until the worst was past and returning to set up his own successful weaving firm.

A soup kitchen was set up for starving weavers in St Mary's Hall. (Coventry City Council)

Gutteridge struggled on in penury and with the help of his friends published an entrancing memoir of his life, *Lights and Shadows in the Life of an Artisan*, that attracted a measure of national interest in the early 1890s. Shortly before his death he was awarded £70 from the Royal Bounty Fund, an arcane instrument of patronage controlled by the Prime Minister of the day – in this case Coventry's old friend William Ewart Gladstone. Perhaps a case of a conscience being pricked?

Joseph Gutteridge, weaver and author of a poignant memoir. (Coventry City Council)

The Cobden Treaty had consequences for the watchmaking trade too as a flood of cheaper imports from France and Switzerland gave the trade a setback from which it appeared unlikely to recover. Salvation for Coventry looked a forlorn hope indeed, but it was to be embodied first in a small, intense character whose diffident personality harboured serious ambitions.

Francis Skidmore was born in Birmingham, the son of a gold and silversmith who shortly afterwards moved his business to Coventry. The gifted young Skidmore served an apprenticeship with his father in Cross Cheaping, but in 1850 he set up on his own in a yard in West Orchard as an art-metal worker.

Over the next two decades, the Skidmore Art Metal Company was to become the country's leading specialist in decorative metal, working on some of the most prestigious projects of the age. To the leading architect Sir George Gilbert Scott, Francis Skidmore was 'the only man in the world to carry out my ideas' and when Scott was asked to design and build the Albert Memorial in Kensington Gardens, Queen Victoria's extraordinary Gothic tribute to her dead husband, it was to Skidmore that he turned for the decorative iron work.

Over the years, Skidmore worked on many of Scott's major commissions – ornamental screens for the new Foreign Office building in London, decorative railings for The Embankment and art metalwork for fourteen Oxbridge colleges and for many of Britain's churches, including a screen for Hereford Cathedral that is regarded as his finest work.

Skidmore's own story ended sadly. His obsessive quest for perfection led him to destroy much work in progress and the business eventually failed. He spent his last years living in poverty in Eagle Street in Hillfields, kept out of the workhouse by a small pension raised by several of the country's leading architects.

Nevertheless, to Coventry he remained something of a hero. At the height of the crisis in the ribbon industry he had employed out-of-work weavers, and the success of his firm, based in a new factory he had built himself in Alma Street, had somehow pointed to a new way forward for a city frantically casting around for a future.

That future came from Sussex, in the shape of a farmer's son with little time for agriculture but possessed of an inventive compulsion that was not far short of manic.

James Starley, born in 1830, ran away from the family farm as soon as he could and by his early twenties was working as a gardener for wealthy marine engineer John Penn in Lewisham, south London. After his employer had acquired a new-fangled sewing machine, Starley fixed it when it broke, made one or two important improvements to it and in 1859 joined the machine's manufacturer, Josiah Turner, as managing foreman at his works in Holborn.

Two years later, the pair moved their business up to Coventry, chosen because they thought the skills of its watch-makers, then suffering a serious downturn in trade, could be switched to making precision components for sewing machines.

After a shaky start, the European Sewing Machine Company, as the partners now called themselves, proved successful. But in 1868 came an epiphany when Turner's nephew Rowley, their agent in Paris, brought back to Coventry a velocipede, pedalling it through the streets from Coventry station to the astonishment of passers-by. The partners recognised an opportunity when they saw it. Rowley was sent back to Paris with orders to sign a contract to import 400 of the machines

James Starley at the age of twenty-three. (Coventry City Council)

into Britain. The firm changed its name to the Coventry Machinists Company to reflect its broadening interests and Starley began to make improvements to the French machine.

In 1871, he designed the Ariel, still regarded as the first true bicycle. Almost casually, he also came up with two inventions that made the bicycle genuinely viable as a means of transport – the differential gear and the tangential spoke. Coventry had the beginnings of a new industry that in time would give it global renown. If ever a single person could be seen as the saviour of a city, the slightly dumpy figure of the man they called the father of the cycle industry was it.

The ribbon industry crash of 1860 had an instant effect on the fabric of Coventry. The brothers Cash cancelled phase two of their innovative Hundred Houses cottage factory at Kingfield, having built only forty-eight. The number of firms in the business fell from more than eighty to less than twenty and departing weavers left more than 800 houses in the city untenanted.

A bold plan by the London and Midland Railway to purchase the site of Coventry Barracks and give the city a central railway station was turned down by the government in 1861. But in the years that followed real progress was made in other areas of city development.

Cash's Hundred Houses project. Only forty-eight were built. (CV One/Coventry City Council)

In 1862 the twenty-year-old Coventry School of Design was turned into a custom-built and rather handsome School of Art. Among those backing it with hard cash was the great designer himself, Sir Joseph Paxton, who had become one of Coventry's two MPs in 1854 and took a fairly close interest in the city's affairs until his death in 1865.

In 1867 the city opened a new market hall to replace the old, a hopelessly inadequate structure that was little more than a shed on brick pillars and properly served neither man nor beast. And in the same year the Coventry & District Co-operative Society opened for business.

There had been a co-operative society on Lockhurst Lane in neighbouring Foleshill since 1832, twelve years before the Rochdale pioneers put the movement on the map, but the Coventry society emerged at a time when

Sir Joseph Paxton, MP for Coventry, photographed in later years. (Coventry City Council)

cheating on price and adulterating food was rife. It stood for a fair deal and was quickly successful.

The city even had its own voluntary fire brigade, started by 'forty or fifty local gentlemen' in 1861 and one of the first in the country. By 1873 it also had a brand new public library, the envy of many other towns.

The man behind it was a Quaker banker and silk broker who had been active in city life since the 1830s. A friend to the poor, and to Liberal MP Sir Joseph Paxton, John Gulson was nineteenth-century Coventry's most influential and effective moderniser. His gift of land on which to build a new library on the site of the old city gaol was only one of many important interventions. He was one of the first to see the desperate need for a hospital in Coventry, gave money to improve the city's water supply, took a leading role in the creation of the School of Art and a Technical Institute and, as mayor in the late 1860s, was credited with steadying the ship in tough times.

The opening of Gulson's new library closely followed another milestone for the modernists, the setting up of the Coventry School Board in 1871. Established under legislation to broaden the educational franchise to include all children up to the age of twelve, the school board was the first step towards sorting out the jumble of private, charity and grammar schools in the city.

Alongside the two older foundations of Bablake and King Henry VIII, which taught the classics and had become effectively grammar schools, there were a number of small private schools and six charity, or 'gift' schools, with vivid black, blue or green uniforms and names that were scarcely less colourful.

Boys from poor families keen to get them into a useful occupation attended either Baker, Billing and Crow's, Katherine Bayley's or Fairfax's school, while girls were pupils at Southern & Craner's, the Freemens' Orphan Girls School or the Blue Coat School, founded

John Gulson, Coventry's most effective nineteenth-century moderniser. (Coventry City Council)

in 1714 and since 1856 perched in a new building atop the ancient cathedral ruins in Priory Row.

By the 1890s, the boys' 'gift' schools had been amalgamated into Bablake, although it was to be nearly another twenty years before Barr's Hill School, initially an academy to train young women teachers, would become the city's first all-girls grammar school.

The grip of the Lammas and Michaelmas lands, strongest along the western edge of the city, had at last been loosened with the final enclosures around 1875. In 1888 Coventry had the opportunity to take a further step in municipal coherence when the Local Government Act of that year created County Councils, a new administrative tier of local government that reflected the growing complexity of managing geographical counties.

All large towns with a population of more than 50,000 were to become County Boroughs, equal in status and rank with the new County Councils. But Coventry's name did not appear on this list, initially at least. Its population at the 1881 census had been recorded as 42,111, probably an underestimate in itself, but by the late 1880s well out of date as the city recovered its prosperity and attractiveness to immigrants.

Fearful of having to bow to Warwickshire supervision and control after hundreds of years of administrative independence, Coventry exploded in outrage. A campaigning committee was set up, MPs and influential supporters lobbied parliament and finally the city was included on the list.

Two years later, without many fanfares, it secured its first modern boundary extensions, drawing in the outlying districts of Earlsdon, Radford and Kingfields. These extensions, small-scale in themselves, were signs of the increasing upwards pressure on Coventry's population figures, due entirely to its new staple industry – bicycles.

James Starley had died, much mourned in 1881, but his imitators as inventive engineers and entrepreneurs quickly saw opportunities in Coventry and were already piling in.

Starley's colleague William Hillman, who had followed him up from Lewisham, had set up on his own as a cycle manufacturer in 1876. From Nottingham came Thomas Humber, from London George Singer, from Leicestershire William Herbert and his younger brother Alfred, and from Wolverhampton Daniel Rudge. From even further afield came Siegfried Bettmann, the son of a Jewish land agent from Nuremberg in Germany, and

The Katherine Bayley school (Blue Gift) band in 1887. (Coventry City Council)

Cycle workers in the early years of the industry, an informal style for what was still a craft business. (Coventry Transport Museum)

later several young Americans, including the formidable Oscar Harmer, who was to become the driving force of Alfred Herbert's machine tool firm. Among the big names, only the Rileys were from Coventry, a ribbon-manufacturing family who had successfully made the switch of trades.

At first the cycle industry adapted itself to the 'cottage industry' style of the city's traditional industries, with small workshops popping up in the spaces left by ribbon weavers and watch-makers. But in 1885, James Starley's nephew John Kemp Starley, who had joined him thirteen years earlier from Walthamstow in Essex, launched the Rover Safety Cycle. It was chain-driven and had two rubber-tyred wheels the same size separated by a diamond frame. In other words it was the bicycle we know today.

Starley had set up his own firm with a business partner, William Sutton, in 1877 specifically to develop bicycles that were safer and easier to ride. Other bicycle designers had been travelling in the same direction, but Starley was the first to get this new idea on to the market and to him went the credit and the explosion in demand for this new wonder.

News of his achievement of 'setting the pattern for the world' was trumpeted by one of the new industry's earliest magazines, *The Cyclist*, founded in

Coventry in 1878 by William Iliffe, son of a printer and bookseller with a shop on Smithford Street.

Iliffe, who had been apprenticed by his father into the ribbon trade, saw that bicycles were the new craze and started up the magazine to record what was happening. He later changed its name to the *Bicycling News* and employed a young Alfred Harmsworth, the future press baron Lord Northcliffe, as his deputy editor.

Iliffe went on to found Coventry's first daily newspaper, the *Midland Daily Telegraph*, in February 1891. From the beginning, its regular weekly column, 'Cycling Gossip', recorded the doings of a trade for which the paper proudly announced that Coventry was already the centre. The first week's column ran a suggestion that members of the city council ought to have their own cycling club and named two councillors often seen around town aboard safety cycles; the inventor himself, J.K. Starley, and George Singer.

Dorset-born Singer, another former employee of marine engineer John Penn in London, was making his mark on Coventry in more ways than one. He was to become mayor of the city three times in the 1890s and back in 1883 he had helped set up a football team for his workers. Fifteen years later, when the game in Coventry went professional, the team became Coventry City Football Club.

Alongside football, rugby and cricket were the staples of Victorian sport and both had made significant progress in Coventry in the second half of the century. While records of cricket matches between teams from Coventry and Leicester went back to the late 1780s, the city's premier cricket club, Coventry and North Warwickshire, had

John Kemp Starley, the man who brought the world the modern bicycle. (Coventry Transport Museum)

Mass production in one of Coventry's cycle companies, under the watchful eye of a bowler-hatted foreman. (Coventry Transport Museum)

been founded back in 1851. Coventry Rugby Club, set up by the public school-educated sons of the city's business elite, with the Rotherhams well to the fore, played its first fixtures in 1874.

At the end of its first week of publication, William Iliffe's *Midland Daily Telegraph* announced that it would be publishing a special sports paper every Saturday to cater for the growing following for sport in the city.

Cycling itself was becoming a serious leisure pursuit for the young men pouring in to work in the factories and workshops of this new industry. Soon, almost every company, church and social institution in Coventry seemed to have its own cycle club, decamping en masse each weekend to the highways and byways of Warwickshire to pedal away a few hours of fresh air and fun.

By the boom years of the mid-1890s there were ninety-five cycle firms operating in the city and the way they were transforming the old place did not please everybody.

In November 1891, a resident of comfortably off Warwick Row wrote to the Midland *Daily Telegraph*, demanding that something must be done:

Instead of the quiet watch-making, ribbon-weaving place it used to be Coventry has become a great centre of a new and important industry of a different class, bringing with it large factories, smoking engine stacks, steam whistles, dangerous steam tram engines, a great increase in the artisan working population and over-crowding of the narrow streets and small old dwellings in the centre of the city.

He had a point, but the age of the noisy machines had only just begun.

Among J.K. Starley's principal rivals in designing a safety cycle was the London-born son of a brass turner, not only a highly inventive engineer, but a visionary and a crook too.

Harry Lawson arrived in Coventry in 1878 and over the next fifteen years worked his way through a number of cycle companies, first as designer and later sales manager. But his first love was setting up and promoting new companies. Lawson was a man who could spot a shift in the status quo from a very long way away, and from engineering developments he heard about on the Continent, particularly in Germany, he could see that something new and very big was coming.

The scale of things to come. The Townend factory, later used by Humber. (Coventry Transport Museum)

In 1895, he set up the British Motor Syndicate to try and monopolise the coming automobile industry by controlling patents. In this he failed but within a year, in partnership with German-born Frederick Simms, he was in possession of the rights to manufacture Gottlieb Daimler's cars in Britain.

The first proposed site for a new factory was Cheltenham, but Lawson was instrumental in getting it switched to Coventry where a burned-out cotton mill in Radford was purchased by another of his partners, the financier and company promoter Ernest Terah Hooley. On 2 March 1897, the first Coventry-built, Daimler-engined car made its maiden run. Within weeks

Harry Lawson, visionary and crook. (Coventry Transport Museum)

there were twenty more. The British motor industry, in the shape of the Daimler Motor Company, was spluttering and popping into life.

Lawson's own future was a good deal darker. Seven years after this triumph, he was to find himself in court, charged with defrauding shareholders. Conducting his own defence, he was found guilty and sentenced to one year's hard labour. His fellow defendant, the wily Hooley, hired an expensive lawyer and got off. Neither man ever featured again in the story of the industry they had helped to found, and it was left to another of Lawson's associates to properly usher in the motoring age.

Henry Sturmey was a schoolmaster turned cycling journalist who had worked for William Iliffe's *Cyclist* magazine, before switching his interest to motor cars. He was a director of the Daimler company and editor of Iliffe's new magazine, *Autocar*, when in the autumn of 1897 he announced his intention to drive a standard-pattern, four-horsepower Daimler carriage from John O'Groats to Land's End.

Sturmey's journey, accompanied by a young company mechanic, Richard Ashley, who was plainly terrified throughout, reads like something out of *Toad of Toad Hall*.

Above A line-up of cars outside Motor Mills, Britain's first car factory. (Coventry Transport Museum)

Right Henry Sturmey, journalist and motoring pioneer. (Coventry Transport Museum)

Stampeding horses and scattering crowds, Sturmey arrogantly brushed off the efforts of local constabulary in a dozen places to book him for driving this coughing, belching monster at the breakneck speed of up to ten miles an hour. At Carlisle, passers-by complained about the smell. At Ambleside, fellow guests at a hotel demanded to know 'why he had brought a thing like that here'. In Gloucester a crowd of women ran away shrieking when he skidded.

Unabashed, Sturmey had a stack of 'What is it?' cards with him, which he flourished at every available opportunity. They explained that the vehicle could not explode because it did not have a boiler, that there were eight different ways of stopping it, and that it was made by the Daimler Company of Coventry and cost £300.

There was a curiously low-key end to Sturmey's pioneering journey as he trundled the last mile or two to the Land's End Hotel. But over rough moorland track and through narrow cobbled street he had boldly been where no horseless carriage had ever been before. He had put the motor car on the map of Britain.

Two years later, Daimlers were out in force when Coventry hosted what was almost certainly the first foreign trade delegation in its modern history.

On a cold day in early December 1899, a convoy of six Daimler cars was lined up at the city's railway station as Sir Chih-Chen Lofengluh, Ambassador plenipotentiary of the Chinese empire in Great Britain, Belgium and Italy, stepped from his train. The two-day visit by one of the Celestial Emperor's most trusted diplomats began awkwardly. The ambassador stepped forward and bowed deeply to the most gorgeously attired figure among his hosts – who turned out to be the town crier, probably the most junior official on the platform. Recovering swiftly from this diplomatic faux-pas, the ambassador astonished his hosts by quoting liberally from Alfred, Lord Tennyson's poem 'Godiva' and expressing his delight at finally seeing the city made famous by Shakespeare's 'duel that never was' on Gosford Green.

At a banquet that night in St Mary's Hall, he noted in his speech the elephant on the city coat of arms and concluded that Coventry had had dealings with the East over centuries. In their determination to make a good impression, his hosts did not disabuse him of this notion.

Among the firms chosen for the ambassador's whistle-stop itinerary over the next two days were the Daimler Company in Sandy Lane, Swift cycles in Parkside, where his son was presented with a bicycle, the watchmakers Rotherhams in Spon Street, and the Stevengraph factory in Cox Street.

The last two were unusual examples of old-established craft businesses that had managed to survive by diversifying. Rotherhams still made watches, but were now beginning to manufacture precision instruments for the fledgling machine tool and automobile industries. By contrast, Joseph William Player, arguably the Coventry watch-maker's watch-maker, produced the most complicated watch ever made in England in 1909, featuring a perpetual calendar and masses of astronomical detail and valued at £1,000. His firm went bust the following year.

The Stevengraph Company had been founded by a resourceful and inventive weaver, Thomas Stevens, who in 1862 patented his ideas for making pictures out of silk and had made an international business out of bookmarks and cards.

Thomas Stevens, Sen
Died October 24th 1888.
Aged 60.

The inventive Thomas Stevens, who diversified while many others went out of business. (Coventry City Council)

Another survivor of the old ribbon-weaving industry, J and J Cash, had benefited from a similar sidestep in the 1870s and now manufactured the nation's woven labels. At one time Joseph Cash had attempted to create artificial silk, helped with financial backing from the forbidding railway magnate Sir Richard Moon, who from his home at Copsewood Grange, just outside Coventry, had ruled the London and North Western Railway with an iron fist for almost thirty years. They failed, but in 1904 there appeared in Coventry a major new employer who could, indeed, make silk that was artificial.

The Courtaulds were perhaps the most prominent example of a Huguenot family who had chosen Britain as a place of refuge, and as the twentieth century dawned they were looking for a site for a new factory to produce artificial silk, or rayon as it was to be called. They found it in Foleshill, newly drawn into Coventry by a second boundary extension in 1899. A handy means of transport was also apparent in the nearby Coventry Canal to distribute the products of their new venture.

Constructed by J.G. Gray, Coventry's premier builder and a man rich enough by the 1920s to purchase Coombe Abbey, the new factory opened for business in 1905. From the outset it employed women, at first mostly the wives and daughters of Bedworth miners.

By 1913 its workforce had grown to 2,000, delighting the *Midland Daily Telegraph* who had expressed concerns that Coventry's increasing reliance on the motor car was making it a one-industry town once again.

The female workforce at Courtaulds was not attractive to the conservative craft unions that had represented many of Coventry's artisans, but political change was already on its way from another direction.

On 6 December 1902, a bitterly cold day, a small group of men had gathered at the Alexandra Café on Ford Street, which sold 'a good working man's dinner, with meat and two veg' for 6*d*. As it happened, they weren't there principally for the food. They were meeting to set up a Coventry branch of the Labour Representation Committee, later re-named the Labour Party.

Within three years, the party had won its first seat on a city council still dominated by the publicans, butchers, shopkeepers and professional men who had controlled civic life since municipal reform in the 1830s.

Coventry's first Labour councillor, watchmaker's son George Poole, had lived in straightened circumstances as a boy and retained a lifelong hatred of injustice that made him a highly effective and determined campaigner. Poole is remembered as the moving spirit behind a long campaign to bring a public abattoir to Coventry, sweeping away the age-old practice of allowing private slaughterhouses to operate, right in the heart of the city.

Their activities – even in the twentieth century herds and flocks were still being driven through the streets – were a challenge to public health, a stinking nuisance and even, on at least one occasion, a threat to life and limb. Back in 1866, poor blind Phoebe Hoggins, a weaver's wife in her seventies, had been gored to death in her own home in Much Park Street by a terrified cow which had broken away from a herd on its way to slaughter.

Poole's first focus as a city councillor, however, was not the public abattoir but public housing. In 1906 he was able to push through a motion pledging the council to action after a special committee had looked into overcrowding in the city. The census of 1901 had calculated Coventry's population to be just under 70,000, almost double the figure of thirty years before and the pace was accelerating as the city's expanding engineering industries opened the flood gates to immigration from bigger cities like London and Manchester.

Coventry's first public housing, aimed at families who could not afford private rents, was a modest terrace of dwellings in the appropriately named

Short Street and forty-eight homes in Narrow Lane in Foleshill, later renamed Kingfield Road.

One of George Poole's associates in this 1907 landmark scheme was a solicitor and Conservative member of the council, Malcolm Pridmore, whose contribution was recognised in the use of his name for a new street when the Foleshill scheme was extended three years later.

Poole's generous and open-hearted nature made him many friends across the political spectrum; another was his one-time employer, the German-born cycle manufacturer Siegfried Bettmann, then a Liberal in politics.

Bettmann had been a councillor since 1903 and in 1913 he was elected Mayor of Coventry, with every expectation of serving two years in office, as was the custom at the time. A world war, however, was to put a stop to that and Coventry would be the worse for it.

As a boy growing up in a comfortable Jewish home in Nuremberg, Bavaria, Siegfried Bettmann was an admirer of all things English. It was this, he would later recall, that brought him as a restless young man to London in 1884 to try his luck in the most exciting city in the world.

Within two years, he was working as an agent for the Coventry Cycle Company, selling their bicycles on the Continent under a company name of his own devising that was English but could be readily understood in many other languages – Triumph.

In 1889 his friend and fellow countryman Mauritz Schulte, who had joined him in business in London, persuaded him that they should move to Coventry and set up a company to manufacture their own bicycles there.

Neither of them were engineers: Schulte was the entrepreneur, Bettmann the financial brain. Initially, they struggled to find backers, but they managed to secure small factory premises on Much Park Street, took on two engineers and before long the Triumph Company of Coventry was ready to join the city's growing roll-call of manufacturers.

By 1895, Bettmann was prosperous and settled enough to take an English wife, Annie Meyrick, and to apply for British citizenship. As he wrote later, he was 'proud to be an Englishman, not only by law, but by marriage and sentiment.'

Something of a political animal, even in childhood, he was nevertheless stunned in the autumn of 1903 when the Liberal Party in Coventry asked him to stand in the Bishop Street ward against a well-known sitting Conservative. Despite widespread scepticism, he won. Coming from Germany, where every city worth the

By 1912 Triumph was successful enough to occupy buildings on both sides of Priory Street. (David Fry)

name had its fine municipal buildings, thea-
tres, concert halls, opera houses, parks and
museums, he immediately joined the ranks
of those trying to modernise Coventry, which
had none of these things.

President of the Coventry Chamber of
Commerce in 1907 and chairman of a local
committee set up to implement Lloyd
George's pioneering pension reforms of 1911,
Bettmann was a figure of growing standing
and influence in his adopted city, and in the
autumn of 1913 he was chosen as its mayor,
becoming the first foreign-born mayor of a
British city in modern times.

Moved to tears by the honour shown him,
he was quick to redouble his efforts as a moderniser. He advocated building a new town
hall, a new technical institute and a large hall

Siegfried Bettmann in his mayoral robes,
proud to be an Englishman. (Herbert Art
Gallery)

for concerts, festivals and conferences. And he pressed hard for the future town
planning of Coventry to be put on a scientific basis, a revolutionary concept outside the great cities.

But by the summer of 1914 war with Germany was looming and, shamefully,
Bettmann found himself characterised as an enemy alien and Shylock, even by
former friends and associates. He was forced to resign from posts like the chair-
manship of the Standard Motor Company and the prospect of a second year in
mayoral office, customary at the time, disappeared. Only the intervention of powerful friends stopped him from being interned as an enemy alien.

Bettmann never entirely got over his bitterness at this betrayal. In the 1920s
he dabbled with Labour Party politics, becoming a friend of Ramsay MacDonald
but turning down the chance to stand for the city council again on a Labour ticket
in 1928.

Between the two world wars he travelled widely and turned his hand to writing,
with an autobiography, travel diaries and translations of Schiller's poetry. For many
years he was still involved in business, only grudgingly accepting retirement at his
house in Stoke Park after the death of his wife Annie in 1941.

On his death in 1951, alongside many charitable bequests, Bettmann left his
papers and memorabilia to the city he had loved. Had he been given the opportunity,
his legacy could have been so much greater.

ten

WAR AND PEACE

On 1 August 1914, Coventry journalist Henry Wilkins began his 'journal of the Great European War' with the sombre words, 'the shadows deepened, the streets were filled with people desirous of hearing the news.'

In fact, Britain's declaration of war on Germany was still three days away, and on that Saturday evening up to 25,000 Coventry people had already left the city, heading for the Bank Holiday highlights of Blackpool or north Wales or Eastbourne. In beautiful weather the prospect of war, however close, was not going to deter the city's new industrial working class, still getting used to the idea of a summer holiday away from home.

In the days that followed, preparations for war moved quickly. Within a week 1,000 army reservists from Coventry were on their way to their mustering points and huge crowds had lined the streets to cheer the 7th Battalion, Royal Warwickshire Regiment as it marched through the city centre to the railway station.

In an atmosphere of growing war fever, 200 boy scouts were deployed to watch places 'where outrages might be perpetrated', such as the gas works, electricity sub-stations, canals and telegraph lines. And following the government's hasty introduction of an Aliens Restriction Act, more than seventy Coventry citizens, mostly German, had come forward to register with the police.

In theory at least they included the city's mayor, and founder of the Triumph Company, Siegfried Bettmann, who was already under pressure because of his German birth. Ironically, two days before war was declared, Bettmann had been asked by the War Department to convene a meeting of motorcycle manufacturers, at which the military made it clear that they wanted a supply line of machines for service in Belgium. He wrote later that he knew at that moment that the fate of Europe was sealed. Over the course of the war, the company controlled by this 'enemy alien' would supply a staggering 30,000 motorcycles to the British Army.

The cause the army was fighting for, at least initially, was 'gallant little Belgium', the first stop on the German route map of conquest in Western Europe. And by October, the first of around 2,000 Belgian refugees were arriving in Coventry, heading for billets in the cavernous spaces of the unused Whitley Abbey, made available to the city by its owner, Colonel Oswald Henry Turville-Petre. The relationship between the refugees and their Coventry hosts remained warm throughout the war, and a plaque expressing their eternal gratitude, paid for by the Belgian government, still hangs in the lobby of St Mary's Hall.

For Coventry's resident German population, however, the atmosphere of uneasy calm did not last. What happened to Rudolf Henninger was not exceptional.

Henninger had been head waiter at the King's Head in Hertford Street, an old inn rebuilt in 1879 and turned into Coventry's best hotel. In the years before the war he had started up a tobacconist's shop on the corner of Charterhouse Road and Northfield Road in the new residential district of Lower Stoke.

A well-known opponent of 'Prussian militarism', he was popular with the workers at Humber's nearby factory. But that counted for nothing when a mob smashed the windows of his shop one night and looted it, only deciding against setting fire to it, with his terrified wife and two children hiding upstairs, because they worried that the blaze might spread to the rest of the street.

The King's Head Hotel, Coventry's finest. (Author's Collection)

Henninger was interned in the Isle of Man, it was said for his own protection, and his Birmingham-born wife returned to her native city and went to work for the BSA company. Her first day there triggered an all-out strike, with her workmates declaring they would work with 'no bloody Huns'. When her badly wounded soldier brother was brought from his hospital bed to reason with them, they threatened to lynch him.

An extreme example, perhaps, but there were plenty in Coventry who disliked the 'foreigners', not just from other countries but also from other parts of the United Kingdom, who were fundamentally changing the old city they knew. And their prejudices were given voice by elderly publican Dan Claridge.

Claridge was a man who had been born at least a generation too late. As the young landlord of the Craven Arms in High Street, once Coventry's premier coaching inn, he had tried to reintroduce a regular stagecoach service to London back in 1874.

It was sporadic at best, an anachronism whose day would never come again, and it had petered out by 1892. Nevertheless, he retained the appearance and the attitudes of a Dickensian sporting gentleman, and in 1915 he was interviewed by a national newspaper journalist visiting Coventry for some wartime colour. 'It's gone, the old Coventry spirit,' he growled. 'It don't exist any more. They say Coventry is more go-ahead than it used to be, but did you ever see people more slack and dawdling than the people you meet today?'

In an attempt to preserve at least the fabric of the old city, if not its atmosphere, a City Guild had been established in Coventry in 1914 to promote public interest in the city's historic buildings and campaign for a proper museum, finally achieved in modest style in 1920.

Among the guild's moving spirits were Mary Dormer Harris, the daughter of a Stoneleigh farmer, who remains one of the most respected of Coventry's historians, and Angela Brazil, writer of girls' school stories, who had moved to Coventry in 1911 to keep house for her doctor brother Walter at their home at No. 1, The Quadrant.

Brazil, who would become the English-speaking world's biggest-selling author for girls between the two world wars, was at the centre of Coventry's cultural and social life for more than three decades. She lived to see the destruction of so much of the history she loved in the Second World War.

Among the 'foreigners' who at first sight had less to contribute was an inventive and hardworking young engineer named Moses Whittle, who arrived from Manchester around the turn of the century to work in the cycle industry.

His son Frank, born in Earlsdon on 1 June 1907, turned out to be an archetype of so many twentieth-century Coventrians, not, perhaps, blessed with the broadest of cultural horizons, but a problem-solver by nature and utterly engineering-obsessed. What set Whittle apart was the stroke of genius that enabled him to invent the jet engine and thereby make the world a smaller place.

The Whittle family moved to Leamington Spa in 1916, but not before little Frank had experienced his first brush with powered flight, while playing with his friends on Hearsall Common. A small plane landed for running repairs to the engine and as it took off again the updraft blew off his cap. From that moment, he recalled in his autobiography, all he wanted to do was fly.

By 1916, Coventry had acquired a huge new network of munitions factories, chiefly spreading north from the heart of the old city, where there were no substantial private estates to get in the way of development.

In 1905, the same year that Courtaulds opened in Foleshill, plans were drawn up for a giant complex of workshops in nearby Red Lane for the Coventry Ordnance Company, which was to spend the war turning out naval guns for battleships and howitzers for the army, alongside ammunition and even tanks and aircraft. The Stoke Heath housing estate, under construction in 1916, was built for their workforce.

Sir Frank Whittle's statue, unveiled in 2006, on the centenary of his birth. (CV One/Coventry City Council)

While some of the munitions manufacturers were new to Coventry (the French machine gun company Hotchkiss, for example, arrived in Gosford Street in 1914 from a Paris under threat from the German advance) the switch of others into war production was simply the next move in a story of rapid expansion.

The Daimler Company had built themselves a new factory in Radford in 1912. Humber, the UK's second biggest car manufacturer at the beginning of the war, had done the same in Stoke four years earlier. The machine tool company that young Alfred Herbert had started back in the 1880s was now one of the country's most important, a fact reflected in Herbert's appointment as the government's machine tool tsar during the war, a role that in 1917 was to earn him a knighthood.

By the beginning of that year, the city's population stood at 127,000, a figure boosted almost entirely by the steady stream of munitions workers being drafted into Coventry from other areas of the country to help the war effort.

Among them were the Canary Girls, an evocative nickname for up to 4,000 women who worked for the firm of White & Poppe, a relatively new name in Coventry's engineering pantheon.

White & Poppe was an engine manufacturer, set up in 1899 by Alfred James White, son of a prominent Earlsdon watchmaker, and Peter Poppe, a Norwegian engineer. But in 1915 the company turned corn fields in Whitmore Park into National Filling Factory No. 10, turning out artillery shells, detonators and fuses by the hundred thousand.

The women who worked there were called Canary Girls because tetryl, the explosive compound they worked with, turned their skins yellow. And the work could be dangerous. Emergency evacuations were not infrequent and at least one worker died when an exploding detonator blew off an arm and the side of her face.

The Canary Girls came from all over the British Isles and wore coloured armbands denoting their country of origin – red for England, green for Ireland, blue for Scotland and pale blue for Wales. They were well paid for their work; one local resident recalled, many years later, that a sixteen-year-old Welsh girl billeted on her family was earning almost £3 a week, a princely wage at the time.

But the hazards of working with dangerous chemicals were not fully understood, and even if they had been, in wartime conditions a blind official eye would undoubtedly have been turned to the risks that the Canary Girls were taking.

Above A naval gun emerges from the giant
Ordnance Works during the Great War. (David Fry)

Right White & Poppe Canary Girls – their work was
hazardous. (Coventry City Council)

As women, they could not count on trade union representation, and it was something of an irony that a perceived injustice done to the male minority of the workforce at White & Poppe should have brought Coventry's munitions industry to a grinding halt in late 1917.

Signs of growing unrest were clear early in the year, when a crowd said to be a staggering 50,000 strong gathered on Gosford Green to demand cheaper food and equal distribution of supplies. In November, management at White & Poppe were accused of refusing to recognise or negotiate with shop stewards representing their male workforce. Within days, workers at most of the big players in the munitions industry – Hotchkiss, the Ordnance, Humber and Daimler among them – had walked out.

At Daimler, the strikers were led by a young shop steward recently arrived in Coventry, who over the next four decades would make a lasting mark on the city.

George Hodgkinson, the son of a Nottingham lace-maker, was part idealist, part ruthless backroom operator, whose early background of Christian socialism did not stop him becoming the most implacable and scheming of opponents.

This was the beginning of a political career that gave him a key role on the city council in Coventry's darkest hour, a lasting reputation as one of the architects of the post-1945 city and, perhaps, an unwanted epithet as the man who should have been an MP and never was.

Despite a wide divergence of views – Hodgkinson described his own men at Daimler as 'largely Tory and reserved, and needed careful handling' – the strike was 100 per cent solid and a compromise settlement was quickly found.

Establishment opinion outside Coventry was outraged. The *Aeroplane* magazine of 5 December 1917 demanded that strikers should be run straight into the army, describing Coventrians in general as the most self-satisfied, self-opinionated, pig-headed and muddle-headed people in England.

The *Midland Daily Telegraph*, and indeed much of the national press, took a more balanced view, arguing that there were clearly faults on both sides and commenting on the 'exemplary' behaviour of the strikers.

The public, however, could be highly critical too. 'Angry of Earlsdon' suggested in the *Telegraph's* letters column that the military casualty lists, running at about 4,000 a day, should be run side by side with the strike news. But significantly, trade union recognition did not come under threat from employers for the rest of the war.

At 1 p.m. on Monday 11 November 1918, the Mayor of Coventry, Councillor Joseph Innis Bates, and the city's Town Crier, struggled through large crowds to Broadgate to announce that the Great War was at last at an end.

By evening, bonfires had been lit in the streets and at least one effigy of the Kaiser set on fire, but the celebrations remained a good few levels lower than wild and there was a thoughtful side to many people's relief. The war had cost the city dear. Of the thousands of men that Coventry had sent to fight, more than 2,600 had never returned. The lives of many more had been shattered by their experiences.

For all its importance as a munitions centre the city had never been seriously threatened by enemy action, although a rudimentary blackout had been observed since early 1916 – on 1 February of that year, it was reported, a performance of *Il Travatore* at the Opera House was conducted by candle and lantern light. Zeppelins made a handful of appearances over the city, the most dramatic on 12 April 1918 when the airship L62, on its way to attack Birmingham, jettisoned bombs on Whitley Common and Baginton Sewage Farm as it came under fire from anti-aircraft guns based in the Wyken area.

Coventry's engineering industries had done well out of the war, and it might be supposed that prosperity and a universal, almost crushing, sense of relief would have led to joyful scenes on Saturday 19 July 1919, earmarked by the government as a national day on which to celebrate peace.

But what began under sunny skies with children's processions, cheering crowds and a peace pageant featuring Lady Godiva, ended with stone-throwing mobs looting shops and battling police in pouring rain – the opening skirmishes of three nights of rioting, the worst in Coventry's modern history.

Over the weekend that followed the city lurched close to anarchy as vicious street fighting left 100 people injured and dozens of businesses smashed and looted. Only the arrival of substantial police reinforcements from Birmingham and soldiers from the Wiltshire Regiment, drafted in from their billets at Radford Aerodrome, finally restored order to a city centre full of barricaded shops and littered with broken glass and discarded missiles.

Blamed initially on drink-fuelled hooligans attacking businesses thought to be German-owned, the riots, in truth, stemmed from much deeper feelings of resentment and discontent. At their heart stood returning soldiers, conspicuous in their khaki uniforms among the stone-throwing crowds.

The Coventry Federation of Discharged Soldiers and Sailors was quick to dissociate itself from the violence, but it had pointedly boycotted the peace celebrations, describing them as a farce at a time when the grievances of its members were not being addressed.

Boarded up shops in Cross Cheaping after a night of rioting. (David Fry)

It was widely believed that the festivities had been monopolised by those who had done well out of the war, while its real heroes faced a chronic shortage of decent housing, poor disablement pensions and little prospect of work in booming factories that had filled their jobs while they were away. Coventry seemed to spend much of the 1920s trying to put right those grievances.

Initially, the city suffered, as did many others, from a recession that followed the sudden end to war production, and its population, 136,000 in 1919, dropped by almost 8,000 in the next two years. But its major firms swiftly switched back to peacetime work and their ranks were bolstered by a new industrial sector – electrical engineering.

The British Thomson-Houston company had been making magnetos in Coventry since 1912. Four years later the General Electric Company opened its first Coventry factory in the grounds of Copsewood Grange in Stoke, and by 1921 the site had become the Peel Connor telephone works. GEC went on to become the city's biggest single employer and by 1939 the sector accounted for 10 per cent of the city's workforce.

Like Courtaulds before them, these new players on Coventry's industrial scene liked to employ female labour, despite the findings of an official report

Women sign on as tram conductors in Coventry in 1915. (Author's Collection)

on women in factories, which had concluded that they were capable of the same skills as men, but had more time off as they found it harder to stomach the monotony!

Women over the age of thirty had been given the vote by the Representation of the People Act in February 1918, and locally there were some small signs of advances for women in Coventry's public as well as industrial life. Coventry had acquired its first female tram conductors in 1915 and by the end of the war it was being proposed that the city should recruit two women police officers.

In 1919, it also gained its first two women councillors. One was Ellen Hughes, who stood for Labour in the Stoke ward. The other was Alice Arnold, born in the Coventry workhouse in 1881 and put out to work in a factory at the age of eleven. Standing as an Independent, she won a seat in the Swanswell ward as a candidate for the Workers' Union.

While many of the women sent to Coventry during the war to work in munitions factories had returned home, the city was still a place where recent immigrants of both genders had invariably been young, placing huge pressures on a housing stock that was hopelessly inadequate. Many temporary dwellings built for munitions workers had to be pressed into service for young families, but by the early 1920s were 'drab and cheerless places'. A way had to be found to kick-start more decent housing.

In May 1925, work started on nearly 140 acres of fields and gardens that had once been Lammas and Michaelmas lands, at Radford, north of the old city. The Radford garden suburb, as it came to be known, was the starting point for a house-building project that was to produce more than 2,500 homes over the next fifteen years. In 1926 the city council bought more than 2,200 acres of land from the Stoneleigh estate, to the south and west of the city. Among the properties acquired was the birthplace of Sir Henry Parkes, who made the long journey from poor Warwickshire farm boy to Father of the Australian Federation.

Alice Arnold as Coventry's first woman mayor in 1937. (Coventry City Council)

Parliamentary approval for a further boundary extension the following year, mainly to the north, dramatically increased the size of Coventry from 4,171 acres to 12,878. It also added 29,000 people to the city's population, although the good folk of Bedworth, who voted to be included, were in the end turned down by Parliament, probably at the behest of powerful Warwickshire landed interests.

For all this unprecedented growth, the centre of Coventry still had the air, and the street pattern, of a late medieval town. A journalist writing in the *London Illustrated News* at the beginning of the 1920s described it as arguably the best preserved medieval city in Europe.

But change was coming here too. In 1918 the Church of England had finally bowed to common sense by separating the exploding industrial dynamo of Coventry from the old, rather sleepy diocese of Worcester and making it the focus of a new diocese, converting the huge parish church of St Michael, one of England's biggest, into a cathedral.

Two years later The Duke of York, the future King George VI, was in the city to open the new Council House, a long-overdue statement of civic pride begun in 1913 on a site that had been left vacant for a full decade before.

Discussions about a separate Town Hall which would give Coventry a city centre performance space came to nothing in the end, but residents did gain a new public park, something else that the city was desperately short of.

It was conceived in 1919 as Coventry's memorial to the loss and suffering of the Great War – an idea that makes it still relatively unusual in the UK. And it was opened in late 1921 on 120 acres of farm land bought from the Gregory family estate at Styvechale, south of the old city.

Six years later, Earl Haig formally unveiled the War Memorial Park's imposing stone cenotaph, accompanied by Coventry's only city-born winner of the Victoria Cross from the recent conflict, Corporal Arthur Hutt, and Mrs Eliza Bench of Foleshill, who had sacrificed four sons to the war.

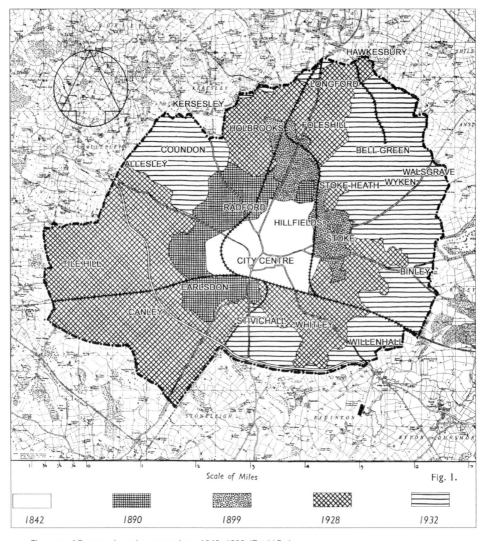

| 1842 | 1890 | 1899 | 1928 | 1932 |

The map of Coventry boundary extensions, 1842–1932. (David Fry)

The interior of Coventry's new cathedral in 1927. (David Fry)

The Coventrian of the late 1920s earned good wages but worked long hours and was still subject to the seasonal lay-offs that had haunted the city's industrial landscape for decades. Many hailed from elsewhere – there had been, for example, branches of the Association of Lancastrians, the Caledonian Corks and the Society of Yorkshiremen in the city since before the Great War.

Curiously, although the population was younger than in many towns, Coventry's birth rate remained lower than the national average throughout the 1920s. This was probably because many immigrants saw their stay in Coventry as short-term and intended to return home before starting a family.

Not many did, for as the 1930s dawned they found themselves living in a place of mounting prosperity, in which newcomers really could leap off the train, get a job in the first factory they tried and if they didn't like it after a day or two, could move on to another.

In Coventry the Hungry Thirties was the decade of the affluent industrial worker. While the unemployment rate in traditional heavy industrial areas like the North-East soared to 25 per cent, in Coventry it remained in the low single figures.

Right The city's new Council House, opened in 1920. (CV One/Coventry City Council)

Below The entrance to Coventry's new War Memorial Park in the early 1930s. (Author's Collection)

The Grove, Kenilworth Road, Coventry.

In late 1937, Coventry would head the rankings in a new national Purchasing Power Index, designed to calculate the spending power of the public. By the end of the decade, almost one in five Coventrians owned a car, a rate of private vehicle ownership that nationally was only achieved in the 1960s.

Of the Big Five British motor manufacturers, only Vauxhall and Ford were not represented in the city. The Rootes Group and Standard were both based in Coventry, while it was at the centre of engine production for Austin-Morris, first at the former Hotchkiss factory in Gosford Street, acquired by William Morris in 1924, and later at a huge new plant in Courthouse Green.

Blackpool-born William Lyons, who brought his modest sidecar business to Coventry in 1928 and went on to carve himself a unique niche in the motoring hall of fame as the founder of Jaguar, was not the only entrepreneur to be enticed to the city.

A decade later, the *Midland Daily Telegraph* was reporting the construction of twenty new factories and dozens more extensions for existing Coventry employers, including an extra 300,000 square feet for the Daimler Company.

For their workforces, these and other Coventry giants, like Alfred Herbert, Courtaulds and GEC, had become more like communities in their own right than mere employers. They offered top-class sports facilities – GEC had its own golf course, while Coventry Colliery at Keresley took on two former members of the Yorkshire 2nd XI to strengthen its cricket team in the 1930s – a wide range of welfare benefits and in some cases real educational opportunities.

They had a place too in the recreational life of those who worked for them. GEC's Social Club, for instance, enjoyed a membership of more than 4,000 and an annual turnover of £33,000 by 1938. Its company dance hall, the biggest in the city, could entertain more than 1,300 dancers at any one time and boasted a soda and ice cream buffet and an illuminated fountain.

The Working Men's Club movement had been slow to take off in Coventry, but accelerated dramatically during the 1930s in the hands of newcomers from more traditional industrial areas where it was already strong.

Alongside a new generation of imposing public houses, serving the new housing estates rapidly being bolted on to the north of the city, cinemas in Coventry moved on from the fleapits of the early 1920s and reached the summit of sophistication in the Rex, opened in 1937 with 2,500 seats, a restaurant, an aviary full of tropical birds and the city's only genuine Wurlitzer.

In 1934, the writer and broadcaster J.B. Priestley had observed this way of life in his state-of-the-nation study, *English Journey*, writing about a ring of factories around the ancient heart of the city and, 'whole new quarters where the mechanics and the fitters and turners and furnace men live in neat brick rows, and drink their beer in gigantic new public houses and take their wives to gigantic new picture houses.'

The Yorkshireman Priestley did not know Coventry at all and he was mightily struck by its appearance: 'You peep round a corner and see half-timbered and gabled houses that would do for the second act of the Meistersinger. I knew it was an old place, but I was surprised to find how much of the past, in soaring stone and carved wood, still remained in the city.'

Not for much longer. In 1931, in the first serious attempt to bend a medieval street pattern to the needs of the city of the car, the city council had bulldozed dozens of homes, factories and shops to create Corporation Street, designed to ease traffic congestion around the northern edge of the old city centre.

In 1937 they went a step further, demolishing wholesale that Meistersinger landscape of Butcher Row, the Bull Ring, Little Butcher Row and Ironmonger Row that stood right at the point where eleventh-century traders had turned the forecourt of the Benedictine priory into a market and in effect created the town.

The Trinity Street scheme was a further measure to combat congestion but in hindsight looks like a grotesque act of vandalism. It was also almost the final act of the old shopocracy that had run Coventry for 100 years, for in November 1937 the Labour Party took power in the city for the first time.

Coventry's new rulers gave the city its first woman mayor, the workhouse-raised Alice Arnold who had been overlooked for the office the year before because, as a life-long Republican, it was thought that she did not possess the right credentials to represent the city in a Coronation year.

They also decided that it was time Coventry had a city architect and chief planner to begin the task of drawing up a blueprint for a new city centre, and within months had appointed the twenty-nine-year-old Deputy County Architect of the Isle of Ely, Donald Gibson. Whether intended or not, this represented a serious challenge for the City Engineer, Ernest Ford, who had been in post since 1925 and had masterminded the Corporation Street and Trinity Street schemes, as well as a long-needed Coventry bypass, opened in 1940 and still taking traffic away from the centre of the city as the A45.

Ford's masterplan for the city centre envisaged 'quieter and more intimate places' with broad vistas and grand spaciousness between Broadgate and the cathedral. Many of his ideas, ironically enough, would end up as part of the

The demolition men already at work in Butcher Row – 'progress' that still looks more like civic vandalism. (Coventry Newspapers)

The congested city centre, photographed from the cathedral tower in 1931. (David Fry)

design of the post-war city centre, but at the time they looked conservative and traditionalist, compared to Gibson's radical plan for a traffic-free shopping centre and carefully delineated development zones. And Gibson was to enjoy the support of both the new ruling Labour group and, later on, the Minister of Works, Sir John Reith.

As Gibson and his young team of architects and planners were starting work on their plan for a new Coventry, the city was welcoming King George VI, who in March 1938 came to inspect progress on a network of new shadow factories, including a secret aircraft manufacturing facility at Whitley and a new aerodrome at Baginton.

The government's idea of building camouflaged industrial facilities around the edges of major urban centres as re-armament gathered pace had found three enthusiastic advocates among Coventry's manufacturing elite when it was first laid on the table in May 1936.

Machine-tool tycoon Alfred Herbert was one. Another was William Rootes, a Kent-born former Singer apprentice who with his brother Reginald had already swallowed up a number of Coventry's well-known car companies, notably Hillman and Humber, in their burgeoning Rootes Group. The third was John Black, the autocratic and ambitious boss of the Standard Motor Company, who liked to use his wartime rank of Captain and would go on to leave his own mark on the city's industrial history in a surprising way.

In total, eight shadow factories were constructed in Coventry under the scheme, in which government built and paid for the new plants in return for companies switching their efforts into war production, principally, in Coventry's case, aero engines.

At the time of the king's visit, the front page headlines of the *Midland Daily Telegraph* day after day reflected the uneasy realities of a march to war. Yet the paper felt able to proclaim, in May 1938, that Coventry was 'not especially exposed to risk of enemy attack' because it lay in the shadow of Birmingham, a much bigger target, and being 120 miles inland presented a difficult bombing proposition to a Continental enemy.

It was a bizarre notion, quickly to be proved tragically mistaken, although the first attacks on Coventry did not come from the expected direction.

At 2.30 p.m. on 25 August 1939, a bomb in the carrier basket of a bicycle left in Broadgate exploded, killing five people, including a bride-to-be who was window shopping for jewellery, a fifteen-year-old shop boy taking his lunch break from WHSmith and the eighty-two-year-old former President of the

Alfred Herbert (centre) and John Black (right), both enthusiastic promoters of shadow factories. (Coventry City Council)

Coventry & District Co-operative Society. The bomb was the bloody climax of an IRA campaign of bombings and sabotage, launched against Britain earlier in the year, which in Coventry had already led to a string of small-scale attacks on telephone junction boxes, electricity substations and even a waiting room at the city's railway station.

The Broadgate bomb remains the single biggest terrorist attack in Coventry's history, yet it was quickly over-shadowed by the declaration of war against Germany, which followed just nine days later.

The man who made and planted the Broadgate bomb was never caught, but by the time two other IRA volunteers, Peter Barnes and James McCormick, had been hanged for the crime at Birmingham's Winson Green prison in February 1940, the phony war was coming to an end.

Coventry's wartime ordeal tends to be crystallised into the Moonlight Sonata raid of 14 November 1940, which destroyed the cathedral, introduced a new word to the German language – *Coventrieren*, to smash the heart of a city – and blew that old medieval street pattern to smithereens. But there were more than fifty air raids on the city, the first of them on 18 August 1940, when high explosives were dropped on nearby residential streets in a bid to strike at the Standard Motor Company's giant works at Canley.

A week later the Rex in Corporation Street, the ultimate cinema-going experience in Coventry, was blitzed flat, fortunately without an audience inside. It had been about to screen *Gone With The Wind*. The first air raid to inflict fatalities came on 28 August when bombs dropped on the Hillfields district killed sixteen people. And on 14 October, Ford's Hospital, one of the city's most beautiful medieval survivors, was severely damaged by a bomb that killed six elderly female residents and two members of staff.

Although the 14 November raid, one of the biggest of the war on any British city, was unparalleled in its ferocity, the two raids of 8 and 10 April 1941 came close. In the first, the city's Coventry and Warwickshire Hospital suffered repeated direct hits, in which more than thirty staff and patients

were killed. In the second, the church of the Greyfriars, for the second time in its long history, lost everything but its spire. Together, the two raids left more than 450 people dead.

Damage to Coventry's industrial infrastructure from more than a year of air raids was enormous, yet, astonishingly, had only a limited impact on war production. Within two weeks of the 14 November raid, 80 per cent of those thrown out of work by the damage inflicted on factories were back at their work benches. Of the 108 factories left without power after the April 1941 raids, half had had it restored within days.

A later claim that Coventry, known to be a compelling target for the Luftwaffe, was sacrificed on the night of 14 November to preserve the secret that the British had cracked the

The burned-out ruins of Christ Church. (Author's Collection)

German Enigma code, has been largely discredited. Only at 3 p.m. that afternoon was the true identity of the night's real target finally revealed. And that was far too late for action.

That said, there is no doubt that Coventry was ill-prepared, at least to begin with, for mass attack from the air.

There were not enough fire watchers to cover every residential street, or enough deep shelters for the population. Weaknesses in the emergency services' preparations were quickly exposed during raids. In the absence of a national fire service, fire crews rushed into the city from other places did not always have compatible equipment that allowed them to hook up to local water supplies, and the idea that the Coventry Canal could be a fail-safe back-up for water to fight the fires disappeared the moment it was hit, early on in the 14 November raid, and drained.

Coventry's anti-aircraft defences, beefed up only weeks before the November raid, were found wanting too. Of more than 400 aircraft involved, only one raider is known to have crashed that night and there is no evidence that it was shot down by an anti-aircraft gun protecting the city.

Questions were later asked too about the city's morale. The fact that at least 50,000 people appear to have left the city each night at the height of the bombing to 'sleep out' has been interpreted as an indication that panic quickly set in. That's unfair and for one thing ignores the necessity for those engaged in war work to get some rest from their labours, something near impossible to achieve under repeated night-time attack.

There was some evidence of looting in the wake of the major raids. The city's Chief Constable recorded just over 500 incidents in his annual report for 1940, and a similar figure for 1941, although in both cases around 80 per cent concerned theft from meters or machines.

Yet it should be remembered that nothing on this scale had ever happened to a British city before. Hindsight is an unforgiving tool but Coventry's stoicism and then recovery in the face of unprecedented devastation must be regarded as nothing short of heroic. More civilians actually died in air raids on Birmingham in the course of the war, yet it was Coventry's searing experience that was transmitted around the world as an appalling testament to the brutality of the Nazis, and the destruction of the cathedral was used, not entirely successfully, to bolster attempts to get America to enter the war.

In 1945, confirmation of Coventry's special status in Britain came in the release of a film, *A City Reborn*, made by the Ministry of Information in

King George VI examines plans for a new Coventry. (Coventry Newspapers)

partnership with Coventry City Council. The government was desperate to avoid the bitter mistakes of 1918 and chose the re-birth of Coventry to epitomise a Brave New Britain, where the returning heroes would have jobs, homes, schools for their children and a comfortable life free from hard times. Scripted by the poet Dylan Thomas, the film starred Bill Owen, in his later years a staple of television's *Last Of The Summer Wine*, as a young demobbed soldier looking forward to a better life in the new city of the working man.

That new city was some time in coming. The wholesale destruction wrought by the 14 November blitz had given real impetus to Donald Gibson's plans for a new city centre, but for the rest of the war council leaders and Whitehall civil servants were at loggerheads over the scale and ambitious nature of his proposals.

A 'Coventry of the Future' exhibition in October 1945 attracted more than 57,000 Coventrians, a fifth of the population, to see the plans. But it was to be 1951 before construction work started on the cornerstone of Gibson's

The forbidding Sir John Black in uncharacteristically relaxed pose with one of his post-war Standards. (Coventry Transport Museum)

plan – five precinct blocks stretching away from the new square, complete with Godiva statue, that had replaced the old Broadgate in 1948.

The city's industrial economy made the transition from war to peace rather more smoothly, fuelled in part by a remarkable agreement that set the bar of earnings among Coventry's skilled engineering workers higher than anywhere else in the country. The Standard agreement, offering a high pay/high productivity package, based on a forty-two and a half hour week, brought together two unlikely allies.

The company's forbidding Managing Director Sir John Black, who had been knighted in 1943, was able to set aside his anti-union instincts to thrash out the deal with the equally forceful Jack Jones, Coventry District Secretary for the Transport and General Workers Union.

Liverpool-born Jones had arrived in Coventry in 1938, after service with the International Brigade in the Spanish Civil War. As a young anti-fascist firebrand he had been waved off to that war by an old firebrand with Coventry connections, founder of trade unions and international agitator Tom Mann, born in Longford in 1856 and sent down the pit at ten.

Jones himself would go on to achieve some notoriety in the 1970s as General Secretary of the TGWU, labelled by his enemies in the press as Emperor Jones, the most powerful man in Britain. But it was in a spirit of compromise that he helped lay the foundations of Coventry's post-war prosperity.

The Times newspaper had first described Coventry as Britain's Detroit way back in 1916, and that comparison began to be made again as in the 1950s the city once more became the focus of those in search of a better life, paying the first five pound note in a peacetime weekly wage packet for shop-floor workers.

In the years immediately before the war, Coventry's rapidly growing population had necessitated a house-building programme that turned out something like 4,000 new homes a year. Now, virgin land, brought into Coventry by boundary extensions in 1928 and 1932, was being covered by a new generation of edge-of-city estates.

Coventry's central redevelopment plans were finally bearing fruit too. Its pioneering traffic-free shopping precinct, the first in Europe, attracted visitors from far and wide, keen to see the future in action.

The Hotel Leofric in Broadgate, part of Gibson's original plan, was described as the finest outside London when it opened in 1955. Coventry had a new circular market and the beginnings of an innovative ring road, to take traffic away from the centre. By 1958, it also had the Belgrade, the first civic theatre to be built in Britain after the Second World War, a city council initiative described by the critic Kenneth Tynan as 'one of the greatest decisions in the history of local government.'

Broadgate from the old cathedral tower in the late 1960s – a scarcely credible contrast to the 1931 view (see page 220) taken from almost the same spot. (Coventry Newspapers)

The Lower Precinct in 1961, part of a city centre to be proud of. (Coventry Newspapers)

Within two years it could also boast a new museum and art gallery, named after Sir Alfred Herbert, who had partly funded it. The Herbert's first director was the Ulster poet John Hewitt, whose enthusiasm for his adopted city was in marked contrast to his fellow poet, and acquaintance, the Coventry-born Philip Larkin.

With these new cultural assets, a prosperous and still growing population and a city centre that was the envy of many other towns, Coventry could greet the 1960s with some confidence.

MOONLIGHT SONATA – 14 NOVEMBER 1940

The single most concentrated attack on a British city in the Second World War began shortly after 7 p.m. on a brilliant, moonlit night, so bright that traffic could move around on the roads without lights.

The Luftwaffe had gathered more than 400 bombers from airfields all over Europe to deliver a knockout blow to one of Britain's major centres of war production. It was said too that Hitler had personally ordered the raid in revenge for an attack on Munich by the RAF. During eleven hours of bombing, the Luftwaffe dropped 500 tons of high explosive, 30,000 incendiaries and fifty land mines. It was also trying out a new weapon, the exploding incendiary.

Within an hour of the sirens sounding, fire-watchers were reporting 240 fires spread across the city. By 11 p.m. all sources of water to fight the fires had dried up, with the mains shattered and even the canal breached and drained. Those trying to save the great medieval church of St Michael's, the city's cathedral, were forced to retreat to save their own lives and shortly after 1 a.m. the roof fell in.

Alongside St Michael's, the only cathedral to be destroyed by enemy action in the Second World War, Coventry lost its central library and market hall, the new Owen Owen department store and the King's Head Hotel, hundreds of shops and public buildings and sixteenth-century Palace Yard, one of the last reminders of its golden age. Its tram system, already considered out-dated, died that night too.

The smell and heat of the burning city reached into the cockpits of the German bombers, 6,000 feet above, and the fire at the huge Daimler works in Radford, which turned fifteen acres of factory buildings into a raging inferno, was one of the biggest of the war in Britain.

Coventry's new Owen Owen store on the eve of war. Along with the city's tram system, it was a victim of the November blitz. (Author's Collection)

Trying to get to work in a city centre that no longer existed. The morning after the November blitz. (Coventry Newspapers)

More than 43,000 homes, just over half the city's housing stock, suffered some damage and around 2,300 were completely destroyed. While Hillfields bore the brunt of the attack, other residential areas like Stoke were badly affected too.

The official death toll from the night stands at 554, with more than 800 seriously injured, but that is a significant underestimate as many people remained unaccounted for.

As dawn broke, hundreds wandered Coventry's streets in a daze, unable to comprehend what had happened. By midday it was as warm as spring and almost dark because of the fires.

Army units who rushed into the city to clear the rubble-choked streets and make buildings safe had to be prevented from dynamiting the cathedral tower. They didn't realise it had been leaning for at least 100 years.

A shocked King George VI made an impromptu visit to Coventry on 16 November and is said to have shed a tear as he stood in the ruined cathedral and surveyed the damage. Three days later, the mass burials began, as fighter planes patrolled the skies above London Road cemetery in case the Luftwaffe returned.

Of all the eyewitness accounts of that horrifying night, the measured voice of firewatcher E.S. Bramwell as he wrote in his official log, on duty in the tower of the Council House, right at the heart of the conflagration, perhaps echoes most strongly down the years.

Fires still burning, unchecked all round the city centre. The devastation is indescribable. Service personnel make their way slowly over the debris. No-one speaks.

My personal feeling is one of sadness. Then, I recall the starlings trilling a few notes of song as I left the Council House this morning. Did the heat of the fires make them think it was Spring, or could this be a message of hope for the future?

The old city was dead, but the spirit of Coventry remained very much alive.

eleven

BOOM AND BUST

Just before 8.30 p.m. on Millennium Eve (31 December 1999) a wheel fell off a camera trolley in the studios where the BBC was filming that momentous night's National Lottery draw.

The draw was live, part of the special rolling coverage of Millennium Eve, and just up ahead was the moment when the queen arrived at the Embankment to see the fireworks and, later on, link arms with Prime Minister Tony Blair in an awkward climax to the celebrations. Technicians needed more time to fix the wheel and the decision was taken to stay with the lottery, scrap the next item in the schedule and then go straight to the Embankment.

And so Coventry's astonishing tightrope walk between two medieval towers, surely the most visually arresting image of the night in Britain, never got a live national audience. By the time it was screened in the early hours, all but insomniacs had gone to bed.

To the 100-strong BBC team who had hired Britain's tallest crane to film tightrope walker Ramon Kelvink as he teetered in a white suit between the parapets of Holy Trinity and the ruined cathedral, it was a disaster that induced tears and apoplexy in roughly equal measure. A prime slot in an historic television event watched by millions had been dashed from their hands.

To experienced Coventry watchers, it was no real surprise. As one senior council officer remarked, 'nothing comes easy to Coventry'.

Back in the early 1960s, such a view would have seemed preposterous. Lots had come easy to Coventry in the decade and a half since the war, and the crowning glory was the dedication of the city's new cathedral on 25 May 1962.

Naturally enough, most people in Coventry had wanted the cathedral that lay in ruins to be rebuilt once hostilities ended. But restrictions on materials and the diversion of skilled labour from the pressing business of putting day-to-day Britain back together again had ruled that out pretty swiftly.

Sutherland's tapestry frames an interior full of great art. (Andrew Paterson)

An idea to fill in Coventry's historic canal basin and build there thankfully came to nothing, and eventually, after much controversy and a surprising degree of bare-knuckle, back room politics, it was Basil Spence's design for a cathedral, built at right angles to the ruins, uniquely facing north, that was chosen.

Edinburgh-based Spence had dreamed of designing a cathedral since childhood but found himself working on exhibition halls for the Festival of Britain. His submission to the international architectural competition that in 1951 gave him the Coventry commission came at a time when his career was at something of a low ebb.

Getting down to detail, he struggled to work out how to incorporate stained glass windows into what was essentially a box-like structure and only 'discovered' the secret in a novocaine-fuelled state of unconsciousness while at the dentist. But another of his ideas, to commission work from most of the significant artists working in post war Britain, gave his new cathedral an enduring parallel identity as an unrivalled gallery of great twentieth-century art.

Graham Sutherland's gigantic tapestry, the biggest in the world when it was made, Jacob Epstein's monumental sculpture of St Michael defeating the Devil, his last major work, and John Piper's luminous baptistry window were merely the headliners, along with John Hutton's beautiful west screen of saints and angels, a work involving so much etching in glass, a hazardous process at the best of times, that it is said to have contributed to his death.

As it rose from the ground, Coventry's new cathedral came to symbolise the recovery of Britain from the Second World War. Four million people came to see it in its first year and the journalist and commentator Bernard Levin surely caught that mood when he called it, 'A boundary stone that marks the divide between one age and another.'

The cathedral's dedication to peace and reconciliation, hammered out in words and charred beams within hours of its predecessor's destruction, had given Coventry a status in Britain and across the world that the pre-war city lacked.

In the Coronation year of 1953, the queen had boosted civic pride further by giving Coventry consent by charter to elect a Lord Mayor each year, instead of just a mayor.

Labour Party veteran Hamblett (Bertie) Cresswell was the first and in 1957 Pearl Hyde became the city's first female Lord Mayor.

The London-born daughter of a publican, Pearl Hyde had arrived in Coventry in the 1920s and had had a good war, earning herself a national reputation for her work as a fearless and hard-working organiser for the Women's Voluntary Service, a calming presence amidst the chaos of the Blitz.

A larger-than life character in more ways than one, she was an influential politician during the post-war years and might have gone on to greater things, had she not been killed in a car crash while on holiday in Scotland in April 1963.

The same fate had befallen the Belgrade Theatre's first director Bryan Bailey, who died in an accident on the

The larger-than-life Pearl Hyde. (Coventry City Council)

M1 in March 1960. One of the shining lights of his generation in theatre, Bailey created a resident company at the Belgrade, featuring young actors of the calibre of Frank Finlay and Richard Briers, and devised for it an ambitious programme, including premieres for *Chicken With Barley*, *Roots* and *I'm Talking About Jerusalem*, a trilogy of plays by an exciting new writer, Arnold Wesker.

He also planted the seeds for a Belgrade project that was to mature after his death. In 1964 the theatre pioneered 'Theatre in Education', the radical idea of bringing theatre directly into the school classroom which fifty years on has spread around the world.

The Belgrade Theatre - ambitious from the start. (CV One/Coventry City Council)

Education was very much on the city's mind at the time. In 1961 the Lanchester College of Technology, thirty years later to become Coventry University, had opened on a site close to the new cathedral. And in the same year the government finally gave the go-ahead to a new university for Coventry, to be built on 200 acres of farmland at Gibbet Hill.

A university promotion committee, led by William, now Lord Rootes, had spent ten years lobbying for a development that in the view of the city's able and influential Town Clerk, Charles Barratt, was 'the one thing required to make Coventry a great city'.

Even though the initial gift of land came from Coventry, the university was to be named the University of Warwick, an uncomfortable compromise that the headmaster of Bablake School, for one, thought was wrong. Why should it not be called Coventry? he asked, a question that has resounded down the decades since.

Lord Rootes, chosen as Chancellor designate, died before he could take up office and was succeeded by Lord Radcliffe, the lawyer who had partitioned India, another flawed compromise that had had much more serious consequences. The first students, 340 undergraduates and 90 postgraduates, took up their places in October 1965.

As 1966 dawned, Coventry folk had plenty to look forward to. Although Coventry's investment in residential tower blocks had been insignificant compared to Birmingham's, the city council were proudly announcing plans to build seventeen-storey blocks in Spon End and on the Stoney Stanton Road.

There was to be a large new city centre hotel, built almost within touching distance of the north end of the new cathedral, and a May completion was being targeted for stage four of the pioneering inner ring road, the stretch connecting Spon Street and the Foleshill Road. Also scheduled to open that spring were two new recreational facilities for the people of the city, the Olympic-sized swimming baths in Fairfax Street, the only one in the West Midlands, and the country park at Coombe Abbey. This was acquired by the city council in late 1964 after passing through a number of hands in the decades since 1923, when the Earl of Craven fell overboard from his yacht, forcing the family to sell up.

Later in the year, the council was planning to open President Kennedy School, the ninth comprehensive school in an authority that had committed itself to comprehensive education perhaps more than any other in the UK.

What was not realised at the time was that 1966 would also be the year in which Coventry's manufacturing output, almost entirely engineering-based, would peak. From then on it would start to fall away. A harbinger of that, for those who cared to look for it, was the fate of the city's aircraft industry, clustered around Baginton and Whitley.

After a war turning out Lancaster, Whitley and Stirling bombers, peacetime prospects looked bright, with the expansion of the Royal Air Force offering new opportunities for a skilled and inventive aviation workforce. In 1947, Armstrong Whitworth Aviation, based at Whitley, had produced the futuristic AW 52, the Flying Wing, and by the early 1960s engineers working for its successor at Whitley, Hawker Siddeley Dynamics, were even beginning to think very seriously about space satellite design.

But the optimism of the early years had already been dented. In 1952, AWA's Apollo, designed and built at Baginton, had failed to measure up to its rival, the Vickers Viscount, and had never made it into production. Later on, Baginton Aerodrome's lack of concrete runways on which to test modern aircraft forced Hawker Siddeley to acquire an airfield that did; Bitteswell near Lutterworth. The government never did invest in space satellite design and in the spring of 1965 Harold Wilson's new administration cancelled three aircraft projects of direct interest to the industry in Coventry, the HS681, the Hawker P1164 and the TSR2.

Baginton closed in July 1965 and Whitley had followed by October 1968, when it was reported that the aircraft industry in Coventry had lost 11,000 jobs in just five years.

At a series of Lord Mayor's Conferences, convened that autumn to consider the city's future, concern was expressed that too much of Coventry's employment and prosperity was now focused on making cars, an industry subject to too many variables. While new jobs were still being created in parts of the industry, the warning signs of long-term decline were already there. As early as 1959 it had become clear that Standard and Rootes, the two Coventry-based members of the pre-war Big Five motor manufacturers, were heading for trouble.

In that year, the Standard Company was taken over by Leyland. This left Harry Ferguson's tractor company, taken on board by John Black in 1946 and housed at the old Standard shadow factory at Banner Lane, to go its own way. By 1967, Rootes had been fully absorbed by the American giant Chrysler, after repeated cash injections from it in the early 1960s.

Some blamed this decline on the policy of successive governments to steer new industrial development away from cities like Coventry and into industrial areas that were struggling. Others blamed a local culture of high wages and poor industrial relations for putting off would-be inward investors in Coventry.

Clearly, there were increasing signs of strife on the factory floor. The old generation of company managers, many of them local men who had risen through the ranks and had something in common with the rank and file, were retiring.

Their replacements were younger executives recruited elsewhere who had no loyalty to company traditions or in many cases, even to Coventry. By the mid-1970s only Alfred Herbert of Coventry's top fifteen employers would have its head office based in the city. The trade unions' trigger-happy response to management aggression, real and imagined, only made things worse. This gave Coventry an unenviable reputation as a place where people were apt to walk out at the drop of the proverbial hat.

In the gathering gloom, there was, however, one bright spot – local sport. In 1961 Coventry City, a football club that had been shuffling along in mediocrity for decades, was suddenly galvanised into brisk upwards movement by a shrewd, energetic and oddly charismatic former footballer, Londoner Jimmy Hill.

In 1967, this master showman, quite happy to plunder cultural references from other worlds, notably the Eton Boating Song and the hunting pink he occasionally donned to entertain the crowds, took them into the First Division in front of more than 51,000 stunned supporters.

Off the pitch, Hill made the Sky Blues a trail-blazer in the world of professional football, pioneering the dedicated match-day programme, a club radio station and, later, the all-seater stadium, among many other things.

By contrast, it was Coventry Rugby Club's adherence to the old virtues of grit and a formidable pack that had made it England's premier club by the mid-1960s, its team packed with internationals.

The Coventry Bees speedway team, founded in the 1920s, won the British League title in 1968, a precursor to many years as one of the sport's leading clubs. The city's athletics and swimming clubs, Coventry Godiva Harriers and the City of Coventry Swimming Club, both produced a number of Olympians.

Coventry's last prominent cricketer had been R.E.S. Wyatt, a former pupil of King Henry VIII School who had captained England in the mid-1930s. But in July 1964, car worker's son Tom Cartwright, one of the cleverest and most accurate bowlers of his generation, won the first of his five Test caps, against Australia.

Cartwright, born in a miner's cottage in Alderman's Green and infused with the principled socialism of his parents, should have played for England many more times, but perhaps lacked the right background in a game still dominated by class. Instead, he went on to become one of cricket's most admired coaches.

The historic fabric of Coventry was doing rather less well. With something of a start, the city had discovered in 1966 that it had only thirty-four buildings left dating from before 1700. The Luftwaffe and 'clearances' going back to the early 1930s, reaching a peak in the post-war policies of comprehensive zoning, had accounted for literally hundreds more.

It was an embarrassment. To save further losses a Townscape scheme was initiated in 1967 to

Tom Cartwright should have played for England more than he did. (Coventry Newspapers)

Much Park Street in 1913, a street full of interest. (David Fry)

move threatened historic buildings from ancient streets like Much Park Street to a new location in Spon Street. The result was a picturesque collection of late medieval timber-framed buildings, their impact sadly diminished by the presence of utilitarian tower blocks at both ends and an eye-level ring road that cut the street in two.

Poor Much Park Street, not long before a thoroughfare boasting 600 years of quirky architecture, became largely featureless, its street frontage given over chiefly to grass.

Large swathes of grass were generally what passed for landscaping among the edge-of-city housing estates created in the 1950s in places like Canley, Tile Hill, Bell Green, Willenhall and Stoke Aldermoor. By the early 1970s many of these places, despite their attractive names, were losing their attraction as places to live.

Experimental building methods like the 'no fines' concrete system had made whole patches of them almost uninhabitable, while communities marooned in a sea of grass with few of the staple facilities for daily life were already experiencing social problems. If the city council hoped that new investment might help, it was in no position to make it happen. A local authority that had been a laboratory for so much social policy in the post-war years, pioneering, among a whole range of things, the smokeless zone and meals-on-wheels, was powerless in the face of an on-rushing global slump.

In 1972 redundancies began to accelerate as the oil crisis loomed. Whole chunks of Rolls Royce's engine business had to be taken into state ownership and its Coventry factories, at Parkside and Ansty, suffered the knock-on effect.

By 1975, Chrysler had to be bailed out to the tune of £162 million, while British Leyland plants in the city were nationalised to save them. By the end of the decade, a study showed, more than 40 per cent of Coventry's working population were now dependent on the government for their livelihoods.

Throughout the 1960s, Coventry's population had continued to rise, peaking at 336,000 in the 1971 census. It would dip by a startling 25,000 over the next decade as Coventry's accelerating economic decline prompted a brain drain among younger, more mobile residents, but the demographics had already triggered a new Parliamentary seat for the city.

Coventry had emerged from the Second World War with just two seats, both held for Labour, oddly enough, by Oxbridge intellectuals and writers rather than graduates of the shop floor. Richard Crossman represented Coventry East and Maurice Edelman Coventry West, and in 1950 they were joined by Yorkshire-born schoolteacher Elaine Burton, who won the new constituency of Coventry South.

In 1974, the Boundary Commission gave the city a fourth Parliamentary seat. Richard Crossman had died in the spring of that year, but Maurice Edelman held on to Coventry North-West until his own death in late 1975.

A wet day in Coventry's pioneering shopping precincts in March 1971. The post-war boom has already lost its sheen. (Coventry Newspapers)

Former Rootes Group convener George Park became MP for Coventry North-East, Newcastle-born left-winger Audrey Wise took Coventry South-West and solicitor William Wilson held on to the renamed Coventry South-East seat.

Wilson is one of only two native-born Coventrians to have held Parliamentary seats in the city since the war. As an MP and a lawyer, he made immigration his special interest, an appropriate speciality in a city that had throughout its history attracted newcomers to put down roots.

In the years before the Second World War, virtually all immigrants to Coventry had been white, mostly from older industrial areas of the UK, in particular the depressed South Wales coalfield. In the late 1930s there were also around 2,000 Irish people living and working in the city, and in a mini census taken thirty years later in the mid-1960s almost 17,000 people gave their birthplace as Eire.

The equivalent figure for the Commonwealth, chiefly the Indian subcontinent, was just over 11,000, roughly similar to those born in the north-west of England and somewhat less than for Scotland.

Generally, Coventry's record on race relations had been a good one. A campaign had to be fought over a colour bar operated by some Coventry working men's clubs in the mid-1960s, but the city's small Pakistani population had been the first in the West Midlands to build their own mosque in 1961 and in 1966 Mohammed Daar started work out on the beat in Coventry, the first ethnic minority policeman in Britain to do so.

The impression of harmony was to change dramatically in the spring and early summer of 1981, with tensions across the country rising and rioting beginning to scar many towns and cities.

On 18 April, a twenty-year-old student, Satnam Singh Gill, was stabbed to death in a motiveless attack by a gang of white skinheads in Coventry's Upper Precinct. Weeks of violent racist attacks, rising to a pitch over the first weekend of June, culminated in the stabbing of Indian doctor Anal Dharry outside a hot potato takeaway in Earlsdon on Sunday, 7 June. He died in hospital eleven days later.

Even before this second murder, shock had given way to a determination to reinforce Coventry's credentials as a place where ethnicity and culture were not provocations, and a march through the centre of the city at the end of May, organised by Asian community leaders and supported by the Lord Mayor, attracted thousands. It was ambushed by white extremists as it passed the new cathedral and there were confrontations with the police as the march ended, leading to seventy-four arrests. But it made the point.

This was, after all, the city of 2-Tone music, which over the past two years had brought black and white youth together in a raucous celebration of British ska.

Its founding band, The Specials, were in fact about to split up, but on 12 June, five days after the attack on Dr Dharry, they released their final single, 'Ghost Town', which seemed to sum up everything about the state of Britain in 1981. Specials founder and songwriter, Jerry Dammers, claimed later that 'Ghost Town' was written after he had witnessed elderly women selling their possessions on the streets of Glasgow, but in truth it could have been written about Coventry.

The city's ugly mood had given it a reputation as a dangerous place after dark. That mood was only intensified by what appeared to be indifference from Margaret Thatcher's government to the plight of industrial centres like Coventry. It was an impression confirmed in June 1981 by the Prime Minister's brusque rejection of a plea, made by city MP William Wilson and backed by the *Coventry Evening Telegraph*, to offer some relief to the city's economy.

In the three years after Mrs Thatcher's election victory in 1979, the number of British Leyland employees in Coventry fell from 27,000 to 8,000. Once-great Alfred Herbert had finally bitten the dust and former workers paraded a coffin through the streets in a mock funeral in 1983.

On top of all that, the bitter miners' strike in the winter of 1984/85 effectively ended Coventry's long history as a centre of coal mining, an industry that over the twentieth century in particular had brought thousands from all parts of the UK to make the city their home.

It is not an exaggeration to say that the slump of the early 1980s represented the collapse of Coventry as a major manufacturing and engineering centre. By the middle of the decade the city's unemployment rate had risen to 16 per cent and there was simply no prospect of new jobs emerging in manufacturing.

To its credit, the city council was already taking steps to make sure that the devastating consequences of relying on a single-industry economy would not happen again. It was putting a lot of effort into building up the city's service sector, principally by developing a chain of business parks strung around the southern and eastern outskirts.

It paid off, with companies like National Grid, Powergen and Barclays Bank moving into the biggest, the Westwood Business Park, to take advantage of leafy surroundings in a well-connected location, at a fraction of the cost of doing so in the south-east.

In a separate development, the council was also instrumental in setting up Warwick Science Park, one of the UK's first, in a joint venture with the University of Warwick, Warwickshire County Council and Barclays Bank.

But it was to be the end of the decade before schemes were brought forward to improve the ageing city centre's shopping core – with decidedly mixed results.

The West Orchards centre, built on the site of a Meccano-like multi-storey car park, opened in April 1991 as a moderately successful and reasonably handsome addition to the city's shopping offer. Cathedral Lanes, by contrast, was an act of desperation that in 1990 blocked vistas around the cathedral area with a lifeless brick shopping centre that never gave Coventry the small specialist retailing it promised. It is now the city centre building most Coventrians would like to see removed.

Even though the city council allowed itself a pat on the back for updating the city centre with these projects, not everybody was impressed. Six years later, The *Lonely Planet* guidebook still felt justified in describing Coventry as 'a dismal cityscape of car parks, ring roads and windswept shopping precincts.'

Yet as the new Millennium dawned, there were some grounds for optimism; with a steadily improving economy Coventry was once more beginning to attract interest from investors and developers. Significant capital investment was secured for the Herbert Art Gallery and Museum, the Belgrade Theatre and the re-branded Coventry Transport Museum, giving all three a scale and an excitement they should have had decades earlier.

Coventry's Millennium project, which followed its inventive Millennium Eve celebrations, was a long time coming. It replaced a grim 1960s car park and shops with a series of spaces that reacquainted the people of Coventry with some of the historic landscapes they had lost, making a real attraction of the city's first cathedral, destroyed by Henry VIII.

The Phoenix Initiative, as it was somewhat gracelessly called, was on the final shortlist for the Stirling Prize for architecture in 2004. This was duly won by the Gherkin in the City of London, yet another monument to overweening pride among bankers. Yet, for its clever reworking of landscapes ancient and modern, many felt that the prize should have been Coventry's.

The Ricoh Arena, opened the following year, at last gave the city the sort of conferencing and events space it had always lacked, albeit at a detached location on its northern boundary. It also became the new home of Coventry City Football Club, an ill-fated move that appears to have accelerated the club's

Capital investment gave the Herbert a widely admired new extension. (CV One/Coventry City Council)

The city's Millennium project, a clever blend of ancient and modern. (CV One/Coventry City Council)

David Moorcroft, world record holder, in full flow. (Coventry Newspapers)

long decline since the glory days of May 1987, when the Sky Blues turned over Tottenham Hotspur in one of the most exciting FA Cup finals ever seen.

Coventry Rugby Club has shared the football club's fall into the third tier of their sport, while the city's speedway team have lost their once inalienable right to win everything.

Only in the shape of the ice hockey team, Coventry Blaze, who moved to Coventry in the year 2000, has sporting success regularly attached to Coventry's name. The city has also produced, in athlete David Moorcroft, one of the best-known figures in British sport.

A former pupil of Woodlands School, a hotbed of sport that has also produced England rugby heroes Neil Back and Danny Grewcock, as well as rising star Tom Wood, Moorcroft remains the last non-African to set a world record at 5,000 metres. His astonishing feat in knocking nearly six seconds off the existing record back in 1982 is arguably the greatest single sporting achievement by a native Coventrian and helped open up new career opportunities for him in first broadcasting and later sports administration. He was Chief Executive of British Athletics for ten years until 2007.

The previous year, back in his home city, Peugeot had brought down the curtain on all those decades of volume car production in Coventry by closing its manufacturing operation at Ryton, with the loss of 2,000 jobs. The London black cab, something of a misnomer as it has always been made in Coventry, is the last vehicle produced in any numbers in the city and has had to be rescued from collapse by Chinese investors.

Severn Trent Water's £60 million operating centre, opened in the autumn of 2010 with 1,700 jobs attached, at last brought serious service sector investment into the city centre, a long-held aspiration for Coventry. But if that looked like a door opening, the recession that appeared on the horizon in 2008 has slammed it firmly shut again.

With unemployment creeping steadily up to and beyond 8 per cent and development, except in student housing, temporarily paralysed, Coventry's weaknesses as a place without a strong identity on the national map, which the upwardly mobile have tended to avoid, have been exposed.

The city council, acutely conscious that the city had slipped out of the top fifty in the retail ranking lists, turned to Venice Beach, California master-planners Jerde, who were more accustomed to working with high-rise cities outside Europe. Their ideas for reinventing Coventry city centre generally baffled rather than inspired, but in any event the recession that struck in 2008 put any firm plans that might have followed on hold.

As Coventry looks forward, much now depends on its two universities taking up the role once played, in inventiveness and job creation, by the major

Severn Trent's £60 million investment in Coventry city centre. Much more is needed. (Coventry Newspapers)

The city at dusk. Much now depends on a new dawn. (Andrew Paterson)

engineering companies. It is no coincidence that the innovative and business heart of Coventry University sits squarely on the Parkside site once occupied by early car factories and later Rolls Royce.

Coventry may not yet feel entirely comfortable with being a university town, but while its specialist engineering sector flourishes, the mass employment manufacturers will not be returning. The city has bounced back from bad times so often in its long history that to characterise its current struggles as somehow terminal would be utterly premature. But in a global economy in which every distant and unknown outpost is a competitor it's going to be extra tough this time.

In the 1945 film *A City Re-born*, the young soldier and his girl are looking, wide-eyed with excitement, at Donald Gibson's plans for a Brave New City as the narrator intones, 'Coventry is going to be a place to live in where people can believe how pleasant human life can be.'

It is going to take another rebirth to make that happen.

THE PEACE DIVIDEND

Within hours of the air raid that destroyed Coventry's fourteenth-century cathedral, the instinctive reactions of two men pointed the way to its future as a global symbol of peace and reconciliation. Cathedral stonemason Jock Forbes, looking down on the devastation from the tower, spotted two charred medieval beams lying in the rubble roughly in the shape of a cross and bound them together. And the cathedral's Provost, Richard Howard, felt compelled to have the words 'Father Forgive' inscribed on the stone wall behind the altar.

The words were intended as a plea encompassing all mankind, not just those who had destroyed the church, and the Charred Cross remains one of the potent symbols of the cathedral's ministry of international reconciliation, alongside a Cross of Nails originally fashioned from medieval roof nails.

The impulse to look forward in friendship and not backwards in revenge found an echo within Coventry's civic leadership. In 1944 they sealed a friendship pact with the martyred Russian city of Stalingrad, the first of its kind in the world, and in 1947 entered into another formal link with the north German city of Kiel.

The approach had initially come from civic leaders in Kiel who wanted to pay tribute to an official with the Allied occupying powers they much respected, Coventrian Gwillyn Williams. It was sealed with a personal visit to the devastated seaport city by Provost Howard.

To right-wing elements in the national press, making a formal friendship link with Kiel, just two years after hostilities had ceased, smacked of fraternising with the enemy. But for Coventry it was the next logical step in a process that, in sixty-five years, has given it, in name at least, twenty-six twin towns and cities around the world.

In 1955, Coventry won an international peace prize from the fledgling Council of Europe as the city that most exemplified the new European ideal of friendship across national boundaries. The following year, it established what is arguably still its closest twinning relationship, with Dresden.

The cathedral too was quick to reach out to former enemies. In October 1961, sixteen young Germans arrived in Coventry to help build a new International Centre in

Looking into the future. The cathedral's ministry is captured in the words 'Father Forgive'. (Mark Radford)

the ruins. Money to furnish it was given by a Berlin merchant who had lost his entire family in an Allied bombing raid.

While the purist might question how a city so closely connected with the engineering of armaments, even into the twenty-first century, can truly align itself with the peacemakers, there is no doubt that Coventry's reputation as a place that looks forward in friendship and not back in anger lives on.

The cathedral ruins exert as powerful a pull on the imagination now as they ever did. After the attack on the Twin Towers in September 2001, New York seriously considered the Coventry model of not rebuilding but leaving the site as a place of pilgrimage.

While the cathedral's international ministry of reconciliation and conflict resolution reaches into the darkest corners of the world's killing zones, the ruins have become a place in which to reflect on the imagery of peace and commemoration,

The cathedral ruins are now a site of pilgrimage. (Chris Ross)

most recently through a memorial unveiled in 2012 to the civilian deaths in war.

But it is not all about the past. The current Archbishop of Canterbury, Justin Welby, himself a former international director at Coventry Cathedral, has decided that its work will play a central role in the way the Church of England as a whole approaches this part of its world-wide ministry.

The profile for Coventry that Jock Forbes and Richard Howard gave shape to, more than seventy years ago, has lost none of its power to inspire.

BIBLIOGRAPHY

Books and Pamphlets

Ashdown-Hill, J., *The Last Days Of Richard III,* The History Press, 2010.

Bassett, S., *Anglo-Saxon Coventry And Its Churches*, Dugdale Society Papers, 2001.

Black, A. & C., *Black's Guide To Warwickshire 1874*, reprinted Country Books, 2006.

Bliss, Burbidge F., *Old Coventry And Lady Godiva,* Birmingham University Press, 1952.

Bottle T., *Coventry's Forgotten Theatre*, The Badger Press, 2004.

Carpenter, C., *Locality And Polity, A Study Of Warwickshire Landed Society 1401–1490,* Cambridge University Press, 1992.

Castor, H., *She Wolves,* Faber and Faber, 2010.

Chancellor, V. (ed.), *Master And Artisan In Victorian England*, Evelyn, Adams & Mackay, 1969.

Christiansen, R., *A Regional History Of The Railways Of Great Britain*, Vol. 7, David & Charles, 1973.

City Annals – composite version used in *Old Coventry and Lady Godiva* (see above).

Clark, P. & Slacks P. (eds), *Crisis And Order In English Towns 1500–1700*, Routledge & Kegan Paul, 1972.

Cole, M.H., *The Portable Queen. Elizabeth I And The Politics Of Ceremony,* University of Massachusetts Press, 1999.

Cooper, H., *Shakespeare And The Medieval World,* Arden Shakespeare, Bloomsbury, 2010.

Corporation of Coventry: Charters, Letters Patent etc, Historical Manuscripts Commission, 1899.

Coss, P., *The Early Records Of Medieval Coventry,* Oxford University Press, 1986.

Coss, P., *Lordship, Knighthood And Locality,* Cambridge University Press, 1991.

Coventry Canal Society, *Coventry's Waterway, A City Amenity*, 1972.

Coventry Leet Book, Vol. 2, trans. Phillip and Jean Willcox & Anthony Divett, Oakleaves Press, 2000.

Davis R.H.C., *The Early History Of Coventry*, Dugdale Society Papers, 1976.

Demidowicz, G., *A History Of The Blue Coat School And The Lychgate Cottages, Coventry*, City of Coventry, 2000.

Demidowicz, G., *Buildings Of Coventry,* Tempus, 2003.

Demidowicz, G. (ed.), *Coventry's First Cathedral*, Paul Watkins, 1994.

Dodge, J., *Silken Weave, A History Of Ribbon Making In Coventry from 1700 to 1860,*
Herbert Art Gallery And Museum, 1988.

Fox, L. (ed.), *Coventry Constables' Presentments*, Dugdale Society, 1986.

Fox, L., *Coventry's Heritage,* Coventry Evening Telegraph, 1945.

Goddard, R., *Lordship & Medieval Urbanisation. Coventry 1043–1355,* Royal
Historical Society/The Boydell Press, 2004.

Gooder, A., *Criminals, Courts And Conflict*, Coventry City Council, 2001.

Gooder, A., *The Black Death In Coventry*, Coventry Historical Association, 1998.

Gutteridge, J., *Lights And Shadows In the Life Of An Artisan*, Curtis and Beamish,
1893.

Harper, C.G., *The Holyhead Road* Chapman & Hall, 1902.

Harris, M.D., *Life In An Old English Town,* Swan Sonnenschein & Co., 1898.

Harris, M.D., *The Story Of Coventry*, J.M. Dent & Sons, 1911.

Harris, M.D., (trans.) *The Coventry Leet Book*, Kegan Paul, 1907–1913.

Hinman, M., *Holy Trinity, Coventry And Its Vicars 1264–2007*, Coventry Historical
Association, 2009.

Holland, C. (ed.), *Coventry and Warwickshire 1914–1919, Local Aspects Of The Great
War,* Warwickshire Great War Publications, 2012.

Hughes, A., *Politics, Society And Civil War In Warwickshire 1620–1660*, Cambridge
University Press, 1987.

Hughes, A. & R.C. Richardson (ed.), *Coventry And The English Revolution – Town &
Countryside In The English Revolution*, Manchester University Press, 1992.

Hulton, M., *True As Coventry Blue,* Coventry Historical Association, 1995.

Hunt, C., *A Woman Of The People: Alice Arnold Of Coventry 1881–1955*, Coventry
Historical Association, 2007.

Hurwich, J., *A Fanatick Town: The Political Influence Of Dissenters In Coventry
1660–1720,* Midland History, Vol. 4, 1977.

Ingram, M., *Bosworth 1485: Battle Story,* The History Press, 2012.

John, T., *Coventry's Civil War 1642–1660*, Coventry Historical Association, 2000.

Kimberley, D., *Coventry's Motorcar Heritage*, The History Press, 2012.

Lancaster, B. & Mason, T. (eds), *Life & Labour In A 20th Century City*, University of
Warwick, 1985.

Lancaster, J., *Godiva Of Coventry,* Coventry Corporation (Paper No. 1), 1967.

Leech, D., *Stability & Change At The End Of The Middle Ages In Coventry (1450–
1525)*, Midland History, Vol. 34, 2009.

Lewis, T., *Moonlight Sonata* Coventry City Council, 1990.

Lynes, A., *George Eliot's Coventry*, Coventry Historical Association, 1970.

Masterman, J., *Coventry And Its Story,* Pitman, 1914.

Maycock, G., *The Triumph Of Siegfried Bettmann*, Coventry Historical Association,
2000.

McGrory, D., *A History Of Coventry,* Phillimore, 2003.

McGrory, D., *Foul Deeds And Suspicious Deaths In Coventry*, Wharncliffe Books, 2004.

McSheffrey, S. & Tanner, N. (eds), *Lollards Of Coventry 1486–1522*, Royal Historical Society, 2003.

Monckton, L. & Morris, R. (ed.), *Coventry – Medieval Art, Architecture And Archaeology In The City And Its Vicinity*, British Archaeological Association, 2011.

Morgan K.O., *The Oxford Illustrated History Of Britain*, Oxford University Press, 1984.

Munden, A., *The Coventry Martyrs*, Herbert Art Gallery and Museum, 1997.

Munden, A., *The Third Spire, A History Of Christ Church, Coventry*, Coventry Historical Association, 1991.

Palmer, R., *Folklore Of Warwickshire*, Tempus, 2004.

Platt, C., *Medieval England*, Routledge & Kegan Paul Ltd, 1978.

Phythian-Adams, C., *Desolation Of A City*, Cambridge University Press, 1979.

Poole, B., *Coventry: Its History And Antiquities*, Taunton, 1870.

Reader, W., *The History And Antiquities Of The City Of Coventry*, Rollason & Reader, 1810.

Redknap, B., *Engineering The Development Of Coventry*, Coventry Historical Association, 2004.

Richardson, K., *Twentieth-Century Coventry*, City of Coventry, 1972.

Richardson, K., *Coventry*, Phillimore, 1987.

Searby, P., *Coventry Politics In The Age Of The Chartists 1836–1848*, Coventry Historical Association, 1964.

Sherwood, R., *The Civil War In The Midlands 1642–1651*, Alan Sutton, 1992.

Smith, A., *The City Of Coventry, A Twentieth Century Icon*, I.B. Tauris, 2006.

Smith, F., *Coventry: Six Hundred Years Of Municipal Life*, City of Coventry, 1945.

Soden, I., *Coventry: The Hidden History*, Tempus, 2005.

Soden, I., *Ranulf de Blondeville, The First English Hero*, Amberley, 2009.

Storey, R. (ed.), *A Shop Steward At Oxford*, University of Warwick, 1980.

Tiratsoo, N., *Reconstruction, Affluence And Labour Politics: Coventry 1945–1960*, Routledge, 1990.

Tuchman, B., *A Distant Mirror, The Calamitous 14th Century*, Macmillan, 1979.

Tugwood, D.T., *The Coventry And Warwickshire Hospital 1838–1948*, The Book Guild, 1987.

Victoria County History Of Warwickshire, Vol. 2 and 8, 1969.

Walters, P., *History In Our Hands*, Coventry Evening Telegraph, 1989.

Walters, P., *Amazing But True*, Coventry Evening Telegraph, 1997.

Warwickshire Feet Of Fines 1284–1349, Dugdale Society, 1939.

Whitley, T.W. *Parliamentary Representation Of The City Of Coventry*, Curtis & Beamish, 1894.

Willcox, P., *The Bakers' Company Of Coventry*, Coventry Historical Association, 1992.

Wood, M., *The Story Of England*, Penguin, 2011.

Yates, J., *Pioneers To Power*, Coventry Labour Party, 1950.

Newspapers and Periodicals

Jopson's Mercury
Coventry Graphic
Coventry Herald
Coventry Standard
Midland Daily Telegraph
Coventry Evening Telegraph

Cuttings

Arthur Heap cuttings 1915–1920
William Andrews cuttings 1900
John Cox cuttings 1878–1900
Coventry & Warwickshire Collection cuttings 1800–1945
University of Warwick cuttings 1961–1967

INDEX